AF262934

MARY SIMS

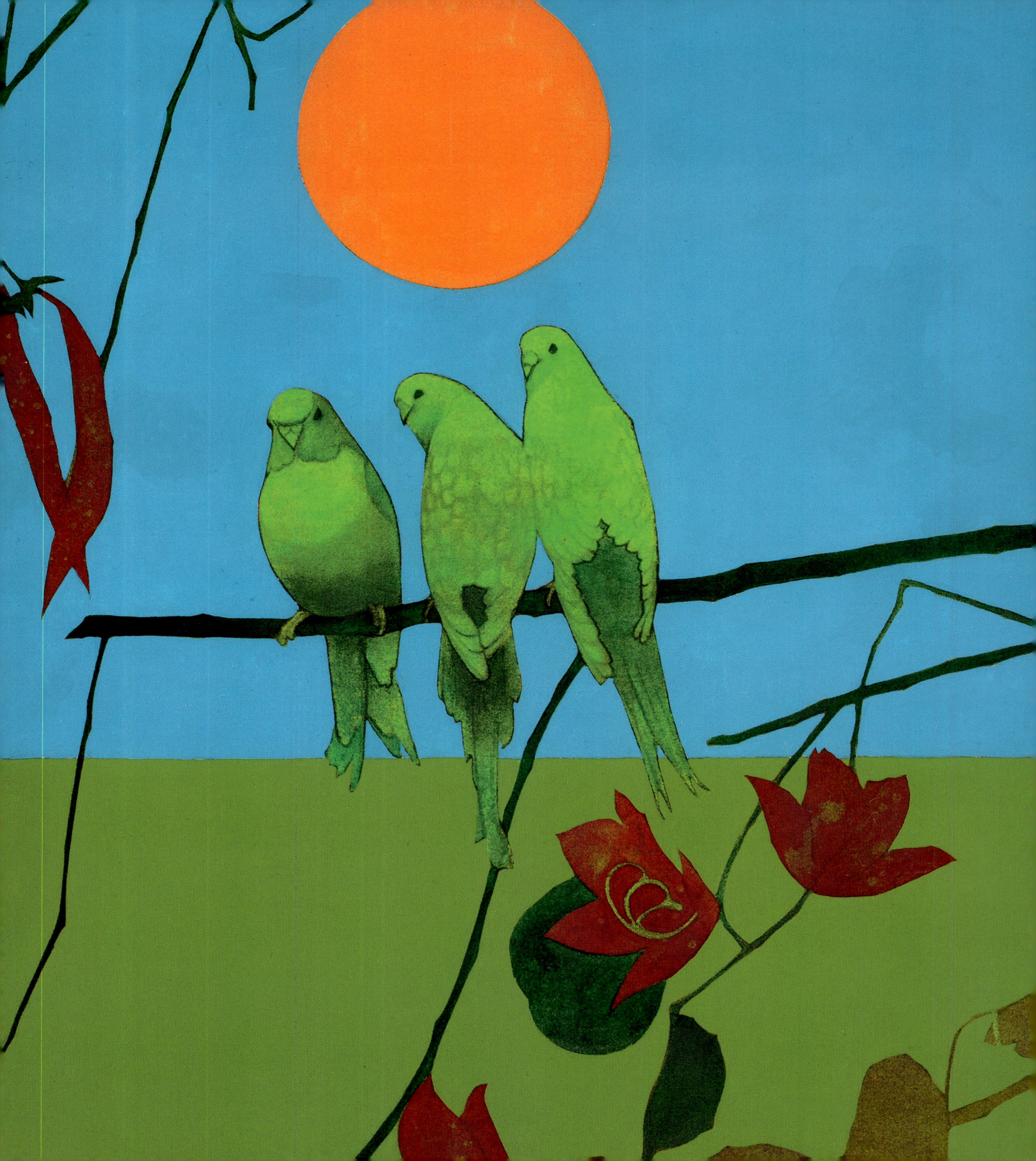

MARY SIMS

A Retrospective

Marina Pacini
Foreword by Kevin Sharp
Dixon Gallery and Gardens, Memphis, in association with D Giles Limited

DIXON
GALLERY & GARDENS

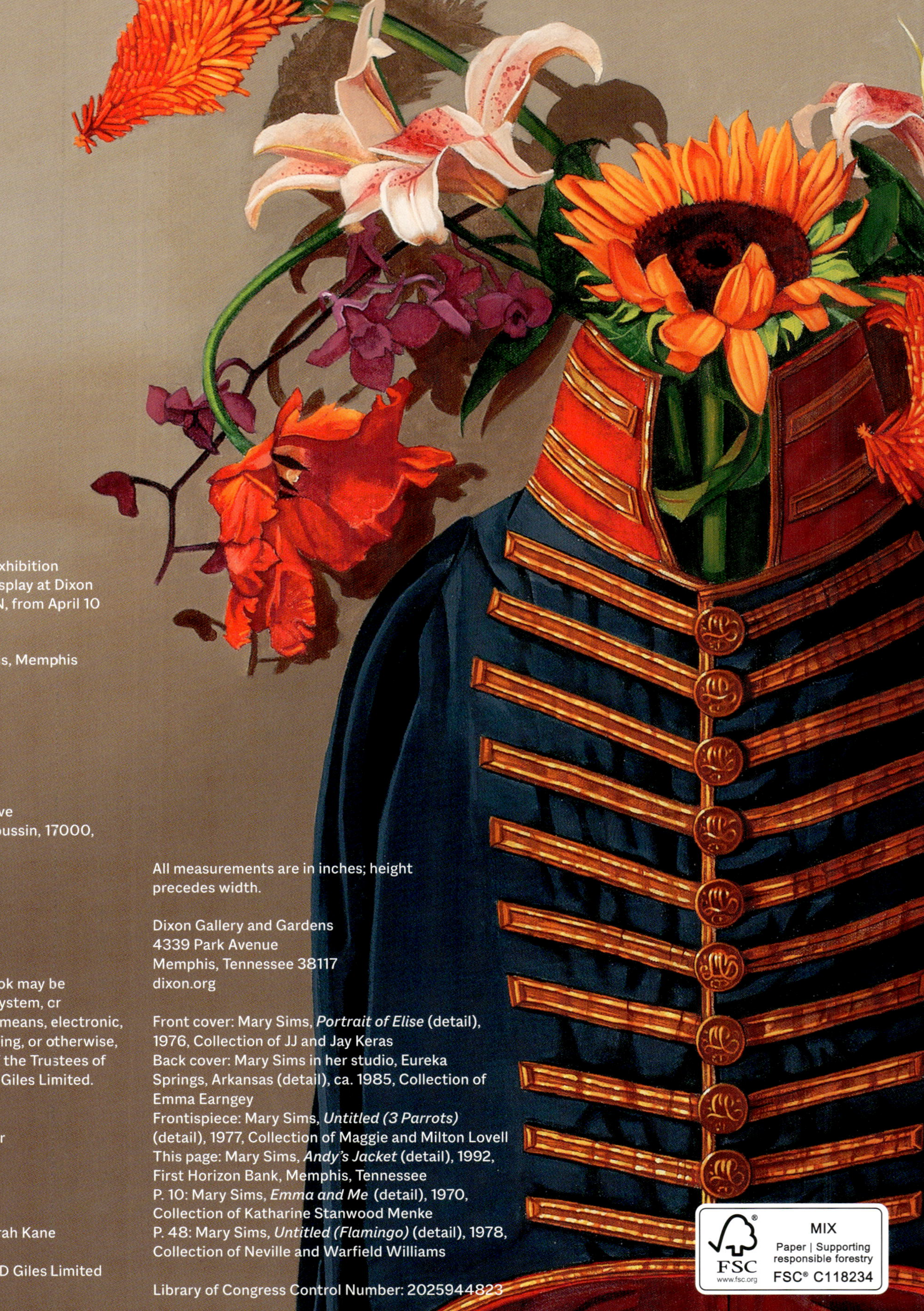

This catalogue accompanies the exhibition
Mary Sims: A Retrospective, on display at Dixon
Gallery and Gardens, Memphis, TN, from April 10
to June 7, 2026.

© 2026 Dixon Gallery and Gardens, Memphis

First published in 2026 by GILES
An imprint of D Giles Limited
66 High Street,
Lewes, BN7 1XG, UK
gilesltd.com

EU GPSR authorised representative
LOGOS EUROPE, 9 rue Nicolas Poussin, 17000,
La Rochelle, France
E-mail: contact@logoseurope.eu

ISBN: 978-1-917273-26-8

All rights reserved

No part of the contents of this book may be
reproduced, stored in a retrieval system, or
transmitted in any form or by any means, electronic,
mechanical, photocopying, recording, or otherwise,
without the written permission of the Trustees of
Dixon Gallery and Gardens, and D Giles Limited.

For Dixon Gallery and Gardens:
Ellen Daugherty, Assistant Curator
Kristen Kimberling, Registrar
Baxter Buck, Photography

For D Giles Limited:
Copy-edited and proofread by Sarah Kane
Designed by Alfonso Iacurci
Produced by GILES, an imprint of D Giles Limited
Printed and bound in Europe

All measurements are in inches; height
precedes width.

Dixon Gallery and Gardens
4339 Park Avenue
Memphis, Tennessee 38117
dixon.org

Front cover: Mary Sims, *Portrait of Elise* (detail),
1976, Collection of JJ and Jay Keras
Back cover: Mary Sims in her studio, Eureka
Springs, Arkansas (detail), ca. 1985, Collection of
Emma Earngey
Frontispiece: Mary Sims, *Untitled (3 Parrots)*
(detail), 1977, Collection of Maggie and Milton Lovell
This page: Mary Sims, *Andy's Jacket* (detail), 1992,
First Horizon Bank, Memphis, Tennessee
P. 10: Mary Sims, *Emma and Me* (detail), 1970,
Collection of Katharine Stanwood Menke
P. 48: Mary Sims, *Untitled (Flamingo)* (detail), 1978,
Collection of Neville and Warfield Williams

Library of Congress Control Number: 2025944823

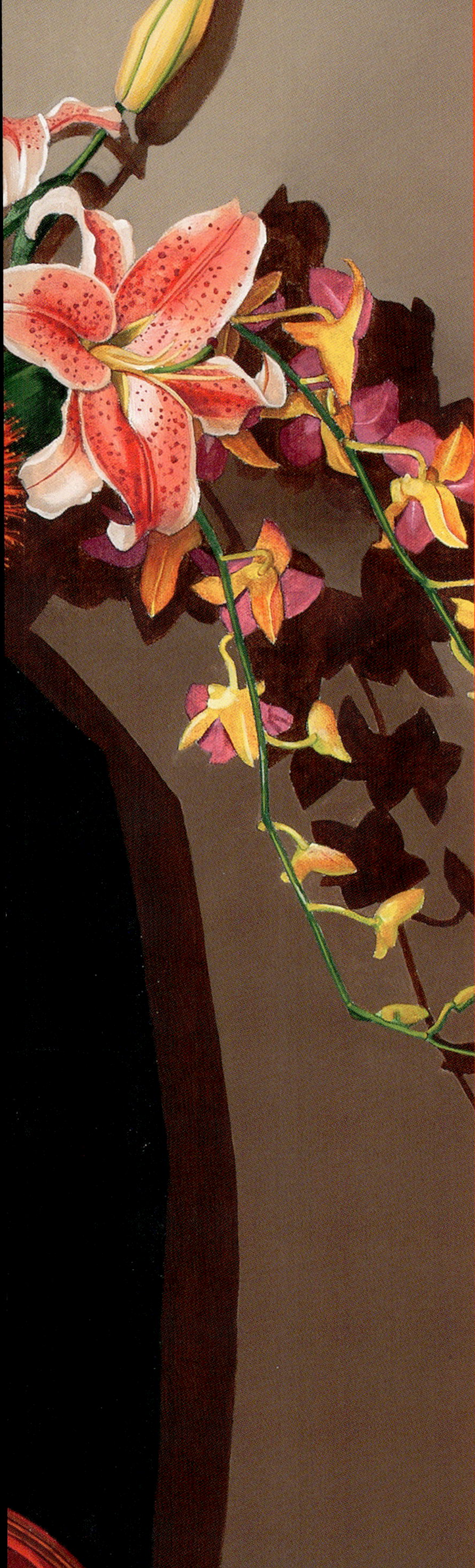

CONTENTS

MARY SIMS

A Memphis Original

Painter and printmaker Mary Sims (1940–2004) was a Memphis original. The works of art in this exhibition, the first museum survey of Sims's extraordinary career, will be something of a revelation even to those who knew the artist and her work quite well. The show moves from her early and elegant intaglio prints of the late 1950s, to spare, optically flat portraits isolated on monochrome backgrounds from the 1960s and 1970s, to monumental later-career canvases that use the Old Testament and ancient mythology as fantastical jumping-off points for rebellious history paintings, and ends with her riotous, maximalist still-life subjects from the 1980s and 1990s that are filled with flowers, animals, toys, and textiles. The thematic arc of Mary Sims's work will come as less of a surprise to viewers well acquainted with her work than the sheer volume of her creative output. Sims, it turns out, was both meticulous in her craft and a prodigious worker. Her consistency and productivity are nothing short of amazing.

Mary Sims was an exceptional draftsperson and colorist who developed carefully organized compositions that were also whimsical and at times even strange. Collectively and individually, her paintings reveal much about the artist, including her idiosyncratic points of view, her sly sense of humor, and her irreverence. In *Mary Sims: A Retrospective*, the Dixon Gallery and Gardens in Memphis celebrates the artist as the distinctive late twentieth-century Southern force of nature that many in this city and beyond remember her to be. The paintings she produced throughout her career and even her earliest etchings reveal both a knowing contemporary sophistication and an unmistakable sense of cool.

This retrospective exhibition and its accompanying publication would not have been possible without the help of many admirers of Mary Sims and friends of the Dixon. First, we would like to thank Marina Pacini, former Chief Curator of the Memphis Brooks Museum of Art, who brought her usual dedication and commitment to this long-overdue Mary Sims project. Marina's deeply researched and valuable essay explores Sims's career through the lens of the artist's biography, which provides essential context for appreciating how her sometimes quirky personality, unconventional lifestyle, and bohemian circle of friends contributed to the originality, shrewdness, and surprising charm of her paintings.

Few have had a more indelible relationship with Mary Sims herself and her work than David Lusk, the owner of David Lusk Gallery in Memphis and Nashville. He was Mary Sims's advocate and friend during the last years of her life, and has continued to be a champion of her work. He still represents her artistic estate more than twenty years after her death and has been an essential part of keeping her memory alive. David has kept her work foregrounded in the context of art in the American South,

women artists of the Southeast region, the influence of Pop Art on Southern
and women in the vanguard of American painting of the 1980s and 1990
deeply grateful for the insights, sensitivity, and experience David has broug
project, and we very much appreciate his wise and supportive contributio

Julie N. Pierotti, the Dixon Gallery and Gardens' Martha R. Robinson
championed this exhibition from the very beginning and has overseen ev
of it with vision and grace. Ellen Daugherty, assistant curator, Kristen Kin
the Dixon's registrar, and Jeff Goggans, preparator, all made important contr
to *Mary Sims: A Retrospective*, including the supervision of photography, a
transportation of the works to the Dixon, and designing layouts for the ex
We are grateful to this small but potent curatorial department for their out
work on this and every exhibition organized and staged at the Dixon,
there have been many.

Developing and planning *Mary Sims: A Retrospective*, both the exhibi
the accompanying catalogue, has been possible only through the gener
kindness of many in the Memphis area and beyond. At this time, we g
acknowledge those who have supported the show with loans of special wo
from their collections. We thank Julian Anthony, Lon Anthony, Stevan
and the partners, lawyers, and staff at Black McLaren Jones Ryland & Grif
Katherine and Adrian Blackney, Betsy Bradley, Cynthia Bringle, Kathe
Stephen Bush, Holly and Paul T. Combs, Lawrence and John Cowart, Meg
Crosby, Anne Curtis, First Horizon Bank (Paula Beale, Clarissa J. Connift
Davis, Philip Fieler, Vernon Stafford, and Lockie Wade), Audrey Taylor G
Aubrey Hampton, Jim Herbst, Amy Amonette Huber, Carissa Hussong ar
Lusk, John Jerit, Rose M. Johnston, Elizabeth Jumet, JJ and Jay Keras, Gail
Sue Langford, Carol LaRocca, Maggie and Milton Lovell, Dianne and Myr
Susan Mallory, Grace Megel and Sarkis Kish, Memphis Dermatology Clin
Birmingham), Memphis in May International Festival (Mack Weaver),
International Airport (Laura Rainey and Glen Thomas), Katharine Stanwoo
Meg Menzies, Rodgers Menzies, Lynn Meyer, Lance Oliver, Sara O'Rya
and Penn Owen, Parker Phillips, Warren Phillips, Rhodes College (Ann
Angelia Brittain, President Jennifer M. Collins, Kristen Hunt, and Rosie
Roger Ross and Trae Winston, Beth and David Skudder, Allison Read Smit
and Fred W. Smith, Dolph Smith, Robert Donovan Smith, Carey and Brad
St. Mary's Episcopal School (Janell Sewell and Albert Throckmorton)
Thompson, Ainslie and Hardy Todd, Muffy and Michael Turley, Brier Smith
Terry Twyman, Urban Art Commission (Lakeisha Edwards), Elizabeth a
Wagerman, Neville and Warfield Williams, Libby Wunderlich, and Mor
Philip Zanone. We are grateful to all these admirers of the work of Mary S
delighted by your kind responses to our project.

The ambitious exhibition program at the Dixon Gallery and Gardens is ge
supported by individuals, foundations, and corporations in the Memphis cor
and beyond. For making this project a reality, we thank the Joe Orgill Fam
for Exhibitions, which helps underwrite every show the Dixon produces

Kevin Sharp

We also offer our deepest appreciation to Kathy and Ben Adams, the Armstrong Company and Robin and Tom Watson, Susan and Damon Arney, Amelia and Mike Bailey, Kathy and Jack Blair, Fran and Rusty Bloodworth, Suzanne and Paul Burgar, Alice and Phil Burnett, Kate and Michael Buttarazzi, Marilyn Rhea Cheeseman, Holly and Paul T. Combs, Jane and Mike Coop, Brenda Crain, Robert B. Dodge and Patti McNeil, Karen and Preston Dorsett, the William B. "Billy" Dunavant Jr. Foundation, the Theodore W. and Betty J. Eckles Foundation, Andrea and Doug Edwards, First Horizon Foundation, Marylon Rogers Glass, Amanda and Nick Goetze, Jenny and Ellis Haddad, Martha and Mike Hess, Julie and Rob Hussey, Rose M. Johnston, Anne and Mike Keeney, Nell R. Levy, Kay and Jim Liles, Gloria and Doug Marchant, Debbie and Chip Marston, Mabel and Phil McNeill, Snow and Henry Morgan, Brandon and Joe Morrison, Nancy and Steve Morrow, Opus East Memphis, Irene Orgill, Gwen and Penn Owen, Linda Pelts, Chris and Dan Richards, Trish and Carl Ring, the Scheidt Family Foundation, the Mary and Jeff Simpson Charitable Trust, Irene and Fred Smith, Kaki and Vince Smith, Barbara and Vernon Stafford, Dorothy Stevenson, Susan Adler Thorp, Ainslie and Hardy Todd, Shirley and Bob Turner, Adele Wellford, Neville and Warfield Williams, Barbara and Lewis Williamson, and Lucy Woodson and Bob Berry.

In alternating years, the Dixon Gallery and Gardens and the Memphis Garden Club work together to present the *Memphis Flower Show*, a Garden Club of America sanctioned exhibition and competition and one of the highlights of our spring season (in even-numbered years). In April 2026, gifted designers from across the country will convene in Memphis for three days and produce floral designs at the Dixon inspired by the works we have assembled by Mary Sims. The *Memphis Flower Show* is complex and as ambitious in scope as the Mary Sims exhibition that will be its point of departure. For their collaborative spirit, dedication, and energy, we would like to thank Memphis Garden Club and especially Elizabeth Coors, its President in 2026, and Emily McEwan and Muffy Turley, the *Memphis Flower Show* co-chairs. Their embrace of Mary Sims's work as the basis of the 2026 flower show and indeed the enthusiasm of the entire membership has been gratifying and sustaining.

Countless logistical details go into the organization of any major fine art exhibition, including *Mary Sims: A Retrospective*. Not the least of which is commissioning, gathering, and assembling photography for the catalogue you now hold. We wish to thank Baxter Buck for the hours he spent traveling across the Mid-South making images for this publication. Additionally, Greg Smith provided expert help with photography at David Lusk Gallery in Memphis. The editorial team of *River City Lifestyle*, especially Christian Owen, and the photographer Uday Sripathi, graciously gave permission to reproduce a photograph originally published in the magazine. Other photographers, Tim Burleson in Asheville, North Carolina, and Rick Rhodes in Charleston, South Carolina, provided meaningful assistance at crucial times in the project. Finally, Julian Anthony, Lon Anthony, Sarah Anthony, Emma Earngey, Naomi Mezey, Jackie Nichols, Gary Green and Pat Sims, and Don Williams generously shared photographs with the Dixon for this publication.

This ambitious exhibition catalogue has very much benefited from the talented people at D Giles Limited, its publisher in the United Kingdom. The Dixon has been

working with D Giles since the start of the pandemic in 2020, and the book
produced together during challenging periods and moments of upswing hav
conceptually sound, elegantly designed, and beautifully made. Moreover, t
as publishers has helped make the Dixon even better known internationally
excellent efforts once again on this our fifth book together, we particula
Dan Giles, Liz Japes, Allison McCormick, and Louise Ramsay—they have s
in making *Mary Sims: A Retrospective* yet another beautiful and compelling pu

At its core, the Dixon Gallery and Gardens is an outstanding group
dedicated to making the institution the very best it can be. We are e
grateful to the staff and volunteers of the Dixon who are eager and coll
contributors to this and every project we undertake and exhibition we
We are very grateful to Christan Allen, Melvin Avendano, Juliana Bjorkl
Blair, Marlin Burnwatt, Olivia Burton, Savannah Carodine, Cindy Co
Daugherty, Jenny Duggan, Chris Emanus, Erika Fuller, Wanda Gaines, Jeff
Dan Goodwin, Rebekah Hedges, Braden Hixson, Gail Hopper, Susan Johns
Jones, Robert Jones, Shawn Jones, Kristen Kimberling, Sarah Lorenz, Kyle
Jorden Miernik-Walker, Lacy Mitcham, Morgan Monroe, Norma Montesi
Perez, Julie Pierotti, Adam Queen, Kristen Rambo, Hannah Reasons, Della
Litzy Roman, Christine Ruby, Margarita Sandino, Corkey Sinks, Dale Skag
Stobbe, Rachel Sturch, Dorothy Svgdik, Stephanie Valentine, Cameron
Shawna White, Jessie Wiley, and Charlene Williams. You are a wonder
and you have done it again. Thank you.

Everything the Dixon produces from plantings in the gardens, to e
programs, to exhibitions is overseen by a highly committed and engag
of Trustees. At this time, we would like to express the gratitude of the in
to these wonderful people and all they represent at the Dixon and in th
Memphis community. We offer our sincerest thanks first to the Executive Co
led by Amanda Goetze and including Larry Crawford, Mike Keeney, Harriet M
and Vernon Stafford. We also thank trustees Ben Adams, Thomas C. Ada
Alspaugh, Markova Reed Anderson, Jack Blair, Rusty Bloodworth, Rob C
Melanie Burroughs Cole, Paul T. Combs, Elizabeth Coors, Brian Dotson, Am
Doug Edwards, Gaylan Fitzpatrick, Ellis Haddad, Buzzy Hussey, Peter Ka
Anne Keeney, Heather Koury, Harsh Kumar, Suzanne Mallory, W. Neely
III, Chip Marston, Estella Mayhue-Greer, Allen Morgan, Brandon Morris
Morrow, Erick New, Mary New, Penn Owen, Carita Palmer, Rob Park, Steve
Chris Richards, R. Lemoyne Robinson, Elkan Scheidt, Darnell Settles III, Su
Thorp, Hardy Todd III, Gil Uhlhorn, Sharon Johnson Wheeler, Willis Wi
Barbara Williamson.

Mary Sims: A Retrospective represents a marvelous opportunity to shine
light on one of the many great visual artists to have come out of Memphis, T
We are grateful for this excellent community we call home, and for the
and creative people who have enriched it over the years, including Mary

Kevin Sharp
Linda W. and S. Herbert Rhea Director
Dixon Gallery and Gardens

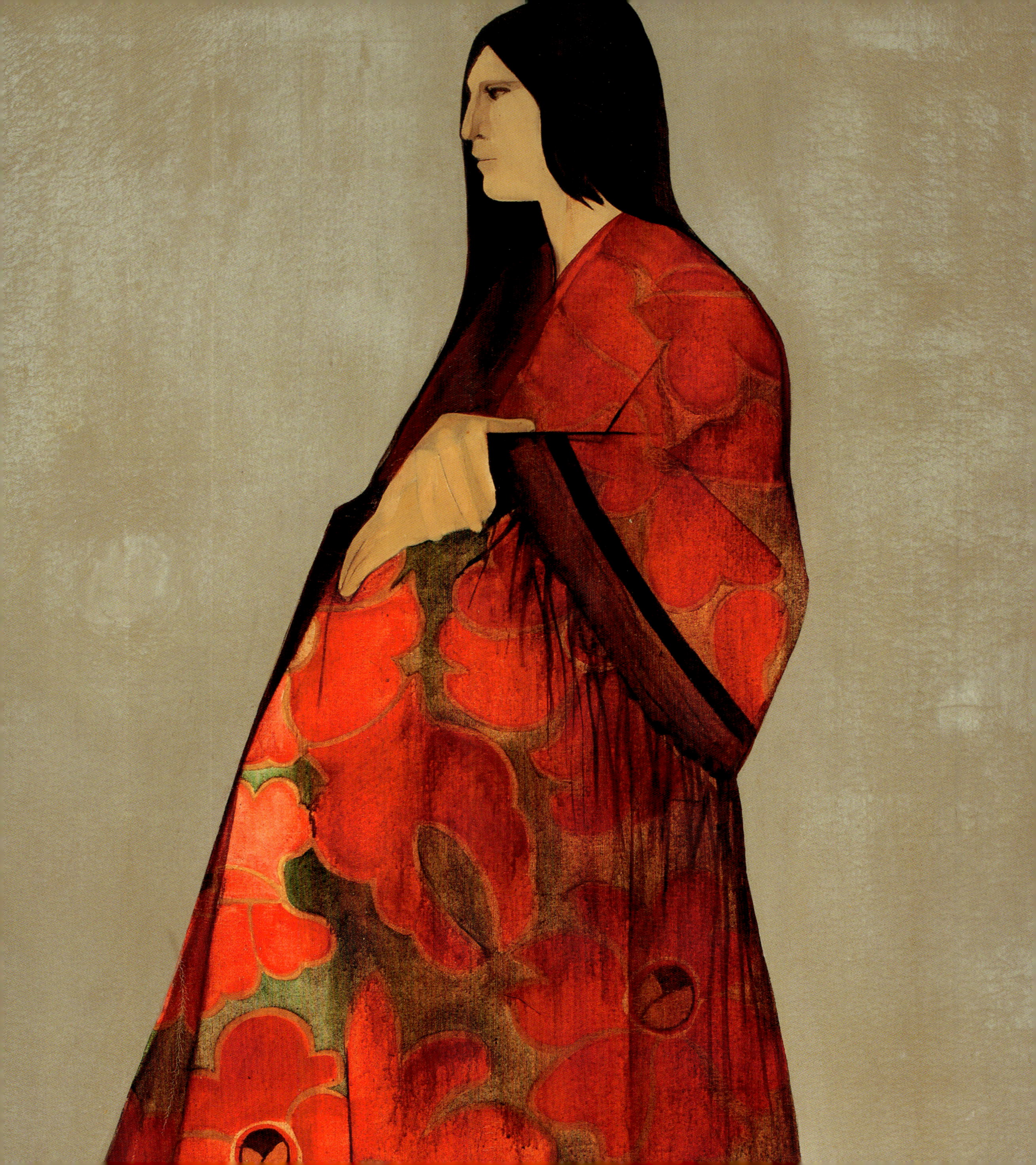

MARY SIMS'S MULTIPLICITY

Marina Pacini

Because what I really want is that everyday thing. I want to paint, I don't want to stand in a roomful of great paintings that I did. I want to paint.[1]

Mary Sims, 1973

To the people who knew her, Mary Adelyn Sims Mezey Radakovic Earngey (1940–2004, Fig. 1) was a multitudinous character.[2] An artist of natural ability, she was funny, tempestuous, energetic, small, single-minded, refined, potty-mouthed, hard-working, focused, and formidable. She was also an accomplished singer, a great cook, an excellent storyteller, and a considerate friend, among other things. What she was *not* good at was documenting her art or her life. She left some clippings and letters, a limited photo archive, and no checklists. She rarely signed and scrupulously refused to date paintings, making it difficult to chart the evolution of her distinctive style and to write a biography of her. And "a" biography is key; she was many different things to many different people, and no one essay could comprehensively capture her blithe spirit. This essay attempts to reveal some facets of her personality and history, and to parse the development of her art making.

Beginning in childhood, and over the course of her decades-long career, Sims experimented with various media, styles, and subjects. Nevertheless, in 1968 she

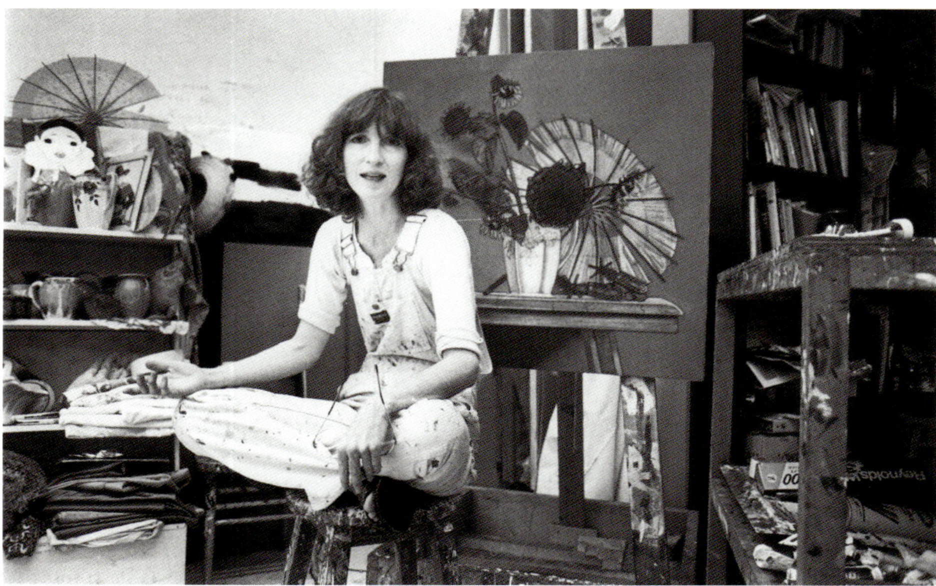

Fig. 1
Mary Sims in her studio, Eureka Springs, Arkansas, ca. 1985. Collection of Emma Earngey

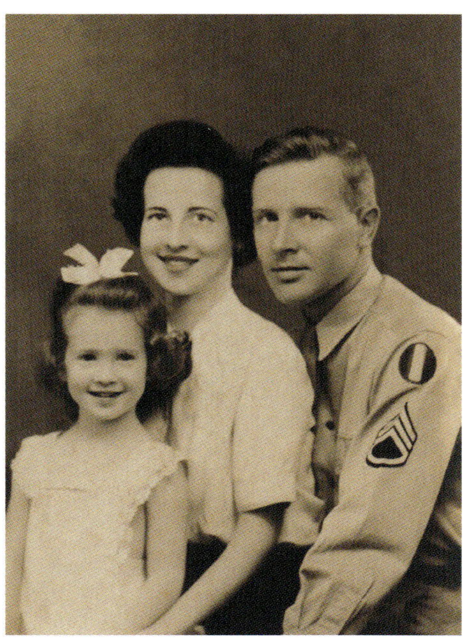

Mary Sims with her parents, Gayle and Lydel
Sims, ca. 1945.
Collection of Emma Earngey

developed what became her signature style and created a distinctive body
Describing her paintings as representational does not do justice to her
of an almost hyper-realism, with her subjects—whether human, animal,
or plant—receiving an attention to detail that resulted in truthful (if al
portraiture, as well as glimmering surfaces of bold color and intriguing

She repeatedly reiterated her love of the visual, emphatically at the
of the written word. She went so far as to claim in the text she wrote for her
that she was not good at writing.[3] This is ironic as she was known and a
the colorful and effusive language she employed—her father would intro
as a longshoreman.[4] Perhaps it was that emphasis on storytelling that helpe
her keen understanding of which details matter and how to compose a v
would keep viewers engaged. Her biblical series was straightforward sto
but many of her other works could be described as narratives as well.
of language and the arts was inherited from her parents, Gayle and Ly
who provided models for what a rich cultural life could be. The influen
family's wit and sense of humor are evident both in her personal life an

Beginnings, 1940–1958

Mary Adelyn Sims was born in Jackson, Tennessee, on October 18, 19
an educated and artistic family (Fig. 2). She stated that she was "the prod
environment. . . . I was raised in an extremely articulate and literary ho
My parents read and played great music to me on the piano and recor
Both my parents were in love with the arts which allowed me to feel lik
be or do anything I ever wanted. This is the greatest gift a parent can give a ch
sister Pat was born in 1952.

Without doubt, the biggest influence was her father, Lydel Sims (1916–199
stints in Nashville and Jackson, he was hired by the Associated Press in
in 1940. From 1949 to 1985 he published *Assignment: Memphis*, a daily fr
column for the *Commercial Appeal*. His ruminations on local goings-on, rid
tall tales were must-reads; it was suggested that the column was proba
by more Mid-Southerners than anything since *Gone with the Wind*.[7]

Mary's mother, Gayle Gladys Munroe Sims (1916–1993), was also artistic.[8]
many women of her generation did not have careers outside the hom
studied painting at the Memphis Academy of Arts (later Memphis Colleg
played the piano, had exhibitions, and volunteered on political campaig
was precocious, ambitious, and hard-working. In a 1978 interview, she

I started saying I was going to be an artist when I was three years old
as I could talk. . . . [W]e moved around a whole lot. . . . Daddy was in
and I never had just friends in a normal situation where they would
Mary come out and play today?" And so I just had to come up with my c
world that had a lot to do with Rapunzel and Cinderella and stuff lik

By the time she was nine, she had begun taking classes at the Memphis Academy of Arts.[10] Among the early awards she won was regional honors in a national art contest sponsored by Hallmark Cards. While attending Whitehaven High School in South Memphis, she worked with the Front Street Theatre in a variety of capacities, including assistant stage manager, later admitting that rather than noting the stage blocking she was drawing the cast and flowers.[11] That lapse did not prevent her from getting a solo exhibition at the theater when she was seventeen or from painting sets for some of the productions.[12] She graduated from Whitehaven in 1958.

Studies and travel, 1958–1967

In 1958 she packed her bags for the State University of Iowa (today the University of Iowa, Fig. 3) with plans to study with Mauricio Lasansky (1914–2012), an internationally recognized printmaker. What she experienced was frustration with her work.

> If you're insecure, you get this wonderful strength of being the best 9-year-old artist you know. And you begin following this pattern of protecting your ego, which makes it impossible to learn. When I got to Iowa, by virtue of my 9-year-old talents I was put into an advanced life-drawing class instead of a basic drawing class and into a printmaking workshop where everyone else was a graduate student. . . .

> At Iowa, I could do the best 20-second line drawing you ever saw, and that's where I was—peaking out on a 20-second line drawing. When I left, I realized that there were people there who had walked [in] off the street at age 18 and learned more than I had.[13]

Among the other classes she took during her first two years at Iowa were painting, history of costume design for the stage, Baroque art, and prints and composition.[14]

Despite her later harsh assessment of her work while at school, she was included in the inaugural Invitation Print Show at the Brooks Memorial Art Gallery (today Memphis Brooks Museum of Art) in April of 1960.[15] The exhibition comprising fifty printmakers included such recognized artists as Will Barnet (1911–2012), Leonard Baskin (1922–2000), and Isabel Bishop (1902–1988). Along with fellow Memphian Ted Faiers (1908–1985), Sims was singled out in the *Commercial Appeal*, in her case for a "straight-forward self-portrait" and the study *Three Birds* (Cat. 1).[16] The latter work presents her subjects in a variety of poses across the bottom half of the paper. Printmaking was highly suited to her talents as a draftsperson. Note the bird on the left where the repetitive span of lines conveys the attempt to take flight. Also characteristic of printmaking is her effective use of gradations of black and the contrast of solid versus sketchy areas to differentiate the birds, resulting in a dynamic image. As would become a hallmark of her work in paint,

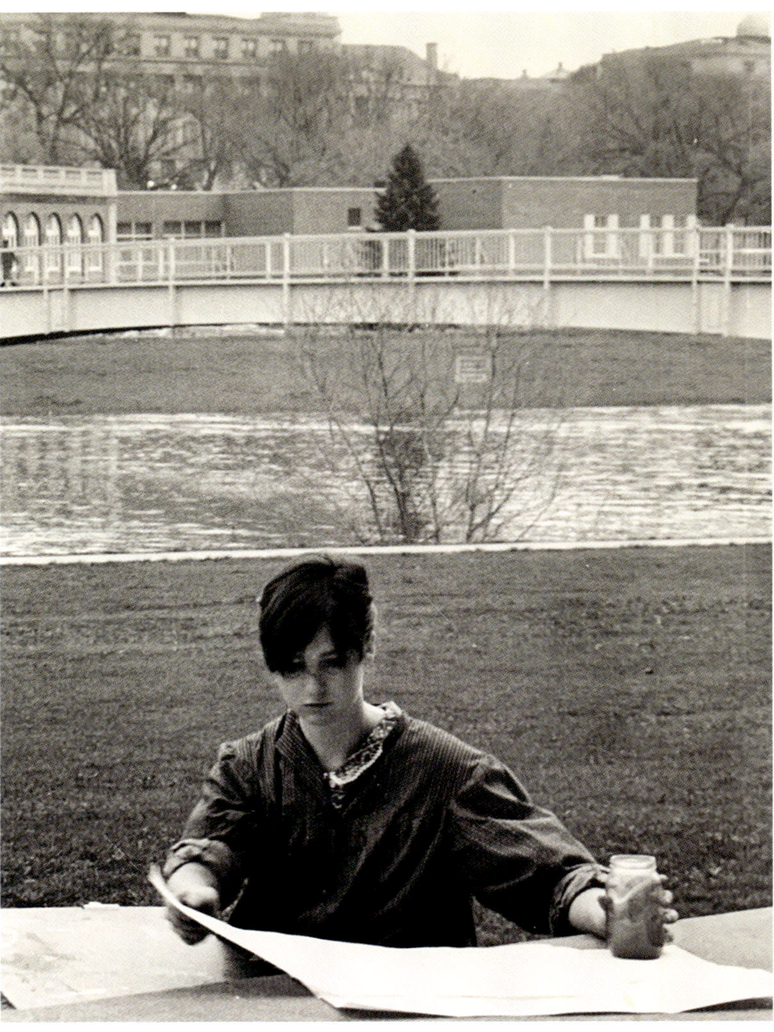

the compositional balance between the seemingly empty background
subjects is essential to the success of the print.

That July, she was in a two-person show with Charles Inzer at the 2-
in Memphis, exhibiting both intaglio prints and paintings. The exhibi
reviewed in the *Commercial Appeal*, beginning what would become a lor
of articles that covered her art, life, and family in newspapers and ma
across the region. Although her father's position at the paper may have
the door, it was her increasing abilities that cemented the attention. Ac
to the review, her subjects were "semi-self portraits" and a large oil of
of children [Cat. 2], vaguely based on a snapshot she once saw, [tha
a suspended moment in time."[17] The five children, of various ages and s
very loosely painted with little detail and little interest in anatomy. T
is thin enough that the texture of the canvas is readily apparent, and

areas it literally drips. Brushstrokes are visible as well throughout, especially in the barely delineated faces of the children.

If Sims was disappointed with her training, she found compensation through a community of like-minded artists, writers, poets, and a theater group.[18] Among the people she met was the poet Robert Mezey (1935–2020), whose last name was added to her transcript. Although there was never an official ceremony, they presented themselves as married.[19] Both singers, they performed folk songs as Bob & Mary.[20]

Mezey was awarded a Jones Fellowship from Stanford University and, in the fall of 1960, the couple moved to California.[21] There is little information on what Sims was doing during this period, although she was driven to work and was known for her alacrity in finding ways to paint when in a new city—she'd make pigment out of beets, a brush out of a T-shirt.[22] And she took a class with the painter and printmaker Nathan Oliveira (1928–2010) at the California College of Arts and Crafts.[23] Unhappy in his work at Stanford, Mezey and Sims decamped for Mexico.[24] By the summer of 1961 they had moved in with her parents in Memphis. That fall, Sims had an exhibition of large paintings of children, flowers, and a "non-sensual odalisque" at the 2-3 Gallery, as well as a group of smaller oils at the Book Shelf shop.[25]

Among the works at the 2-3 Gallery was a portrait of Mezey (Cat. 4). While still loosely painted in oil, the facial features are better defined and the figure is identifiable, unlike the children from the previous year. Working primarily with a limited palette of greens, she enlivened the image with the contrast between the dark shirt and the lighter pocket and collar interior. Patches of green surround his nose and eyes. His reddish hair, too, stands out against the brushy planes of the background. Mezey looks fixedly at the viewer. The result is a muted yet vital likeness.

Sims's relationship with Mezey ended soon afterwards. By the spring semester of 1962 she was re-enrolled at Iowa, and among the classes she took over the next four semesters were introduction to photography, introduction to art theory, and several sections of individual instruction, as well as a class on Greek drama.[26] All of her courses would be reflected in her future endeavors. In 1963, she received her Bachelor of Fine Arts, and once again a relationship determined her next path.

In the spring of 1962, Sims became romantically involved with poet and fellow student Charles Wright (b.1935). Within a few months of his receiving a Fulbright Scholarship to translate poetry in Rome from 1963 to 1965, she joined him as his fiancé.[27] While there, she took private lessons and painted landscapes and portraits.[28] Her progress is evident in an image of the Italian countryside (Fig. 4). The hills and buildings are smoother than in previous works; although the brushstrokes are still clearly visible, they are less patchy. She focused on capturing the sunshine and architecture of Italy—the bright white light flooding the scene illuminates the arches on a hillside bound by a sky reduced to a hazy band over a flat blue sea. The quality of her work was recognized through a one-person show at the Galleria Trevi in Rome.[29] At the end of the two years, Wright and Sims returned to the United States and determined that they were not suited to each other.

Sims then enrolled at Tulane University in New Orleans for a master's degree (Fig. 5). Over three semesters from 1965 to 1967 she took classes in Northern Renaissance

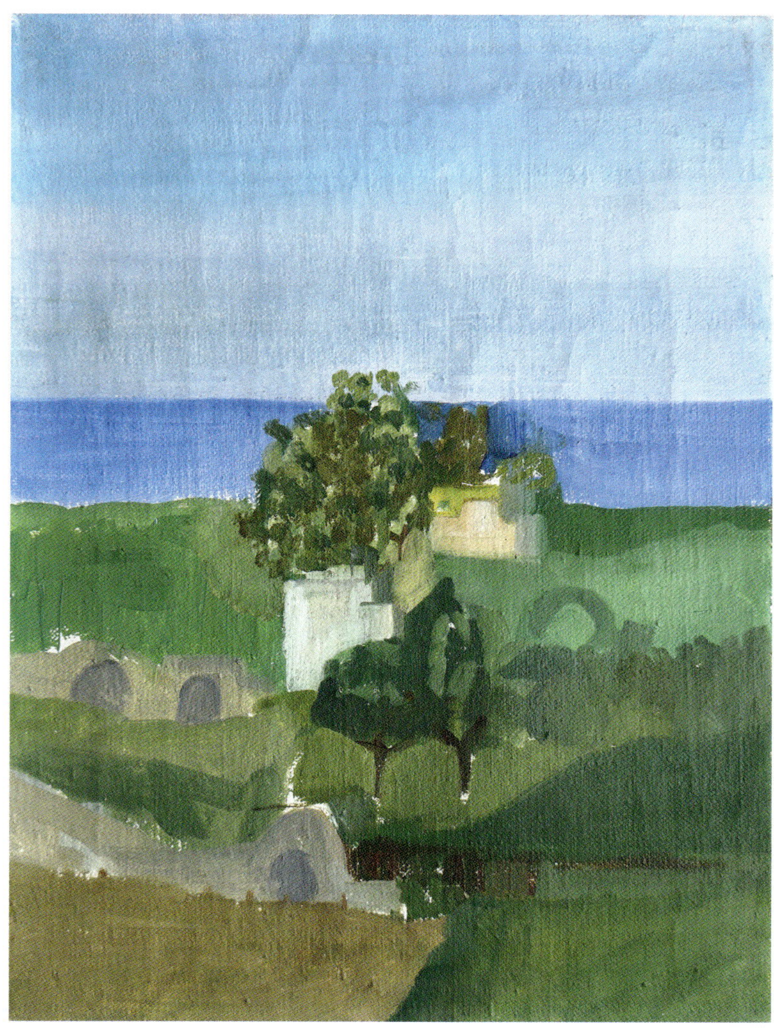

and Northern Baroque art, as well as drawing and painting, but focused
on printmaking—seven out of eleven classes.[30] Three of the latter were with
(1922–2001, who also had studied with Lasansky at Iowa) including relief, int
planographic methods for two semesters, as well as an advanced course i
problems in printmaking.[31] In short, she continued to build on her studies

Despite the emphasis on printmaking, she was painting, including
of Don Williams, her boyfriend at the time (Fig. 6). Loosely and thinly
with evident brushstrokes, the work is tightly organized. Williams sits
in an homage to James McNeill Whistler's *Arrangement in Grey a*
Number 1 (1871), better known as *Whistler's Mother*) slightly off-cente
left. The black vase sitting on a shelf—which humorously breaks the ed
image—anchors the right side of the canvas, while the tan vase and t
table frame the left. The work is a study of greens and browns. This b

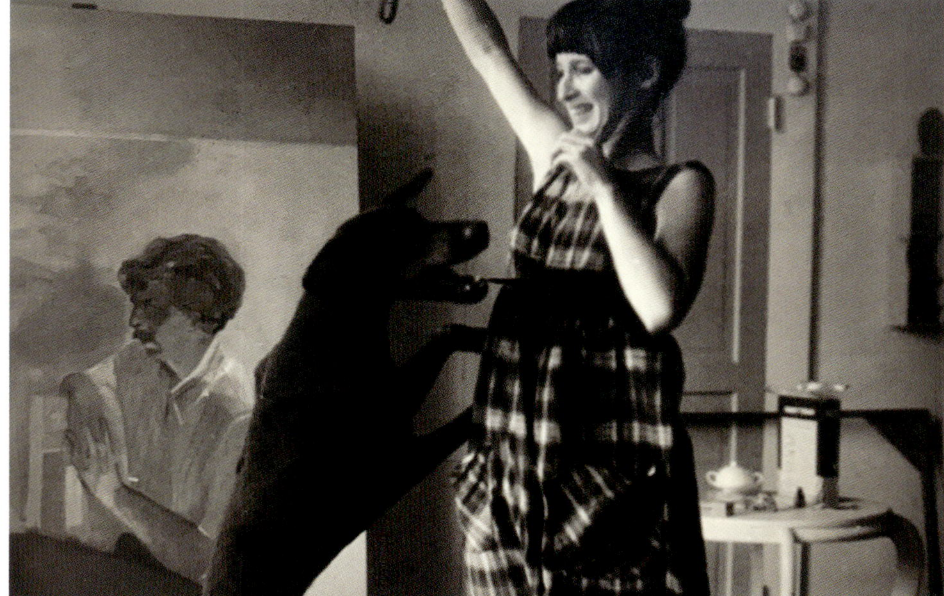

of objects and colors, along with figures set against an empty ground, would become an important element of her later works.

And it was a painting that brought her next acclaim—*Three Ladies* won a $125 prize in 1966 at the Brooks Memorial Art Gallery's *Mid-South Exhibition*, which was juried by the well-regarded figural artist Jack Levine (1915–2010).[32] This success was followed by a July exhibition at the Lowe Gallery in New Orleans, and in the fall a two-person exhibition with George Ford at the Orleans Gallery that included oil florals and portraits, prints, and drawings.[33]

Another relationship soon intervened. On a trip home during the spring of 1967, she and Chicagoan Theodore (Ted) Radakovic met when they were visiting mutual friends at the Front Street Theatre.[34] They returned to their respective homes, but within a few weeks Sims visited Radakovic and the couple married at city hall. They lived in New Orleans until she received her Master of Fine Arts in May and then moved to Chicago.

In search of a signature style, 1968–1975

When Sims's and Radakovic's car broke down on a visit to Memphis in the spring of 1968, they decided to stay.[35] Sims was hired to teach painting and printmaking at Southwestern at Memphis (today Rhodes College) while Radakovic pursued a Master of Fine Arts in the theater program at Memphis State University (today the University of Memphis).

Sims—or, as it stated in the *Commercial Appeal*, "really Mrs. Radakovic. . . the young Memphis artist continues to paint under her maiden name"—had a solo

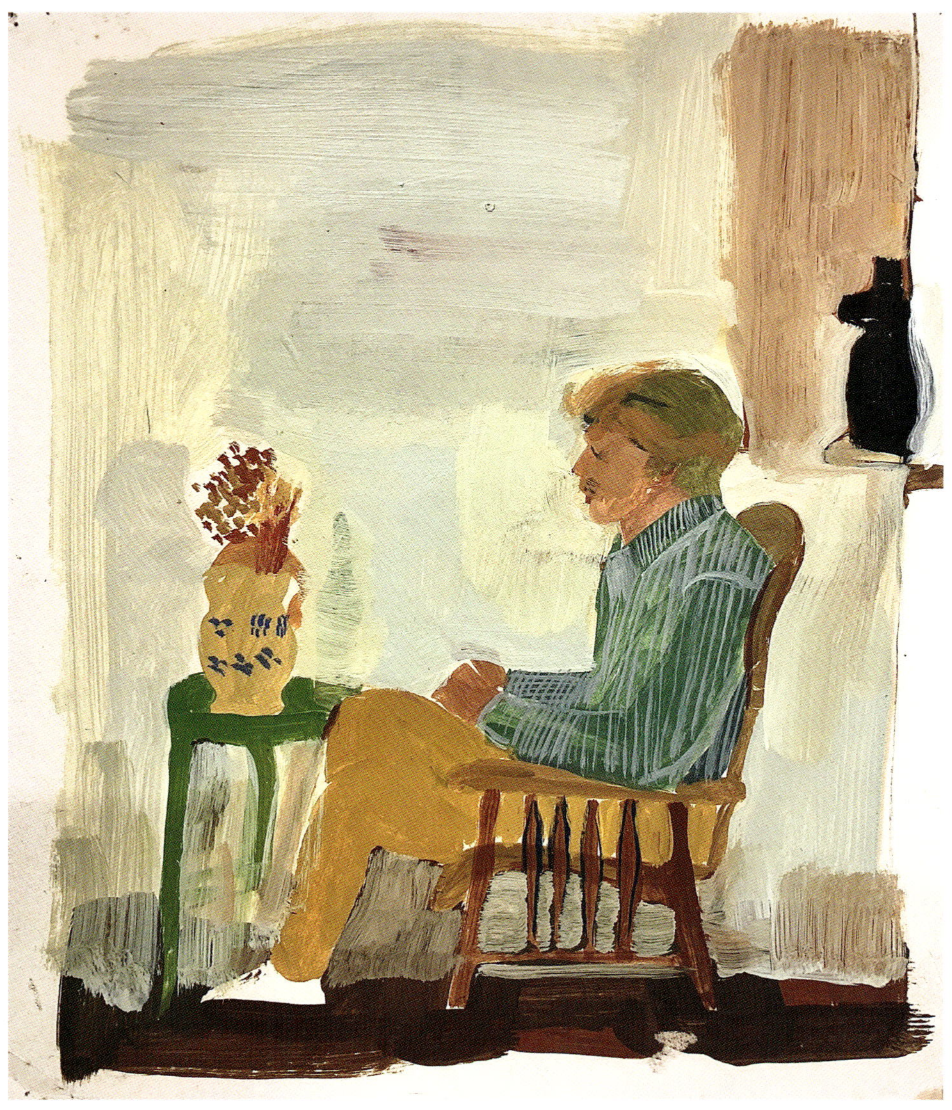

exhibition in June at the recently opened Great Expectations Gallery.[36] Included was a series based on family snapshots from her mother's photo album of women and children in vintage clothing and hats (Cat. 5). In the review she was quoted as saying: "It's not just that these pictures are old—I love the shape of these clothes. Miniskirts aren't fun to do. I always liked those hats that Grandmother made for Mother, and those puff sleeves on the dresses." She also exhibited "sparkling, light-hearted bouquets in her floral paintings." Her interest in costumes and florals would very soon be transformed into a new body of work.

While experimenting with painting, Sims also developed her hands-off teaching style. She recounted, "I was not a good teacher at all. I had so many teachers with preaching messages that I went in the opposite direction. The great teachers are the ones who suck you further in and then say now you're on your own."[37] Despite her concerns, her students revered her. Valerie Berlin, who signed up for printmaking as a freshman in 1970, characterized Sims as:

> the most unteacherlike teacher. When I first walked in, she had on a paint spattered apron that had sleeves and tied in front. She was smoking and had her feet on the table. . . . She taught the techniques of printmaking, informed students about materials and how to use them, and let us do our thing. She was unorthodox and would find something good in whatever anyone did.[38]

Essentially, Sims the teacher would be recognizable to anyone who knew her before or after her stint in the classroom—vibrant, colorful, mesmerizing, and usually with cigarette in hand.

Along with sculptor Lon Anthony (b. 1934), painter Carroll Cloar (1913–1993), and painter and printmaker Ted Faiers, in the fall of 1968 Sims was included in an exhibition at the Great Expectations gallery. Her self-portrait at work in her studio (Cat. 6) was singled out in the review.[39] The large canvas is bisected by a wall that cuts the room in half, and along which the right edge of her painting rests, creating a shallow space on the left. Seen from behind, she works on a large landscape, which is ironic given how few she produced over her career. On the right, the deeper side of the room encompasses old-fashioned rockers, a wicker couch, and some of her artworks hanging on the wall; the one to the left looks like one of her rare Italian landscapes. The whole back wall disintegrates from a blue wash to blue drips that peter out before reaching the floor, while other areas are covered with more thickly applied pigment. The painting—a view of an artist at work on her craft in a tightly organized, but homely space—is arresting. One can imagine sitting on a rocker, periodically checking on her progress.

Discussing her post-Iowa trajectory in a 1973 exhibition catalogue, Sims recounted her efforts to escape her facility in drawing:

> In the line things I had it to a high grade of slickness. The actual worth of it might have been fairly small but they were really slick and prissy looking. So what I had to do was actually break down every polished, finished thing I had . . . sort of like if you had a cut on your leg and the surface healed over before it was healed inside and you'd have to break it open and make it look all nasty again and let it heal from the bottom up. Well, I had to toss off that little surface talent I had and start all over again.[40]

The essay analyzed her time in Italy making "ugly" things for eight to ten hours a day, attempting to break free of lines. It continued through her studies at Tulane. By the time she returned to Memphis in the late sixties, she was painting loosely, and "trying to understand all that I would eventually want to leave out of my work." She continued:

One summer day (about 1969) I was still working in this liquid, juicy line, and not really liking it much but slogging along. I picked up a stick of charcoal and started to draw on the canvas, and felt like. . . screw it, I've had it. I've done this apprenticeship and now I'm going to start on what I really think I am seeing. And it was just probably the high point of my whole life.[41]

This was the beginning of what would become Sims's personal style, which was not surprisingly based on her printmaking. In an application for a grant in 1980, she detailed that process:

[M]y painting technique is a simulation of the printing process. . . . [T]he first stage of my work is to complete a charcoal under-drawing with charcoal shading. The under-drawing approximates etching a copper plate, as the shading does aquatint. After making the charcoal permanent with a fixative, I then "run on" color much the same as a printing press—yellow followed by blues, getting greens from the overlays. Smaller areas requiring more "solid color" are "hand painted" like a print. Basically, my technique is printmaking without the conventional printmaker's tools. My style of painting is my own. . . .[42]

The actual date of the transition is most likely late 1968 for, by March 1969, her solo exhibition at Southwestern included examples that reveal the beginning of the trajectory towards her signature style. Besides a shift from oils to acrylics, the canvases featured life-size (or close to) figure/s sketched in charcoal, washed over with a thinned coat of raw umber, with the flat background completed last. Her practice of finishing the grounds last was both unusual (most often such flat areas would be done first) and painstaking as it required essentially outlining all the objects. Although not enormously challenging in these early works, her technique became extraordinarily complicated as the paintings grew increasingly complex.

This new style is exemplified by her self-portrait *For Cynthia* (Cat. 7). Sims sits in a chair in a three-quarter view with a vase of dried stems on the tile floor. Her turquoise dress is thinly painted, with the weave of the canvas readily visible through the wash. Despite the dark, flat ground, her tan face, hands, and the plants pop off the surface, creating the illusion of depth. While the image might appear simple, it requires skill to achieve such a harmonious result. Painter Veda Reed (1934–2025), a professor at the Memphis Academy of Arts, summed up one of the important elements of Sims's work, "I have always thought that Mary was a genius at organizing the flat surface space in composition. She never put anything that was superfluous to what she was trying to do and never left out anything that was essential."[43]

Although hung in the hallway of the science building, the Southwestern exhibition was substantial enough to receive a positive review in the *Commercial Appeal* and for *For Cynthia* to be reproduced.[44] Among the other works were portraits, florals, and windows (Cat. 8). The reviewer rightly noted, "Most of the surfaces are flat. Blank, if you like. Shading there is, and a touch of shadow. That matters less than the intensity of the subject. Being autobiographical, Miss Sims peels away

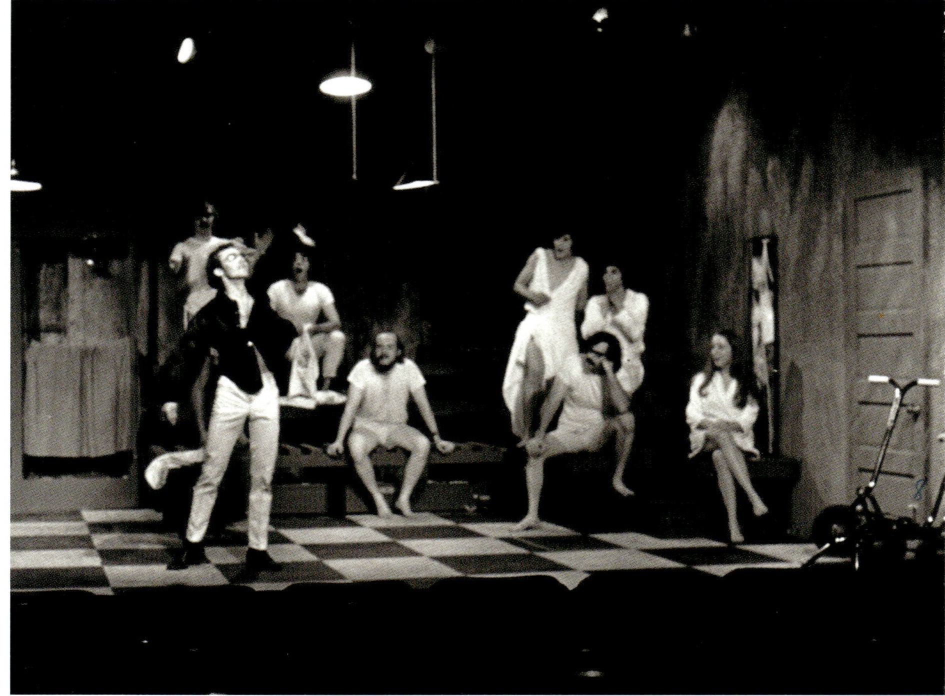

her own skin, and that of her husband (a favorite subject), to look into the minds of two people. The artistic rhetoric, the introspective use of line and color, are as cinematic as the modern movie camera—but the artist has more control."[45] That fall, in a *Memphis Press-Scimitar* article, Sims mused on her work:

> With my attraction to reality, as long as my eyes are open there are all sorts of things nagging at me to paint. It's really like an itch that has to be scratched.... I was always interested in the figure and thought of everything else as what was left. I guess heads are what excites me most. The canvases are getting bigger because I'm working with life-sized people. . . . Then I want them to have as many feet of space around them as possible. I really love space. It's emotional. . . . I think I'm completely an unintellectual painter. The whole thing has got to be visual. It should fail or succeed just visually. [46]

The piece ended with her thoughts about her spring show at Southwestern:

> I walked up and down the hall and just about vomited. They were so far below what I thought they would be. I went home in great depression. Then later I decided if they had been very, very good, it would have been scary. I wouldn't have had a good starting point. In a way it was sort of cheery – a very happy feeling that I would never be satisfied until I die.

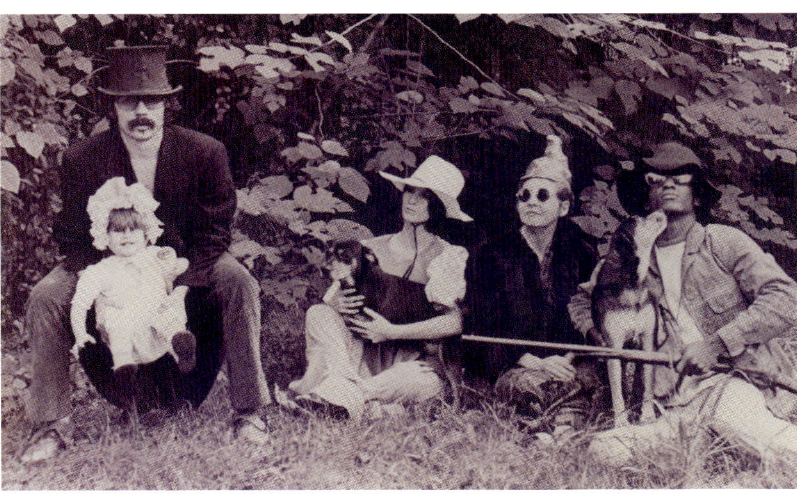

Ted Radakovic holding Emma,
Mary Sims, Gayle Sims, and actor
Larry Riley, ca. 1970.
Collection of Emma Earngey

Fig. 9
Mary Sims exhibition catalogue,
published by the Brooks Memorial
Art Gallery, 1970. Cover Page:
Mary Sims, *The Woman*, cat. no. 5.
Memphis Brooks Museum of Art

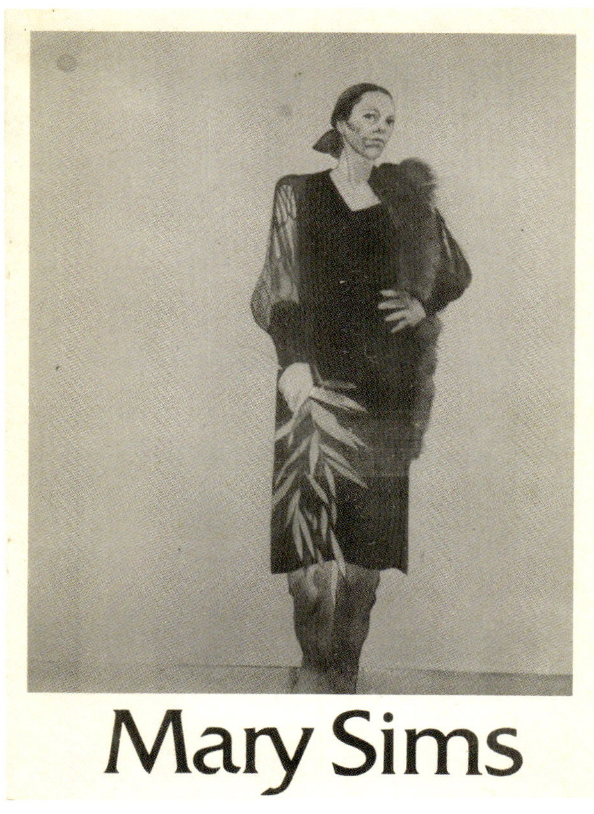

Besides talking about her art, a pregnant Sims noted her baby was due in a month. Soon after daughter Emma's birth the family moved into a craftsman bungalow on Tucker Avenue, across from Overton Park in Memphis' artistic Midtown neighborhood. The house, next door to Circuit Playhouse, was a mecca for artists and theater people. In 1971, Radakovic directed Bruce Jay Friedman's avant-garde play *Steambath* for Circuit, and Sims was tapped to design the costumes (Fig. 7).[47] The off-off-Broadway play, which took place in a steam bath that was revealed to be purgatory, was notable for its language, partial nudity, and bizarre concept, which clearly appealed to both Radakovic and Sims (Fig. 8).

In September of 1969, Sims wrote to Robert McKnight, the director of the Brooks Memorial Art Gallery. She reminded him that when she was forced to turn down his exhibition offer in 1967, he suggested a future date might be possible.[48] The result was an April 1970 solo exhibition, although it was in a lounge rather than in the main galleries. A brochure was printed with several of the eighteen canvases reproduced (Fig. 9).[49] Also notable was that half the works were on loan from private collectors, and most of the rest sold by the time the exhibition closed.[50] In an interview, Sims asserted that she had always painted people and flowers, but "[i]t never occurred to anybody to ask me if I did portraits until last year."[51] At which point, the requests started to flow in.

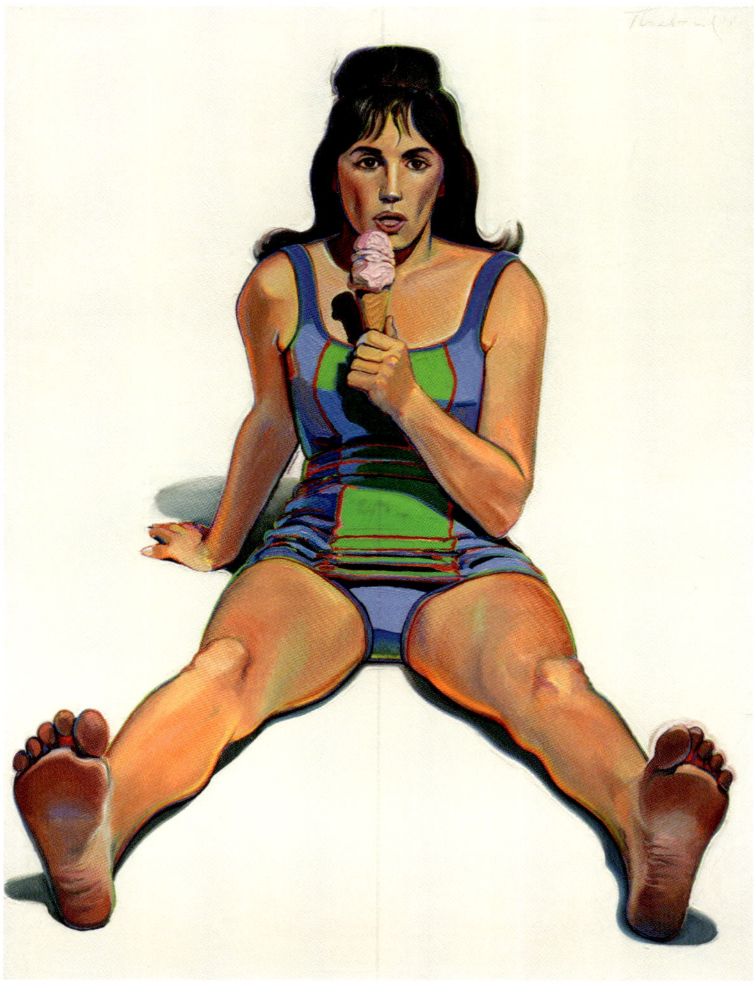

Fig. 10
Wayne Thiebaud (American, 1930–2021)
Girl with Ice Cream Cone, 1963
Oil on canvas, 48 ⅛ × 36 ¼ in.
Hirshhorn Museum and Sculpture Garden,
Joseph H. Hirshhorn Bequest Fund,
Smithsonian Collections Acquisition
Program, and Museum purchase, 1996

As well as three florals, the exhibition included portraits of a pregnant Sims, *Emma and Me* (Cat. 10), and of Radakovic, *The Beggared Outcast* (Cat. 9). The foreword was written by her department chair and friend, Lon Anthony:

For the past year Mary Sims' painting has dealt primarily with the portrait. Portrait as painting, not portrait as flattering near likeness or as detached objective record. Likeness serves her. It is the stimulus to painting but it is the painting itself that is of ultimate concern. Drama frequently results. It is the drama of the visual event; color, tone, the spatial ambiguities of her reduction of these dimensional cues to the two-dimensional reality of the canvas without losing a sense of the palpable.

Guy Northrop's review in the *Commercial Appeal* was laudatory, noting that "The subject is presented as a role player within his particular environment. . . . They

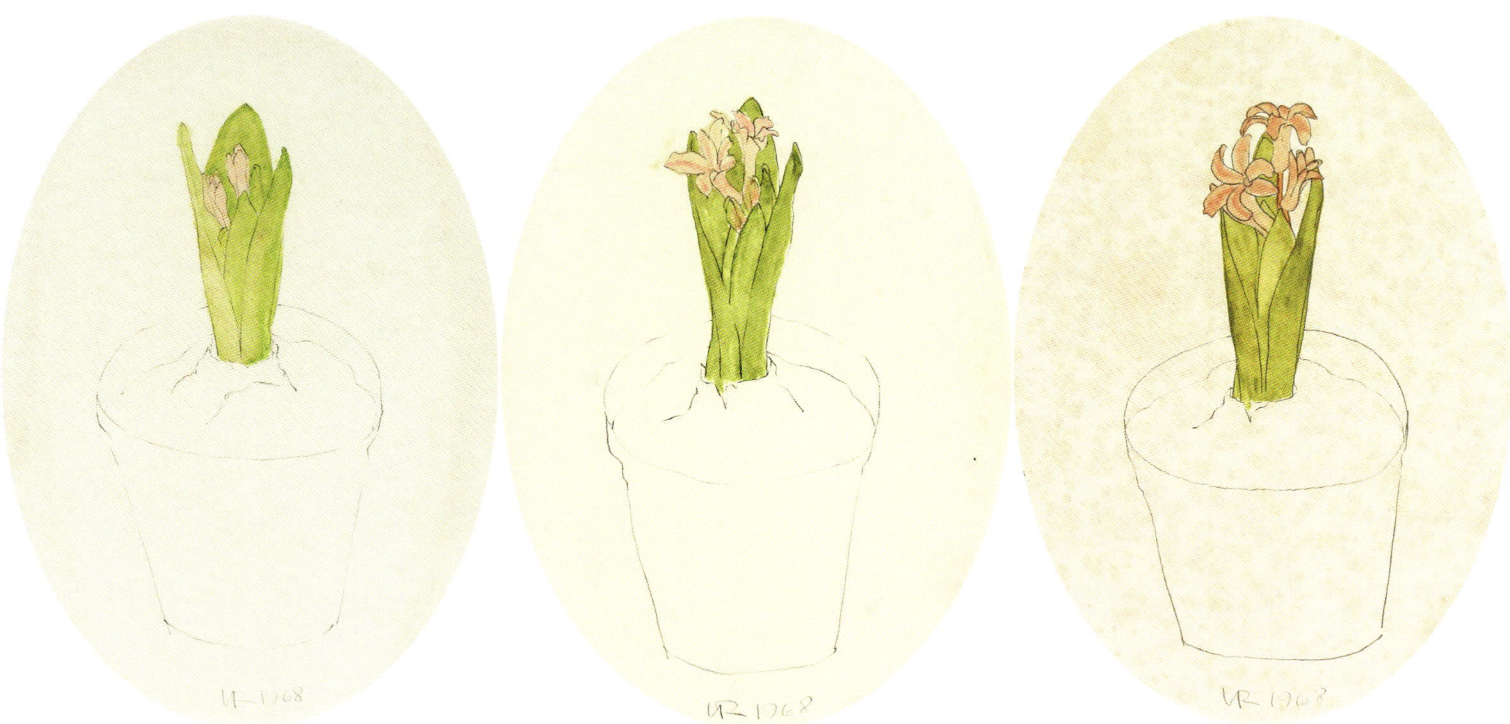

Fig. 11
Veda Reed (American,
1934–2025)
November Flowers, 1968
Graphite and colored pencil
on paper, 10 ½ × 22 ½ in.
Estate of Veda Reed

have style, meaning and are most of all enjoyable whether you know the subject of each scene."[52] He was right that the paintings were appealing whether or not you knew the sitter and also about the importance of role playing. Sims's delight in costumes (hats, clothes) and props (furniture, floral arrangements) transforms the portraits into something closer to theater. Given her early work with Memphis' Front Street Theatre and classes in costume design, these significant characteristics were not unexpected. Nor was it strange that viewers delighted (and still delight) in the colors, textures, and patterns used to define the sitter, as evidenced by Sims's luxurious floral kimono, and Radakovic's shirt decorated with clouds. She and her cast of family and friends are portrayed on flat surfaces that serve to focus the attention firmly on the sitters, who were part of her buoyant and intellectually stimulating life.

Sims was not alone in setting her figures against a monochromatic background. Wayne Thiebaud (1920–2021) produced Pop Art portraits on a white ground in his signature acid-colored, painterly style, a prime example being *Girl with Ice Cream Cone* (1963, Fig. 10). Veda Reed was known for her series of clouds and skies, but she too composed florals on a stark ground, as evidenced by *November Flowers* (1968, Fig. 11). In treatment and tone, Sims's canvases mostly share an affinity with the work of Philadelphia artist Barkley Hendricks (1945–2017). There is nothing to suggest that Sims knew his work; however, in the 1960s, he too began depicting single figures against monochromatic grounds such as *My Black Nun* (1964).[53] He is much better

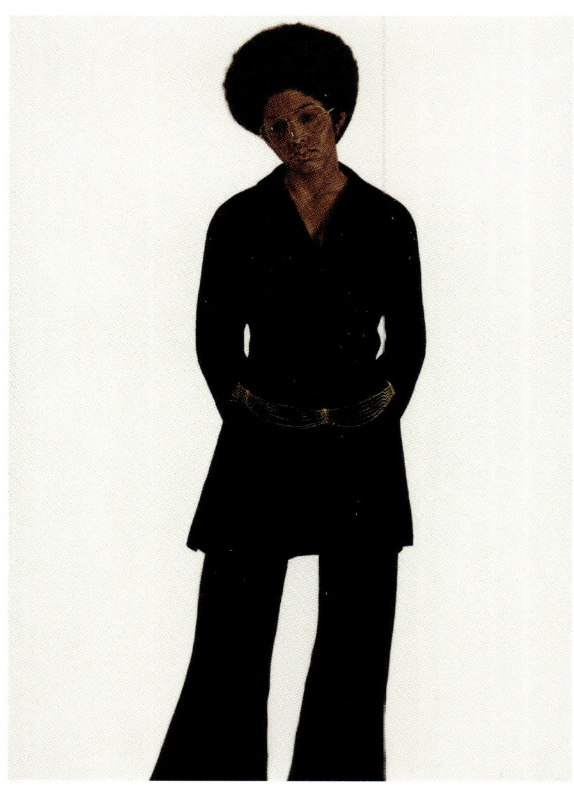

known for later portraits including *Miss T* (1969, Fig. 12), where the figure is placed on a solid ground—often white, although bright colors are also common. The poses, clothes, jewelry, and hats function as important elements in capturing the personalities of his urban Black sitters and as statements of Black pride. None of the above is to suggest that Sims was borrowing from these artists, rather to point out that, as often happens, artists develop similar interests and strategies. In Sims's case, her highly personal method of constructing her images separates her from these other artists, even though the focus on the subject against a plain background unites them. The work of Lasansky, her former teacher, may similarly have provided inspiration. Although many of his prints were complex figural compositions, he completed a series of simple portraits beginning in the 1950s, such as *Self-Portrait* (Fig. 13).

In February of 1972, Sims was in a three-person exhibition with her colleagues Lon Anthony and Biff Elrod (b. 1946) at the Clough-Hanson Gallery at Southwestern at Memphis (Fig. 14). Northrop's review in the *Commercial Appeal* remarked on the amusing nature of some of the works: Robert Gooch in a tree with his son, Jim West on a ladder, and a blue Audrey West (who would later write about Sims) representing the blue moon (Cat. 14).[54]

With an increasing number of sales and a desire to focus on her painting, Sims resigned from Southwestern in the spring of 1972.[55] Among the people who championed her art was John Simmons (1932–2021), who opened more than forty

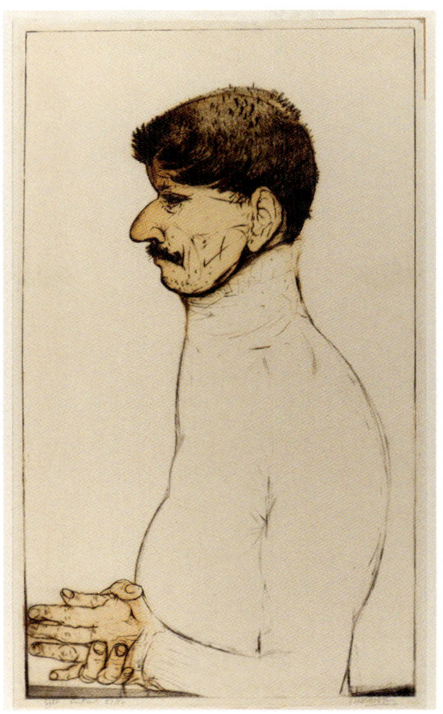

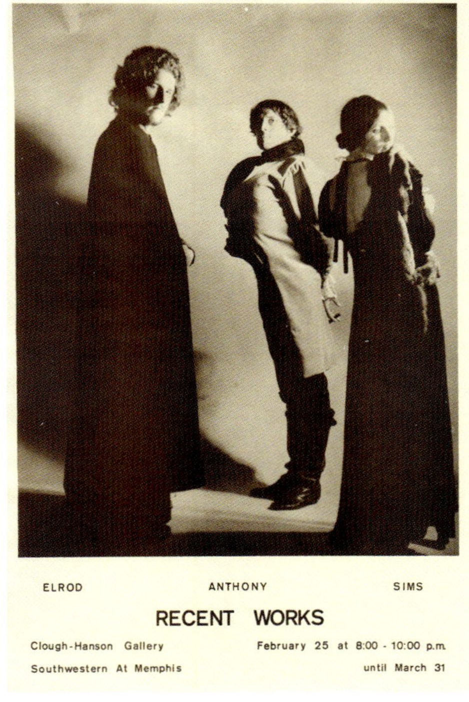

eponymous gift and home accessory franchises across the country. In Memphis, the Sycamore was one of his stores and one of her major outlets. Although a gift shop, the store mounted art exhibitions, and the opening receptions—which were announced in the newspapers as well as through invitations—were well-attended events at which her paintings sold briskly. Initially, Frances Cianciolo, who managed the shop, functioned as Sims's agent, lining up and managing portrait commissions. Usually, Cianciolo was paid in unsold artworks, the "weird ones," which she loved.[56]

Clients were told that they would pay half of the fee up front and the second half upon completion. It was stipulated that if they were unhappy with the result they would not pay the second half, but Sims was adamant about not making any changes when she deemed the work finished. Cianciolo marveled that "strangely enough reverse psychology made people want them more," and only remembered one instance of a couple refusing theirs, claiming they looked like monkeys. Sims's solution to the predicament was to complete a painting of monkeys, which the couple adored and paid for. She subsequently instructed Cianciolo to tell people "that even if they didn't like [the finished work], they would have a fabulous painting that didn't look like a Breck shampoo ad."[57]

Sims became the sought-after artist for the culturally adventuresome people of Memphis (Fig. 15). Regardless of who they were, she would either dress them up at her studio or at their homes with outfits pulled from her trunk or their closets. As Peter Casparian, one of her students, recounted:

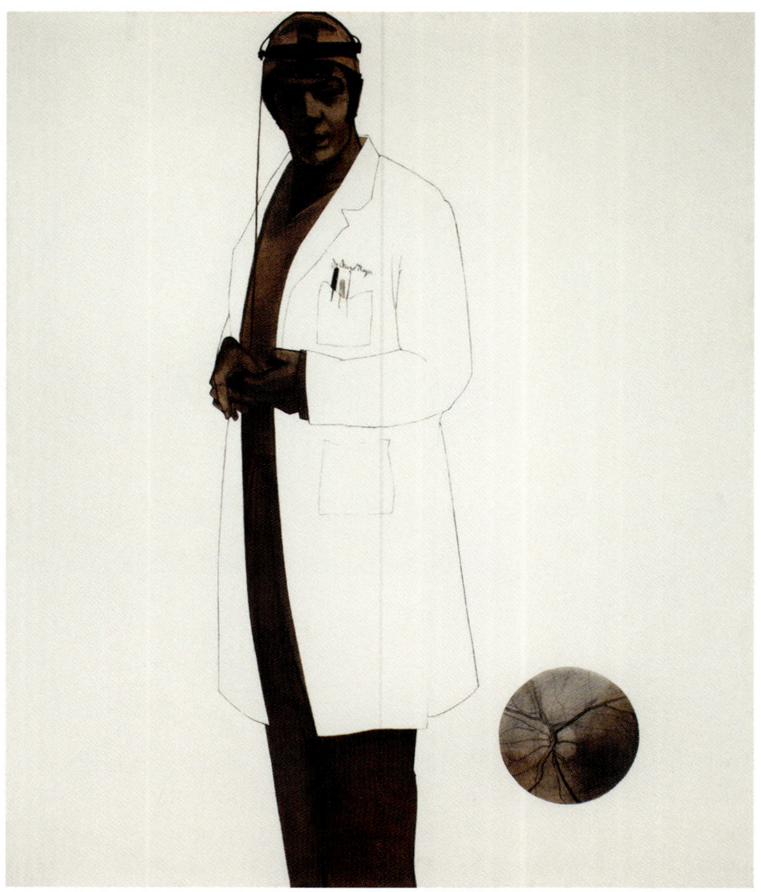

She had a 20-to-30-minute dress up session pulling outfits from her big costume box, and then took a picture. In my portrait she put a sort of night gown tunic over my head, draped doilies around my neck, and had me sit on an old trunk in a quasi-lotus position. So it was sort of whimsical. But she did that to all those fancy East Memphis people, she made them dress up too. It took a certain kind of East Memphis wealthy person to buy her whimsical paintings in the first place, instead of the staid, old south portraits; she was obviously not doing those things [Cat. 20].[58]

She was also completing still lifes that followed the same trajectory as the portraits, becoming flatter and sparer. Which is not to say that they are not mesmerizing in their own right, the stark backgrounds highlighting the simple, elegant compositions (Cat. 16).

For her solo exhibition at the Arkansas State University Art Gallery in the fall of 1973, more than half of the twenty-three paintings were from private collections. They dated from 1970 to 1973 and included portraits, many of children, and bare trees. She started the latter in January, when they were denuded of leaves, believing

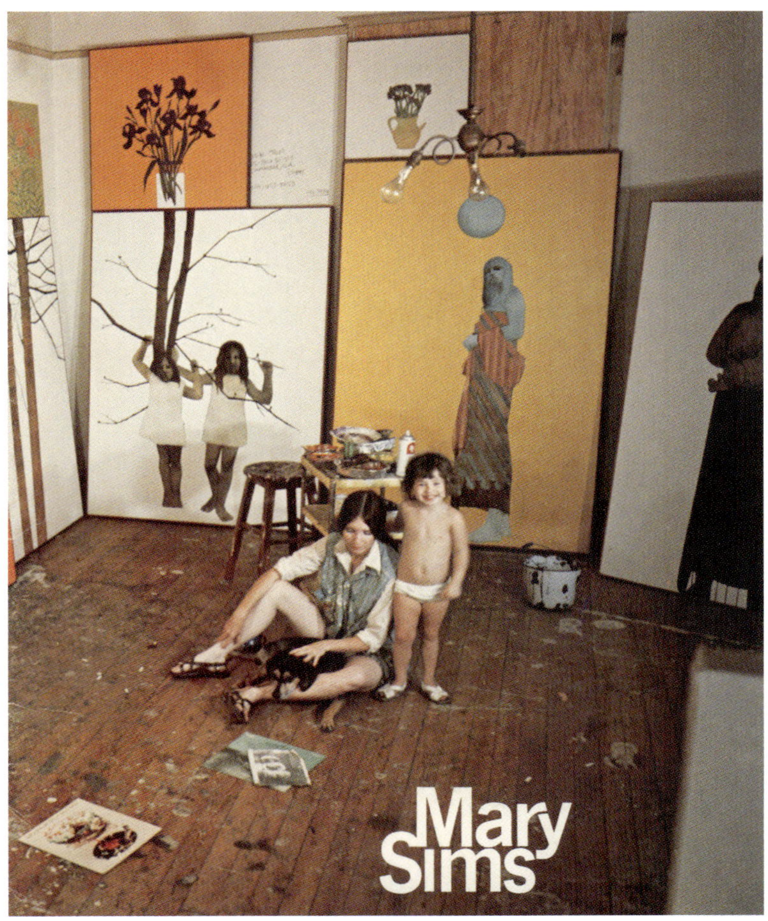

that this was the best way to study them.[59] As with her portraits, she began with the figure, in this case the tree's trunk and branches, finishing the flat ground last. The cover of the exhibition catalogue, a photograph of Sims and Emma in the studio, was carefully staged: the many artworks to substantiate that she was a successful artist; Emma to highlight her motherhood; the music she listened to captured in the Rolling Stones and Bach album covers on the floor; and her whole body in the image to show that she still had great legs (Fig. 16).[60]

In contrast with her professional success, her personal life was in a state of upheaval. Her marriage to Radakovic unraveled in early 1973. Later that year, she met Bill Earngey, the last and best of her love stories. A former marine helicopter pilot, Earngey was trying to decide on a career move.[61] The move he made was into Sims's life; they were married in 1974, with Sims wearing a tablecloth as a veil.[62]

In a *Commercial Appeal* review of her May 1974 Sycamore exhibition, Northrop gleefully reported on a "full-length portrait of a man in frayed shorts. . . . How'd she find the subject? He happened to be the man who installed her gaudy and campy ceiling fan in her blue living room. It was while he was up on a stool doing that

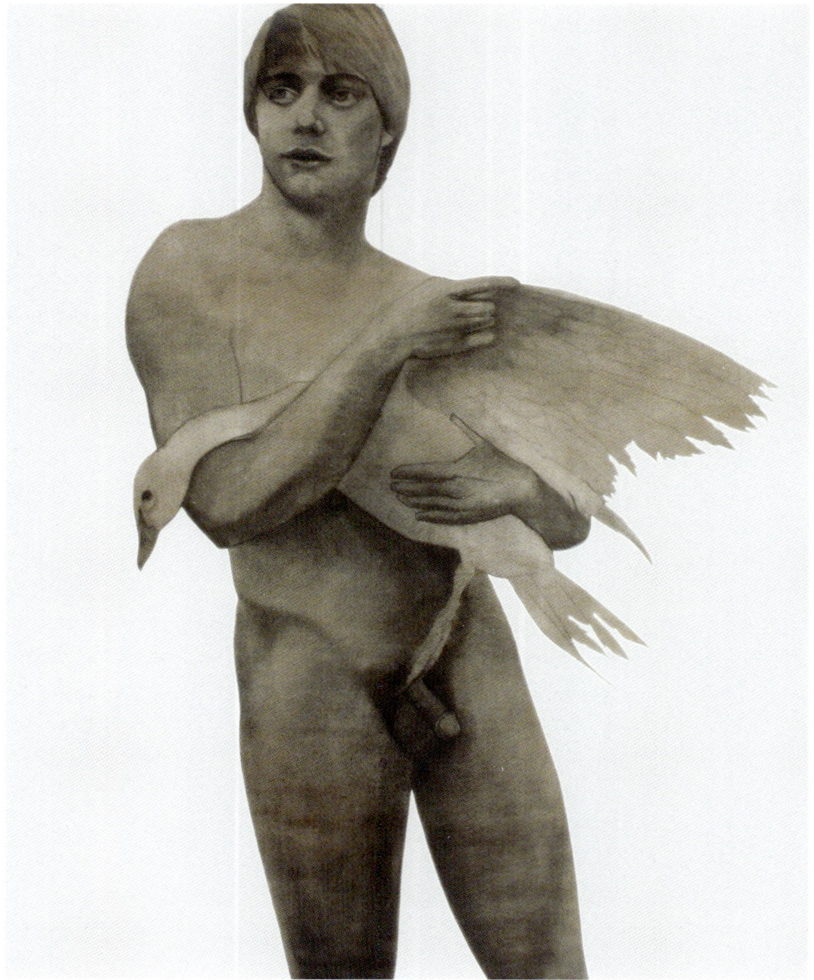

task that she decided he ought to be in pictures. That's the way it is in a Mary Sims show. The subjects are often just the everyday things (or people) you find around the house"[63] (Cat. 17). He also highlighted a recent exhibition in Los Angeles and her sales to such high-profile clients as actor Mary Tyler Moore. In a *Memphis Press-Scimitar* article ostensibly about the exhibition, Audrey West observed some shifts in Sims's personal life that predicted a bigger transformation. West noted Sims's changing fashion sense, describing a move away from wearing "attic-salvaged, granny's fashions that emphasized her demure and helpless appeal."[64] Sims stated:

> The older you get the more you have to pare your life down. I tired of wearing costumes because it became the issue of the evening when I went out. I also tired of trying to be a gourmet cook, so I narrowed that down to two main specialties. One I call "noblesse oblige chili" (just put it in the pot and hope

it obliges you by turning out). The other is black beans, Feta cheese, Greek olives and salami.

Soon Sims determined their social life in Memphis too distracting; in 1975 the family moved to Warrenton, Georgia.

She nonetheless continued to exhibit successfully in Memphis, beginning with a May show at the Sycamore. A laudatory Northrop article in the *Commercial Appeal* characterized it as a homecoming for Sims. He discussed the array of "unusual figure paintings" and florals before describing *Boy with Duck* and *David* (Fig. 17) as "classically conceived"; they were likely the first nudes Sims exhibited, although they were not her first efforts. Overall, the images are spare, elegant, and haunting.[65]

That fall, she had an even bigger triumph. Cianciolo queried Downing Pryor, chairman of the Brooks Memorial Art Gallery's exhibitions committee, as to why the museum only showed the works of Carroll Cloar, when there were many other regional artists, such as Sims, who were deserving of attention.[66] Pryor conceded, and Sims received a letter from Brooks director John Whitaker inviting her to exhibit, noting that additional paintings could be borrowed if she did not have enough on hand.[67] Significantly, this time the canvases would be on view in the Main Hall. She sent a list of objects for the exhibition and said any questions might be answered by her "Memphis agent, Mrs. Frank (Frances) Cianciolo."[68] She also wanted to suggest that watermelon "stuffed with gin" would be great for the opening. In keeping with the festive nature of the paintings, the sitters, including the Memphis artist Dolph Smith (b. 1933) and his wife Jessie (1935–2020, Cat. 18), attended the opening reception in the outfits in which they were depicted.[69] The exhibition, which ran from November 1 through 30, comprised twenty-one works. Included was *Snow White and Rose Red* (Cat. 15), the title of which refers to a Brothers Grimm fairytale.

Her move to Warrenton provided a quiet space in which to work; and work she did. In May of 1976 she had an exhibition at the Sycamore that was primarily paintings based on photographs she had taken on a previous summer trip to Mexico. Northrop wrote positively about the exhibition, noting the many florals and birds, as well as the shift from portraits of people of means to people of few means.[70] *Drop Dead Chic* (Cat. 22), which captured the sitter dressed in Arab costume and riding on an ostrich, was included along with *The Patchwork Kid* (illustrated in the review), *Laughing Woman*, an aging Indian woman, and *Virgin Guadalupe* (Cat. 25).

Recognized internationally, the apocryphal account of the Virgin of Guadalupe is that she appeared to the peasant Juan Diego on a hillside outside of Mexico City saying that she wanted a church erected in her name on the site. To prove the miraculous apparition to the archbishop, Diego unrolled a cloak filled with flowers that tumbled to the floor revealing the iconic image of the Black Virgin standing on a crescent moon, surrounded by a mandorla of heavenly light, angels, and flowers. Although Sims followed most of these conventions, the canvas is clearly hers. The yellow flames of the mandorla have been transformed into a blue that complements the various shades of the Virgin's gown and cloak. She stands on a sliver

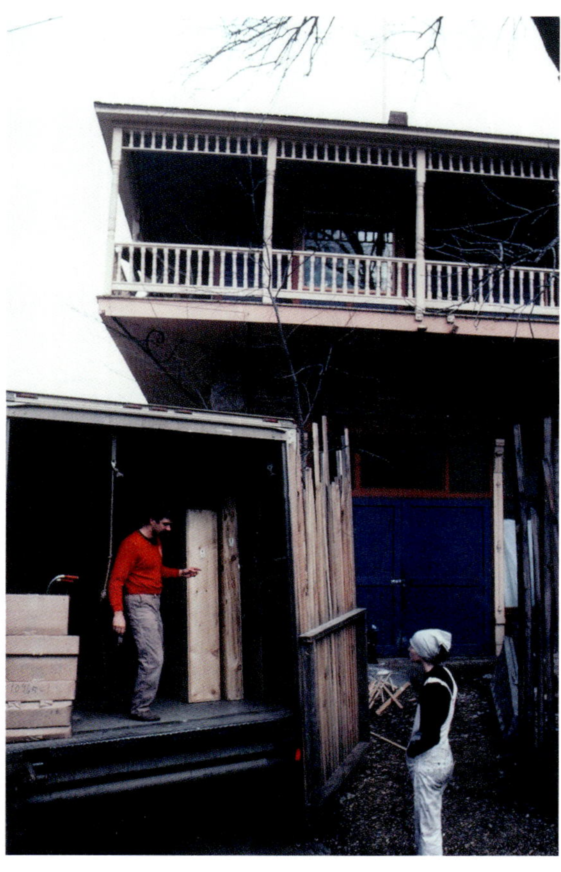

of moon behind several pots of yellow and burgundy flowers that harmonize with the limited palette. In a shift from Sims's normal process, she first washed the ground with a mottled brown and then built the rest of the image on top. This is apparent in the polka-dotted areas of the Virgin's cloak where the variations in the brown pigment are still visible. Hewing to tradition, Sims further darkened Mary's face and hands. The painting reverently reexamines this long-established symbol of Mexican identity.

Eureka in Eureka Springs, 1977–2004

After only a year and a half, in which they found Warrenton unwelcoming and too much of a small town, the Earngeys decamped to Eureka Springs, Arkansas. The springs were among the many that spawned nineteenth-century spa towns by capitalizing on the claims of health benefits.[71] The city underwent a decline during the Depression and then by mid-century began a renaissance. Attracted by the low cost of real estate, artists and hippies arrived, opening craft shops and antique stores that appealed to visitors. Eleanor Lux, a childhood friend who moved

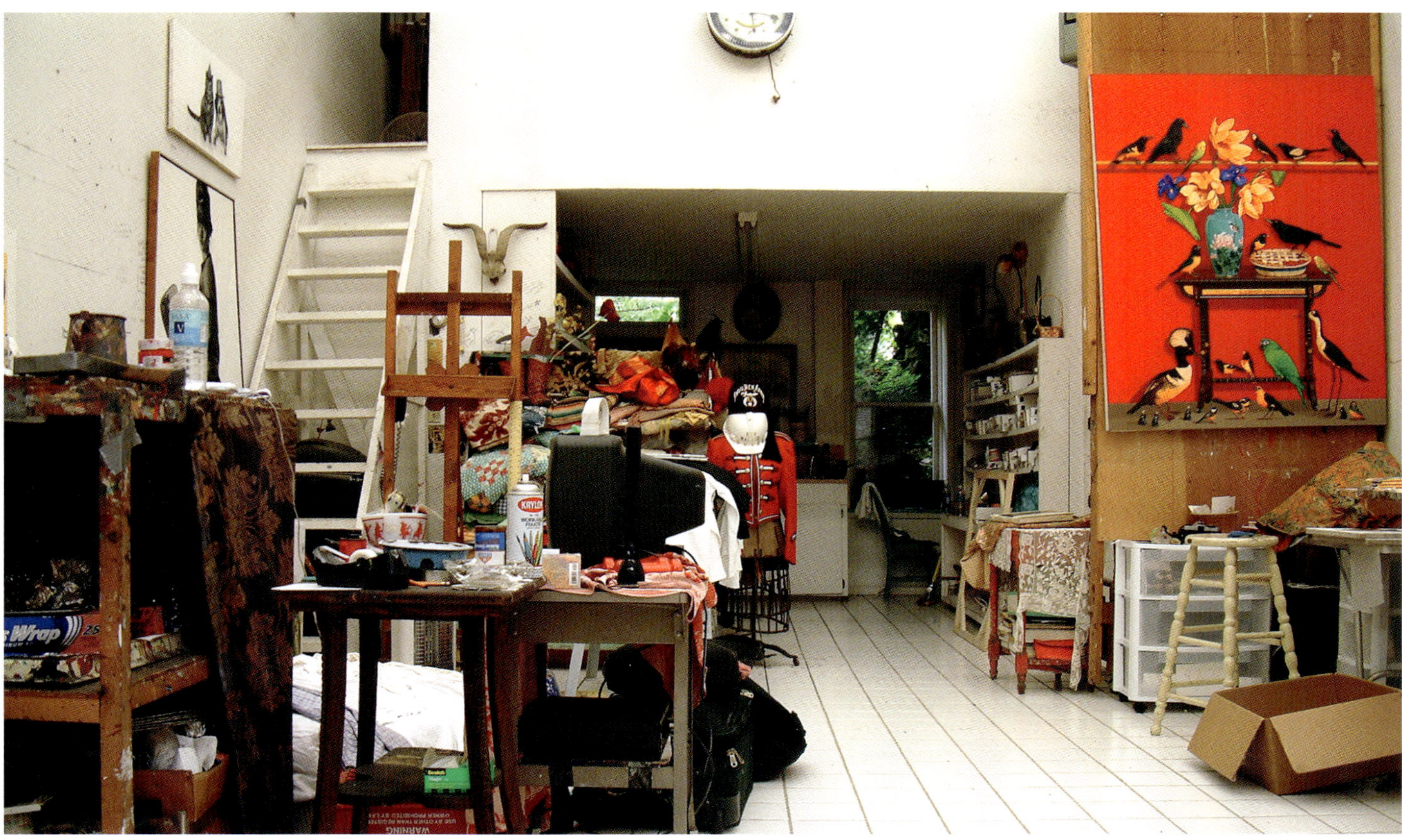

to Eureka Springs in the early 1970s, had introduced Sims to the benefits of the community during a 1973 visit. What she found was not only affordable real estate, but also a beautiful mountainous landscape, a convivial group of like-minded creatives, and a peaceful environment in which to work.

The Earngeys bought a Victorian house that straddled a hillside with the bottom floor providing Sims with a cavernous, open studio space (Figs. 18 and 19). Above, the house and garden became a set designed to accommodate her life with her family, dogs, and friends. It was loaded with ephemera, toys, kitschy objects, plants, and other things that often appeared in her paintings. According to reporter Donald La Badie, "the whole environment has the air of a place in which children have banished the adults and realized their dream of a secret playhouse. That is to exclude the studio. . . . Here, Mary Sims can be found seven days a week."[72]

The Memphis Jewish Community Center approached Sims in 1977 about undertaking a series of paintings derived from the Bible.

They asked what would be religious to me, and I realized if I answered that Vermeer would be religious to me, there would be no common ground. My interest was visual. And I didn't want to illustrate the Bible; I intended to use it, not

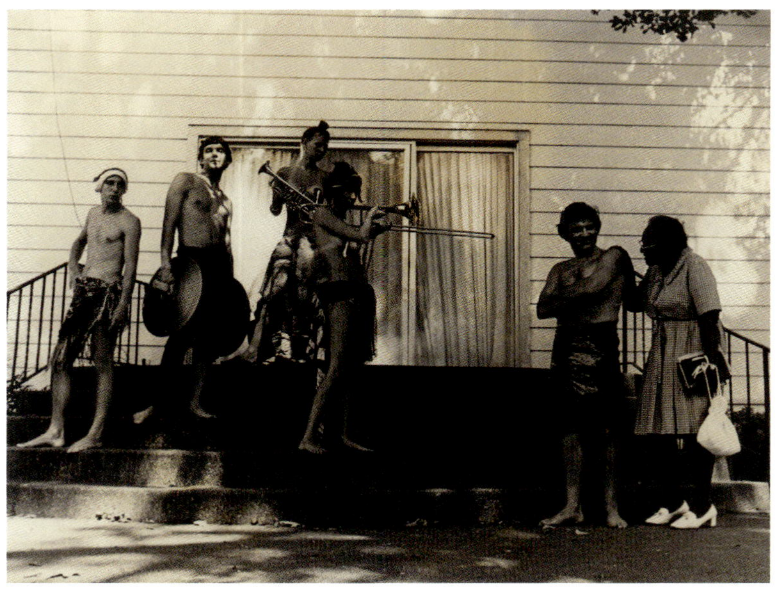

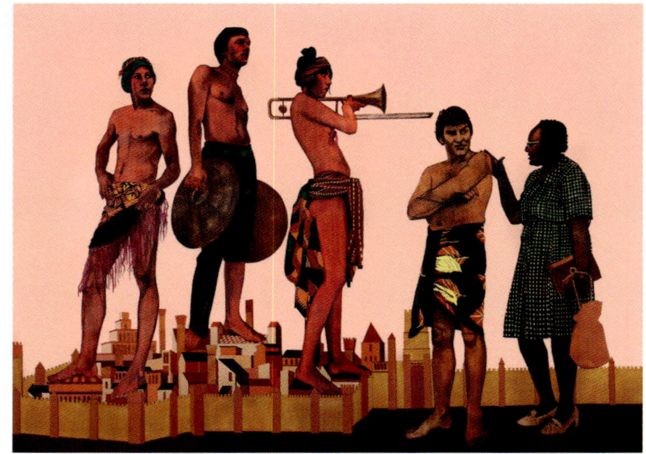

to serve it. I'd always been preoccupied with the real world, and now I wanted a fantasy world of my own. Actually, I think when they finally saw the work they were delighted they hadn't done business with me.[73]

The first three she completed for herself were *A Bride for Hosea* (Cat. 29), *Elijah and Jezebel*, and *Ain't Misbehavin'*, which she exhibited in January of 1978 at Grace St. Luke's Episcopal Church in Memphis. She chronicled the experience with a trace of humor: "I was asked dramatic questions, like 'Why is Elijah wearing jockey shorts?' and 'Why doesn't Job look more frightened if the end of the world is approaching?'"

She accurately characterized herself as having planned like Cecil B. DeMille, the director of such film spectacles as *The Ten Commandments* (1956). "I cast all the roles with people I knew. The paintings were all meant to look like tableaus, not at all like things observed by an unseen watcher. Obviously, everybody was posing." After she orchestrated the elaborate sets with fantastical costumes and unusual props, she shot photographs from which she produced her theatrical extravaganza (Fig. 20).

Although Sims captured many of the salient elements of the scriptural account of Hosea, she transformed many others. Zuma Jones, who was housekeeper for Sims's parents, inspired the series through the biblical stories she told from a Black feminist point of view.[74] Jones, who would appear in several of the other biblical paintings, was cast in *A Bride for Hosea* as the Angel of the Lord. The traditionally male angel is transformed by Sims not just into a woman, but into a middle-aged Black woman, who arrives to tell a white Hosea: "Go, marry a promiscuous woman and have children with her, for like an adulterous wife this land is guilty of unfaithfulness

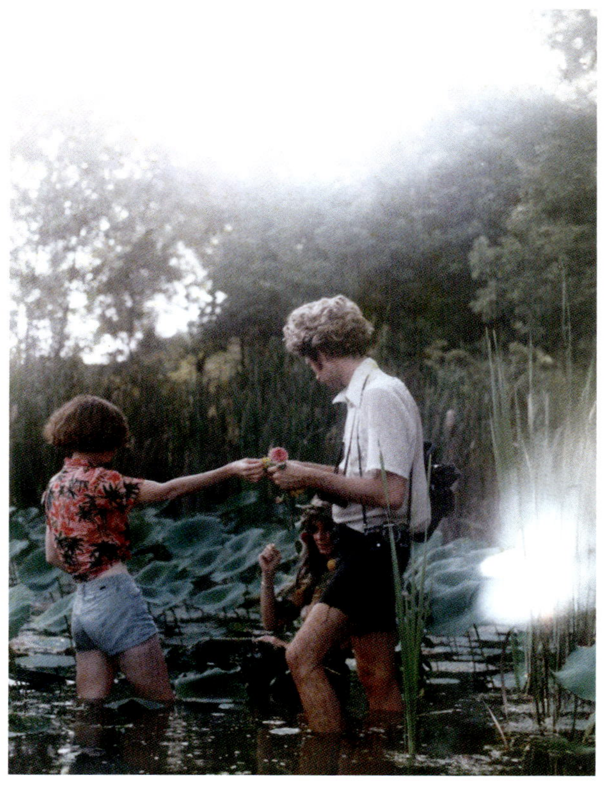

to the Lord."[75] The central woman in *A Bride for Hosea* and the two men to the left represent the three children Hosea had with his wife.

Taking further artistic license with the figures' attire, Sims presents the angel dressed in the conservative clothes of a 1978 housewife—plaid dress, glasses, and sensible shoes—in contrast to the exotic, colorful, and sparse fabrics that barely cover the rest of the figures. Even though the textiles may initially appear closer to historical accuracy, they too suggest contemporary origins—for instance, the print on Hosea's sarong looks like a Hawaiian fabric, and the boy on the far left is draped in a fringed shawl. Incongruously, the woman is about to play a trombone and the man behind her holds cymbals. They stand atop a miniature simulacrum of a walled Italian Renaissance town that serves as their stage. The background, simplified to place all the focus on the figures, is a pale pink that both sets off and complements the colors of the skin, town, and textiles. The image is tied together through the repetition of the turquoise in the clothes of all the figures. The result is both complex and easy to read, tells a story but does not depend upon the story for its success, and actively engages viewers in decoding what exactly is going on.

In a May 1978 exhibition at the Sycamore, Sims unveiled an additional Old Testament painting as well as a series of lyrical and tranquil water lilies. She confided in a 1979 interview that she was afraid when she arrived in Eureka Springs that she had gone as far as she could go.[76] Instead, she decided to focus on flowers and found inspiration at Lake Leatherwood, a peaceful body of water not too far from her home (Fig. 21). Once more, she worked from photographs in creating the large canvases filled with lovely plants floating across the water and over the edges. *Untitled (Lake Leatherwood)* (Cat. 37) is representative of the series she worked on for many years. The surface is highly detailed, sharply focused, and presents a view of the life cycle of the lilies from the upright dark green leaves to the collapsing yellow and red fronds, which appear to dance across the surface. The image begins simply with the silvery, still water in the foreground. Moving back into space, it becomes increasingly complex through the thickening plants along with their shadows and reflections. She had surprised even herself, "Can you believe that perspective and light didn't even interest me until two years ago?"[77]

The water lilies sold well; the biblical series did not because they were, according to Sims, "suicidal designs, too big, religious, and with nudes."[78] She stated that besides being art for art's sake paintings, they suggested that God, as well as man, can laugh. "The ideal buyer was someone with money, a big wall, a healthy knowledge of the Bible and an equally healthy sense of humor."[79]

Unusually given her painting successes, in 1980 Sims applied to the National Endowment for the Arts for a $12,500 grant in the printmaking category. She submitted an honest and funny overview of her life to that moment, stating that she supported her family through the sale of her art and that "[i]t works out about as efficiently as The Children's Crusade."[80] She continued:

I began by staying in school as long as possible. . . .

To raise money for a press, I taught printmaking and painting at Southwestern at Memphis. I bought instead a child and a divorce, quit teaching, and began selling my paintings. That was eleven years ago. Since then, I have been in and out of galleries—The David in Houston, FAR in New York, Adams-Davidson in Washington, D.C. Currently, I'm showing with Gallery Madison 90 in New York, and suing Barbara DeVorzon Gallery in Los Angeles. It's typical. I make it, but not big.

I work ten hours a day, and that's my life. I play a lot of Bach, some early Supremes, and wash my hair if I have time.

There is no indication that she ever acquired printmaking equipment or that she continued to work in the medium. Actually, what she continued to do was to produce large-scale figural compositions, although the figures were not always human.

Included in her October 1980 exhibition at the Sycamore was *Pourquoi Porcine?* (Why Piglike?) (Fig. 22). The giant canvas was Sims's take on the convention of an odalisque in a harem, although she humorously replaced the reclining female nude with an Arkansas razorback hog. In every other way, the painting follows tradition: a hedonistic pose, a variety of ornamental textiles, food, and an attendant—in this case a child wielding a fly swatter instead of a fan. The

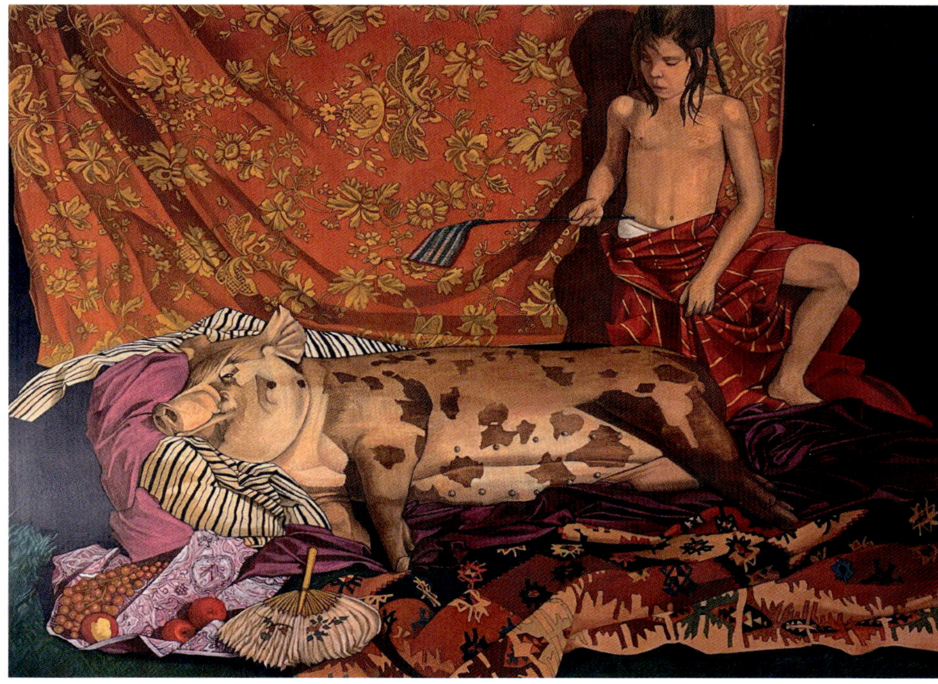

image is about opulence and decadence, although the figure on whom all the attention is focused is an enormous hog. Capturing her subject was no mean feat. As Sims worked from photographs, she began a search for someone willing to tranquilize a pig so that she could stage a tableau and shoot a series of images to work from.[81] In Fayetteville, Arkansas, she found a veterinarian, whose wife was an artist, to agree. In describing the event, Sims recounted:

> Naturally, the veterinarian had thought we were just joking. He said: "Honey, you don't just slip a hog a glass of Wild Turkey with a few hit pills in it. You need to give it a heavy injection and that won't keep it still for very long." Well, his wife said that art had to triumph and they got into a big fight, and she won.

> By the time we got the scene set up and the vet had wheeled his 300-pound pig . . . over in a wheelbarrow and we got it posed, it was dark, and we had to use floodlights. And, of course, by that time the vet had become wildly enthusiastic. He rushed to get his camera and kept jumping up and down and yelling: "By God, it's a Fellini movie!"

> Well, as he'd said, the pig woke up in a few minutes, wondering what in hell had happened, and began to eat the grapes. And that was that.

Pourquoi Porcine? was a commission from Charles Davis, a Pine Bluff, Arkansas, doctor who wanted an artwork for his office waiting room. It says as much about

Sims's clients as it does about her that she was able to fulfill her dream of painting a hog as an odalisque.

Another absurdist play on an art historical convention is *Leda and the Cake* (Cat. 39), Sims's reboot of the mythological legend of the Greek god Zeus, who, in the guise of a swan, impregnated the beauty. While Sims again traffics in the elaborate fabrics that often decorate images of the subject, she turns the story upside down and sideways by depicting Leda in nothing other than a kerchief, apron, and fuzzy blue slippers, with a mixer perched phallically on her pelvis (Zeus?), and a three-tiered wedding cake placed between her legs. Previous permutations of the subject by Michelangelo and Rubens tended to fetishize the lasciviousness of the myth by draping the swan over Leda without obstructing her nakedness. Instead, Sims's canvas has a comic tone: this housewife though barely dressed has still managed to create an imposing confection.

In a 1981 interview in the *Arkansas Gazette*, Sims expressed her thoughts on art, and although the painting she talks about refers to another work that also includes a Mixmaster, the sentiments are still relevant to *Leda and the Cake*:

> I've had a lot of trouble with intellectual views of art and evaluating work in words. . . . I don't care about what anything *means*. I just care about what it *looks like*. If it's a real fine visual image then people will enjoy looking at it. . . . I worship eyes and eyesight. And it undercuts the whole thing to wrap it in words. . . .
>
> I am busy trying to reproduce a series of textures and patterns to look however anyone wants them to look. It's very inarticulate. I have a painting downstairs that's a Mixmaster, two giant shells, fabric and a spotlight. It doesn't mean a damn thing, but I like the way all those things look together.[82]

Caring what things looked like was evident in her 1983 solo exhibition at the Clough-Hanson Gallery at Southwestern at Memphis that consisted of still lifes and charcoal-on-canvas portrait drawings. As noted by the critic Donald La Badie in the *Commercial Appeal*, "She has always been a highly individual personality and artist. With this show, she reaches a new plateau of technical excellence. There is a fresh certainty, strength and downright audaciousness in her sense of color and composition. These are paintings and drawings that confront and challenge the viewer; if they could speak, they might say: 'Take it or leave it, kiddo.'"[83]

Olive Oil and Orchids (Cat. 43) exemplifies her still lifes from this period. While La Badie rightly observed that her earlier works began to include "unexpected elements" such as false teeth and snakes, she had expanded the confounding selection of objects in the new images. A chair and basket of flowers are paired with a can of olive oil, a man's vintage tie (think James Cagney), and a cardboard coffee cup. Typically, the objects are rendered in painstaking detail. Her love of textiles and patterns is evident in the tie, fan, and shoes, not to mention the surfaces of the cans and box. She introduced far greater three-dimensionality through the extensive use of shadow, evident through the silhouette of the basket of flowers that add a decorative touch to the background. Intriguingly, the dark blue/black right side of the canvas becomes a baroque play of shadow that is difficult to unpack—what and how is that created? It may be the chair, but it is nonetheless mysterious.

Also shown at the Clough-Hanson Gallery was a new series of portrait drawings. Sims acknowledged that, because of her early facility, she mistrusted herself and quit drawing, other than as the first stage of a print or a painting. That was until she was induced by Hooks-Epstein, her Houston, Texas, gallery, to produce evocative and haunting pared-down charcoal-on-canvas portraits.[84] The method allowed her to offer less expensive commission options—they were smaller and took less time because they were drawn, not painted. *Let the Wild Rumpus Begin* (Cat. 42) is an excellent example; it is both a striking likeness of the child but also reflects Sims's sense of play. Like a character in Maurice Sendak's *Where the Wild Things Are* (1963), he looks like he's ready to jump up and raise a ruckus, as implied by the title. The work also exemplifies Sims's improved ability to capture a likeness.

Sales in Memphis flourished, with additional venues opening to exhibit her work. One supporter was Alice Bingham, who had shown Sims's drawings at a Junior League event in 1968 and commissioned a portrait of her children in 1970. Bingham opened a gallery in 1979 and exhibited Sims's work between 1984 and 1995 in a succession of spaces: Alice Bingham Gallery, later Bingham Kurts Gallery in Memphis, and Schmidt-Bingham in New York City.[85] She recounted working with Sims:

> Her work, of course, was sought after. From the beginning, it was easy to sell. Mary was certainly not a great business person; all she wanted to do was paint. I remember her telling me once: "Lots of people want to be artists, they want to stand in a gallery and look at their paintings on the wall." But Mary said, "All I want to do is be in the studio and paint." I loved that. I found her choice to be the core belief of true artists. . . . Her place of joy was in her studio.[86]

Sims was aware of her good fortune. "People supported me wonderfully there. When an artist works in an area more people are able to follow the work. People in Memphis have been able to follow my thoughts. My work there has been seen so long they can trust the flight of my imagination."[87]

Not every exhibition was lavished with praise; a 1988 exhibition at the Alice Bingham Gallery received mixed reviews. While *Deborah, Sweet Little Sixteen* (Cat. 48) was applauded in both the *Commercial Appeal* and the *Memphis Business Journal*, the still lifes were critiqued in the latter newspaper.[88] Edwin Howard lamented in the *Journal* what he felt was the now contrived and excessive inclusion of surprising elements, as evident in *Orchid Gut Bomb (Nothing Succeeds Like Excess)* (Cat. 46). Howard was not wrong in noting the increasing complexity, which was quite distinct from her early, stark images of a single vase or pot of flowers. What had also changed was the surfaces themselves, which were now smoother, sharper, and more tightly painted. Sims was also becoming more adept, and for some viewers these changes were not necessarily positive. Examining *Orchid Gut Bomb* begs

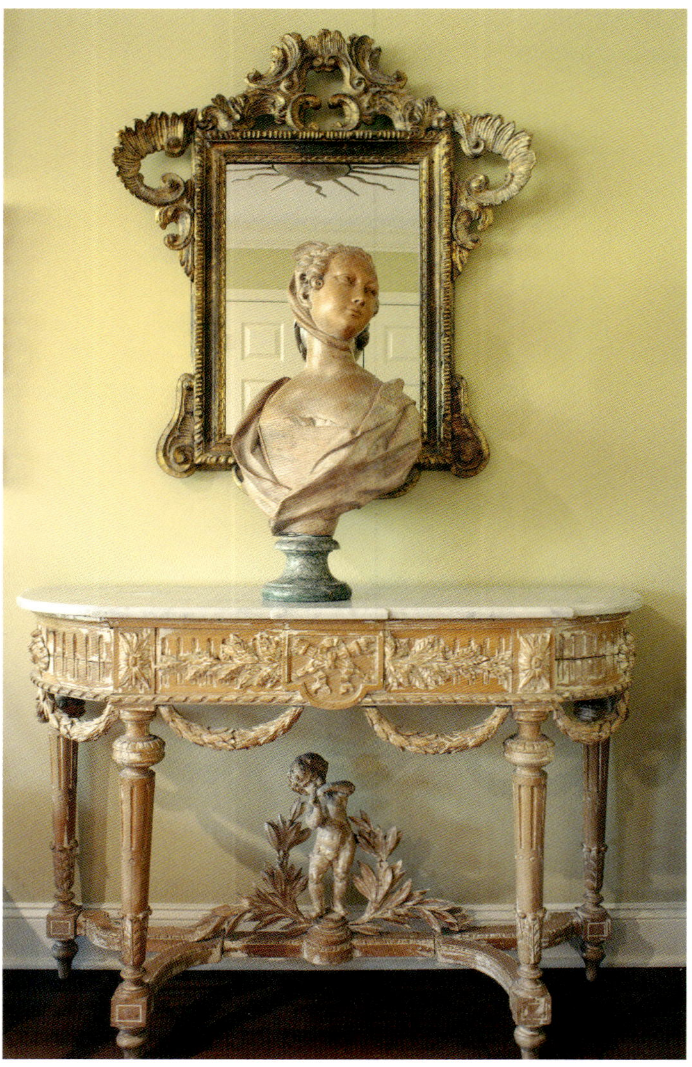

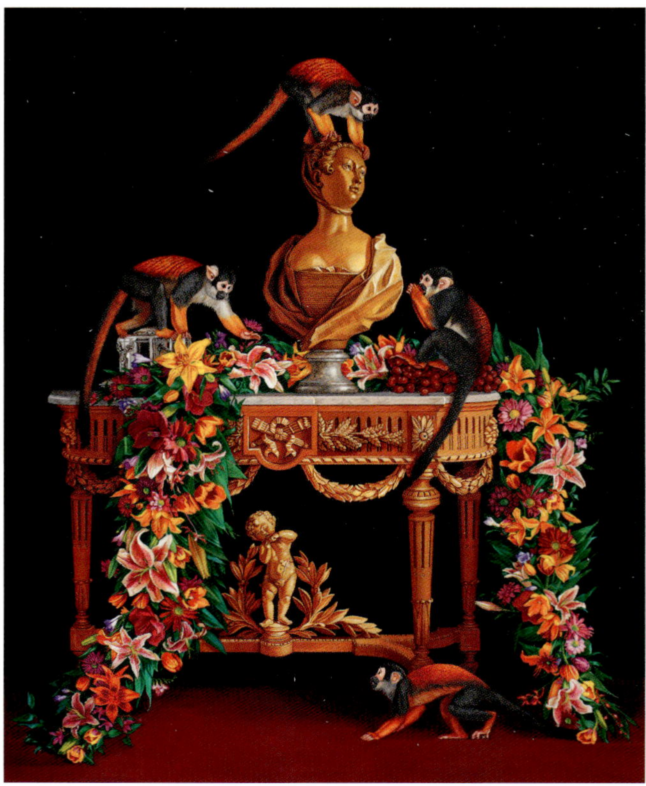

the question of what underlay the shift in reception of her work. Although there are artichokes, grapes, and apples, which are not unusual in a still life, there are no frogs or kitschy ceramics. Displayed on a black backdrop and sitting on an elegant kimono, the still life is a virtuoso performance.

Her infatuation with textiles, and more specifically clothing, resulted in another shift, reflected in a 1992 exhibition at the Bingham Kurts Gallery. "Some clothes are better looking than the people—we all know that, so I'm painting my favorite subject's clothes."[89] This new series of hyper-realist "portraits" focused on shirts, jackets, dresses, and hats surrounded by other still-life objects—flowers, baseballs, and fruit. There are no people, as evident in *Andy's Jacket* (Cat. 52), in which the artist revels in the luxurious fabrics and gold braiding topped by a colorful bouquet.

     Mary Sims's Multiplicity

In 1993, Opera Memphis extended a welcome invitation to produce the stage sets and costumes for their production of *Beauty and the Beast*.[90] For Sims it was a gift, taking her back to her days at the Front Street Theatre, while offering her the opportunity to build on the classes she took in theater design at the State University of Iowa. The results were lauded in the press and were hailed as the "real stars" of the production.[91] She also designed the poster for the production (Cat. 53). The painting—an elegant arrangement of multi-colored flowers sitting on a turquoise fabric pedestal, and highlighted by a lemon-yellow background—is lush, riotous, and typical of Sims's floral works. The only actual reference to the opera is the subtle reflection of the cat-like beast in the pewter vase.

A lover of animals, Sims had long painted a wide menagerie, from birds to frogs and dogs—although they were often presented in elaborate surroundings or with the usual unlikely mix of still life objects. In 1994 she undertook an in-depth study of primates, traveling to zoos and spending hours taking photographs.[92] "It's the hardest bunch of subjects I've ever dealt with in my life. . . . These are not generic monkeys, these are specific portraits. . . . I just started thinking how much fun it would be to paint monkeys. I'm so dumb I thought maybe the zookeepers would just open up a cage and let me in." Instead, she had to shoot through bars, dirty glass, or other barriers, and the monkeys did not always want to perform. The results are such fine portraits that the zookeeper in St. Louis could identify Samantha, a spider monkey who appeared sitting on a chair next to a vase of flowers. A 1995 *Recent Paintings* exhibition at Kurts Bingham Gallery in Memphis included her *Show Me Your Monkey* series. The highest profile sale was *Cheetah Cherry Pie*, sold to author John Grisham, just one of her celebrity fans.[93]

Busting Out (Cat. 54) is a baroque feast that combines flowers with primates. Interior designer and friend Rodgers Menzies had advised Sims that packing her works with kitschy items made them less desirable to the people who could afford them and that employing antiques and beautiful objects would appeal to a wider audience.[94] Taking his advice to heart, for *Busting Out* she photographed an opulent bust and table in his collection as the basis for the confection (Fig. 23). She could not and did not completely bow to respectability; there is a monkey balancing on the bust's head, two others are interfering with the fruits and flowers on the tabletop, and one final monkey is on the floor about to leap. That they are as colorful and visually appealing as the rest of the painting is obvious; but their antics and looping tails give them greater life, not to mention how incongruous they are in that setting, all of which serve to underscore who the real stars are.

In 1995, Sims moved to the David Lusk Gallery in Memphis, where she regularly exhibited her work for the rest of her life.[95] *Five*, an exhibition in 2001, brought together five examples each from themes that were important to her: portraits, still lifes, wildflower bouquets, pets she had costumed, water lilies from Lake Leatherwood, and scantily attired figures from the charcoal *Hoochie Coochie* series. Even though all the works were recent, it was an astute summation of her career that underscored her long-time commitment to her chosen subjects and to her singular style. The road from 1968—the year she shifted away from loosely

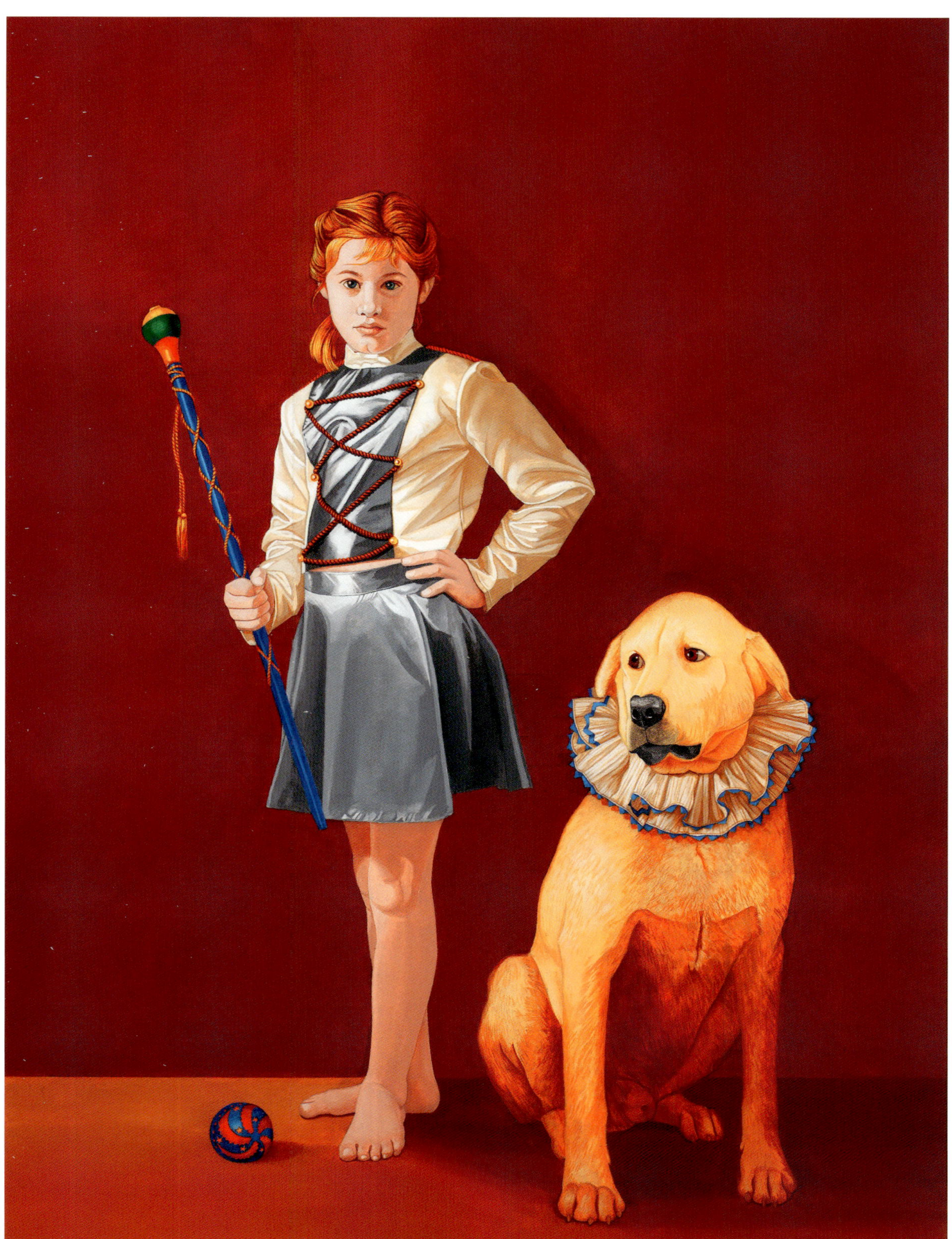

Fig. 24
Mary Sims (American,
1940–2004)
Leader of the Pack, 2001
Acrylic on canvas,
53 × 40 in.
Private collection

Fig. 25
Mary Sims (American,
1940–2004)
That's All, Folks!, 2004
Acrylic on canvas
40 × 30 in.
Private collection

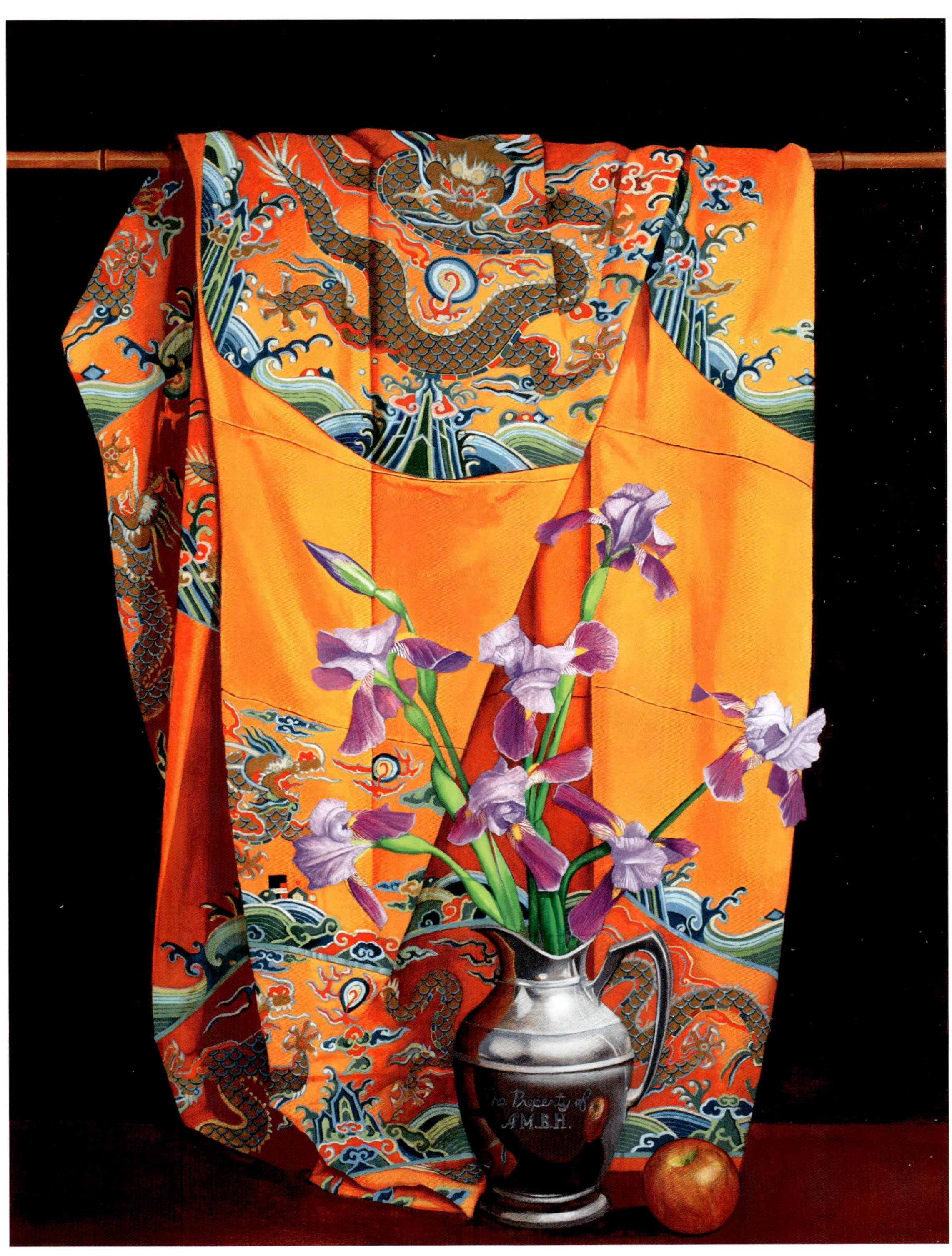

painted, romanticized oils towards realistic acrylics—to the present was powered by a vision that wedded a love of the real with pleasure in surface patterning and the conjoining of incongruous objects. Her style, as evidenced in *Mutual Consent (Portrait of Jessie and Dolph Smith)* (Cat. 18) from around 1972 and *Leader of the Pack* (Fig. 24) from 2001, evolved from looser, charcoal and wash-based portraits, to tight, highly detailed works in acrylic. But there is no doubt that they were created by the same hand. In both, the sitters are defined not solely through their faces, but also through their dress and props, highlighted by the plain, shallow background.

In 2004, Mary Sims was diagnosed with lung cancer. Earngey suggested they take a trip to Rome, but she wanted to stay home and work.[96] Typical of Sims, *That's All, Folks* (Fig. 25) was among her last paintings, the title a nod to Looney Tunes cartoons as well as to her own imminent passing. Found on her easel when she died, it includes a prized kimono, a trademark red apple, and a silver pitcher of irises in front of a dark ground.[97] Less complex than many of her later still lifes, it is a lovely summation of her aesthetic.

At a certain point, Sims decided to stop treatment and settled back in her bed to connect with friends and family, who regaled her with stories. She choreographed her sendoff, asking Earngey to buy Roman candles. With her closest friends surrounding her, she gave them out, asking that when she died, they shoot them off the house's wraparound balcony, which they did on May 19, 2004.[98]

Endnotes

1. Guy Northrop, *Mary Sims: Recent Paintings* (Jonesboro: Arkansas State University Art Gallery, 1973), unpaginated.

2. This essay would not have been possible without the generous support of Mary Sims's family, friends, and collectors who participated in informative interviews and shared photographs. My thanks to Pat Sims, Emma Earngey, Elijah Langdon, Lawrence Anthony, Valerie Berlin, Cynthia Bringle, Bill Broder, Jack Byrne and Dick Turner, Peter Casparian, Frances Cianciolo, Carol DeForest, Beth Edwards, Biff Elrod, Patrick Gordon, Alice Bingham Gorman, Sally Graflund, Erin Harmon, Lyn Jerit, Eleanor Lux, Susan Mallory, Steve McKenzie, Kate Menke, Rodgers Menzies, Naomi Mezey, Mary Mhoon, Jackie Nichols, Shannon Perry at the Memphis Brooks Museum of Art, Theodore Radakovic, Veda Reed, Veronica Sales at the Tennessee State Library and Archives, Bill Short, Dolph Smith, Don Williams, and Charles Wright. I am deeply grateful to the Dixon Gallery and Gardens for providing an ideal venue for presenting a Mary Sims retrospective and the opportunity to publish this essay. And most especially to David Lusk and Carissa Hussong, who embarked on this journey with me. Last but certainly not least to my in-house editor David McCarthy, who keeps me on the straight and narrow.

3. Mary Sims obituary, *Commercial Appeal* (Memphis, TN), May 22, 2004.

4. Lyn Jerit, telephone interview with the author, November 23, 2020. One of Sims's oldest friends, Jerit stated: "Mary swore #1 effortlessly and #2 imaginatively—these were original combinations of profanities, punctuated with dramatic hand gestures. I attribute all of it to the time she spent in Italy." Her prowess was legendary; for example, friends Jack Byrne and Dick Turner in an interview with the author on May 17, 2021, claimed that she "cussed like a sailor."

5. Kini Kedigh, "At Home with Art," *RSVP Magazine,* June 1996.

6. The following biographical information on Lydel Sims is from William Thomas, introduction, in Lydel Sims, *Assignment: Memphis* (Oxford, MS: Yoknapatawpha Press, 1982), xiii–xvii, and from Sims's obituary by William Thomas, "Going…but Columnist is Not Likely to be Forgotten," *Commercial Appeal*, June 4, 1995.

7. Thomas in *Assignment: Memphis*, xiii.

8. Pat Sims, telephone interview with the author, December 15, 2020.

9. Northrop, *Mary Sims: Recent Paintings*.

10. Ibid.

11. Guy Northrop, "Character of Touliatos Caught in Life-Size Sims Portrait," *Commercial Appeal*, July 30, 1972. Front Street Theatre was an Equity theater that attracted national actors.

12. The information about her exhibition comes from *Mary Sims*, Brooks Memorial Art Gallery, Memphis, Tennessee, April 2-30, 1970, the brochure for her solo exhibition. The information about the painted sets comes from Northrop, "Character of Touliatos Caught in Life-Size Sims Portrait."

13. Donald La Badie, "The Artistic Whims of Mary Sims," *Commercial Appeal*, June 24, 1979.

14. Transcript from the State University of Iowa. Estate of Mary Sims. David Lusk Gallery, Memphis.

15. The museum's name will change in 2026 to Memphis Art Museum.

16. Guy Northrop, "Brooks Opens Fine Print Show," *Commercial Appeal*, April 3, 1960.

17. Guy Northrop, "Mary Sims and Charles Inzer Share Art Opening At Gallery Today," *Commercial Appeal*, July 17, 1960.

18. Bill Broder, telephone interview with the author, May 12, 2021.

19. This fact has been corroborated by many people, including Robert Mezey's daughter Naomi who stated in a May 11, 2021, telephone interview that her father often talked about getting a divorce for his common law marriage to Mary.

20. Pat Sims, December 15, 2020. According to Pat, they sang traditional folk songs like "The Fox Went Out on a Chilly Night."

21. See creativewriting.stanford.edu/about/history-stanford-creative-writing-program for a history of the program. Accessed June 8, 2021.

22. Ted Radakovic, interview with the author, May 25, 2021. Although he knew her later than this period, it was plain that her patterns of hard work developed early.

23. This information comes from Sims's application for a National Endowment for the Arts (NEA) grant submitted for 1981-82. Estate of Mary Sims.

24. Broder, May 12, 2021.

25. Guy Northrop, "Living with Art—Twin Exhibitions Held By Mary Sims," *Commercial Appeal*, September 17, 1961. Northrop noted: "The former Memphian is a Memphian again, having moved back from San Francisco this summer with her husband, Lamont Prize-winning poet Robert Mezey."

26. Transcript from the State University of Iowa. Estate of Mary Sims.

27. Charles Wright, telephone interview with the author, May 23, 2021.

28. Margaret McKee, "Profile on Art: Mary Sims Radakovic, There Are All Sorts of Things Nagging at Me to Paint—An Itch That Has to Be Scratched," *Memphis Press-Scimitar*, November 21, 1969.

29. Brooks Memorial Art Gallery Newsletter, April 1970, Mary Sims object file, Memphis Brooks Museum of Art.

30. Tulane University transcript. Estate of Mary Sims. Four of her upper-level printmaking classes were listed as taught by staff. Information from *Bulletin Tulane University Graduate School* (New Orleans: Tulane University, 1965–1966, and 1966–1967).

31. Jim Steg website, www.jimsteg.com/about-printmaker-jim-steg, accessed January 18, 2022.

32. Guy Northrop, "Living with Art—Mid-South Exhibition Leans Toward Tradition," *Commercial Appeal*, February 27, 1966.

33. Alberta Collier, "Orleans Gallery to Open Exhibition," *Times-Picayune* (New Orleans, LA), September 25, 1966.

34. Radakovic, May 25, 2021. The following discussion of their time together is from this conversation.

35. McKee, "Profile on Art: Mary Sims Radokovic."

36. Guy Northrop, "Living with Art—Sims Exhibit To Open at Great Expectations," *Commercial Appeal*, June 23, 1968. The article details the sources for the paintings as well as describing the recently opened gallery.

37. Kedigh, "At Home with Art."

38. Valerie Berlin, telephone interviews with the author, January 12, 2021, and August 24, 2021.

39. Guy Northrop, "Miscellany of Memphis Artists at Great Expectations," *Commercial Appeal*, October 20, 1968.

40. Northrop, *Mary Sims: Recent Paintings*.

41. Ibid.

42. Application for 1981–82 NEA grant.

43. Veda Reed, telephone interview with the author, March 3, 2021.

44. Guy Northrop, "Autobiography is Heart of Mary Sims' Art," *Commercial Appeal*, March 9, 1969.

45. Ibid.

46. McKee, "Profile on Art: Mary Sims Radokovic."

47. Jackie Nichols, telephone interview with the author, December 8, 2021. The following information about *Steambath* is also from the same conversation. After Sims and Radokovic moved out of the bungalow, Circuit Playhouse took over the space and used it for costume storage and rehearsals.

48. Mary Sims Radakovic to Robert McKnight, September 3, 1969, Mary Sims 1970 exhibition file, Memphis Brooks Museum of Art.

49. The April 1970 Brooks Memorial Art Gallery Newsletter noted that the exhibition was in the Lounge. For Sims's exhibition, the museum printed a small brochure illustrated with three paintings and including a checklist. *Mary Sims*, Brooks Memorial Art Gallery, Memphis, Tennessee, April 2–30, 1970. The newsletter and brochure are in the Mary Sims object file, Memphis Brooks Museum of Art.

50. The 1970 exhibition file includes lists of all the loans and receipts for the paintings sold, making it possible for the new owners to collect the works that Sims delivered to the museum. Mary Sims 1970 exhibition file, Memphis Brooks Museum of Art.

51. Margaret McKee, "They're Portraits Second—Paintings First," *Memphis Press-Scimitar*, April 17, 1970.

52. Guy Northrop, "Sims Portraits, Yee Birds Add to Memphis Art Scene, *Commercial Appeal*, April 5, 1970.

53. For an authoritative text on Hendricks, see Trevor Schoonmaker, *Barkley L. Hendricks: Birth of the Cool* (Durham, NC: Nasher Museum of Art, Duke University, 2008). All the images referred to here are reproduced in the exhibition catalogue.

54. Guy Northrop, "Living with Art—Memphis State Students Win Attention, Awards," *Commercial Appeal*, February 27, 1972.

55. Sims and Anthony negotiated for Radakovic to teach a photography course instead. William Bowden to Mr. and Mrs. Ted Radakovic, March 31, 1972. Mary Sims file, Rhodes College archives.

56. Frances Cianciolo, telephone interview with the author, February 23, 2021. The information about the Sycamore and Sims's relationship with Cianciolo is from this phone call.

57. Ibid.

58. Peter Casparian, telephone interview with the author, March 16, 2021.

59. Guy Northrop, "Living with Art—Tree Forms Fascinate Mary Sims," *Commercial Appeal*, May 6, 1973.

60. Emma Earngey, telephone interview with the author, October 20, 2021.

61. Vernon Tucker, "Bill Earngey, a misfit's misfit," *Eureka Springs Independent* (AR), August 31, 2016. The obituary, which captures Earngey's personality, details his "divorce" from the military due to having ingested large quantities of LSD, his writing projects, and efforts to protect the city from overdevelopment.

62. Emma Earngey, text message to the author, June 17, 2022.

63. Guy Northrop, "Mary Sims, Fred and Friends Combine for a Show," *Commercial Appeal*, May 19. 1974.

64. Audrey West, "Cinderless Cinderella Dusts Canvases with Magic Touch," *Memphis Press-Scimitar*, May 20, 1974.

65. Guy Northrop, "Mary Sims To Open Homecoming Show," *Commercial Appeal*, May 18, 1975.

66. Cianciolo, February 23, 2021.

67. Downing Pryor to Mary Sims Earngey, September 18, 1975, and John Whitlock to Mary Sims Earngey, October 1, 1975, 1975 Mary Sims exhibition file, Memphis Brooks Museum of Art.

68. Mary Sims Earngey to Jack, undated, Mary Sims exhibition file, Memphis Brooks Museum of Art.

69. "Musical Opening Planned for Mary Sims Exhibit," *Memphis Press-Scimitar*, October 17, 1975.

70. Guy Northrop, "Mary Sims is Back with a Mexican Touch," *Commercial Appeal*, May 30, 1976.

71. Donald La Badie, "Eureka Springs' Art Blossoms in the Direction of Crafts," *Commercial Appeal*, April 13, 1980.

72. La Badie, "The Artistic Whims of Mary Sims."

73. Ibid. The following information about the beginning of the series comes from this article.

74. Pat Sims, email to the author, November 17, 2021. "She was much more than a housekeeper—she was like my second

mother and our family's guardian angel—providing moral support, endless generosity, and words of wisdom . . . . I know that Zuma was very religious, and she and my sister must have discussed biblical stories."

75. Hosea 1:2.

76. La Badie, "The Artistic Whims of Mary Sims."

77. Ibid.

78. Margaret Arnold, "Portrait of an Arkansas Artist," *Arkansas Times*, March 1981.

79. Ibid.

80. Application for 1981–82 NEA grant.

81. Donald La Badie, "Porcine Parody Hogs Sims Exhibition," *Commercial Appeal*, October 31, 1980. This was not the only time she "hired" an animal to sit for a painting. In 1982 she was asked to create a large (14 x 7 ½ ft.) cowboy painting for a bar in Texas. She wanted a horse to be at the bar and was told that they would go upstairs but down was another matter. Fortunately, the bar in Eureka Springs was on a hill and had a second door that led to stairs leading up to Main St. Donald La Badie, "Mary Sims' Humor Flowers in the Funniest Places," *Commercial Appeal*, July 25, 1982.

82. Mary Sims, "Looking at Art—1: Artists Tell Us How," *Arkansas Gazette* (Little Rock, AR), July 31, 1981.

83. Donald La Badie, "Weekend Hopping with Art," *Commercial Appeal*, November 18, 1983.

84. Donald La Badie, "Another Occasion," *Commercial Appeal*, October 23, 1983.

85. Alice Bingham Gorham, interview with the author, February 26, 2021.

86. Ibid.

87. Charles Kaufman, "Sims' Sense of Fun Colors Her Still Lifes," *Arkansas Gazette*, November 19, 1982.

88. Frederic Koeppel, "Eye, Heart, Mind United in Deborah," *Commercial Appeal*, April 8, 1988. Edwin Howard, "The Visual Dimension: Mary Sims Paintings," *Memphis Business Journal*, April 18–22, 1988.

89. Bingham Kurts Gallery press release, February 1992, Mary Sims object file, Memphis Brooks Museum of Art.

90. Edwin Howard, "Story Behind Sims' Designs for Opera," *Memphis Business Journal*, September 6–10, 1993.

91. Whitney Smith, "'Beauty' Glows in World Made Vivid by Artist Sims," *Commercial Appeal*, November 22, 1993.

92. John Beifuss, "Artist Captures Menagerie of Monkeys on Canvas, Builds Wild 'Portrait' Gallery," *Commercial Appeal*, May 12, 1995.

93. Linda Romine, "Animals in Art: Sims' Exhibition Shows Off Her Monkeys," *Memphis Business Journal*, May 22–26, 1995.

94. Rodgers Menzies, interview with the author, February 16, 2021.

95. Sims started working with Lusk in 1991 at the Bingham Kurts Gallery, later Kurts Bingham Gallery, and joined the David Lusk Gallery when it opened in 1995.

96. Ed Hicks, "Legacy: Mary Sims Says 'That's All, Folks' in Postmortem Finale," *Memphis Business Journal*, November 5–11, 2004.

97. None of Sims's friends was able to identify either the initials or the pitcher.

98. Menzies, February 16, 2021.

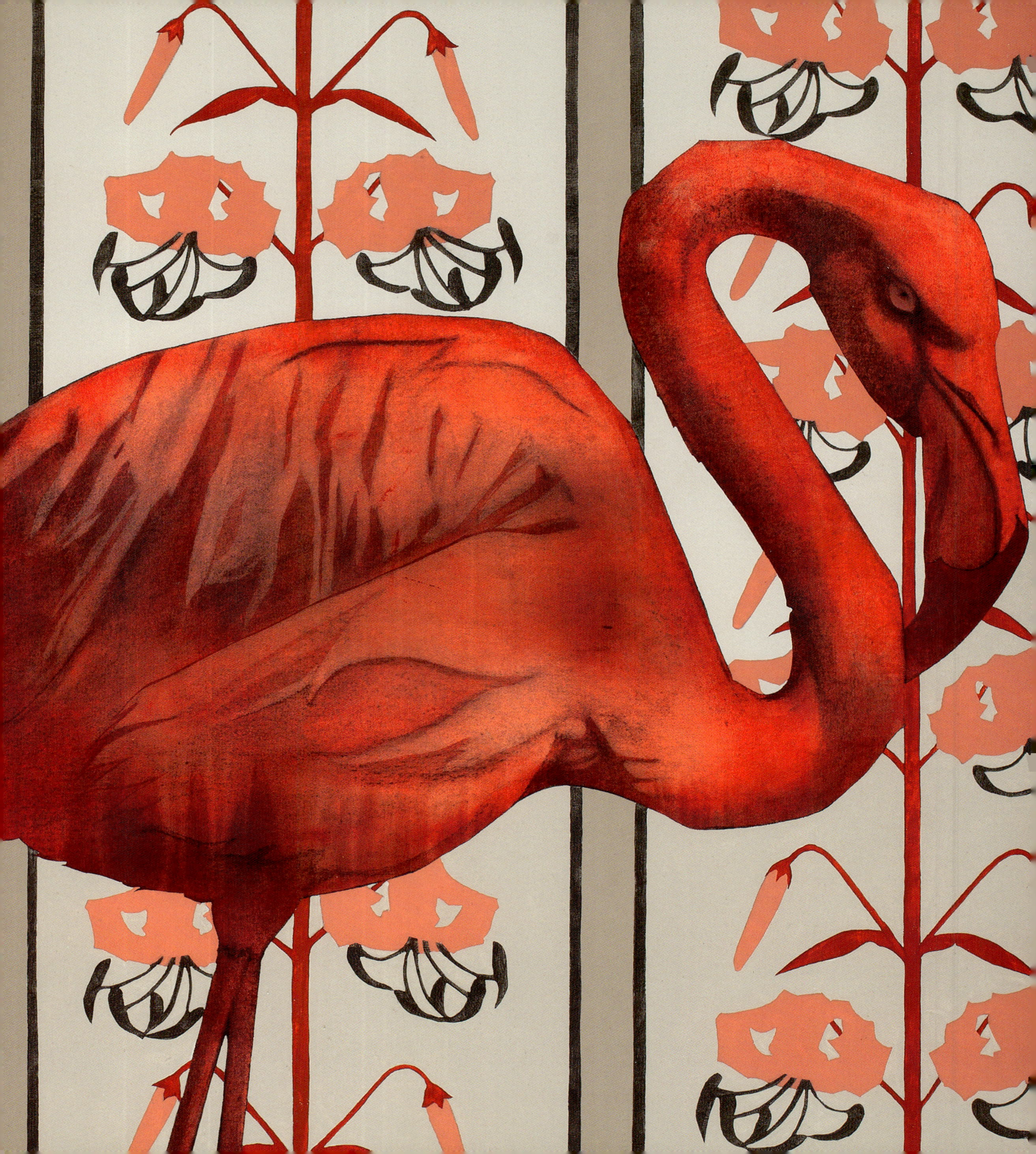

CATALOGUE

Three Birds, 1960
Etching
13 × 18 ¼ in.
David Lusk Gallery, Memphis and
Nashville, Tennessee

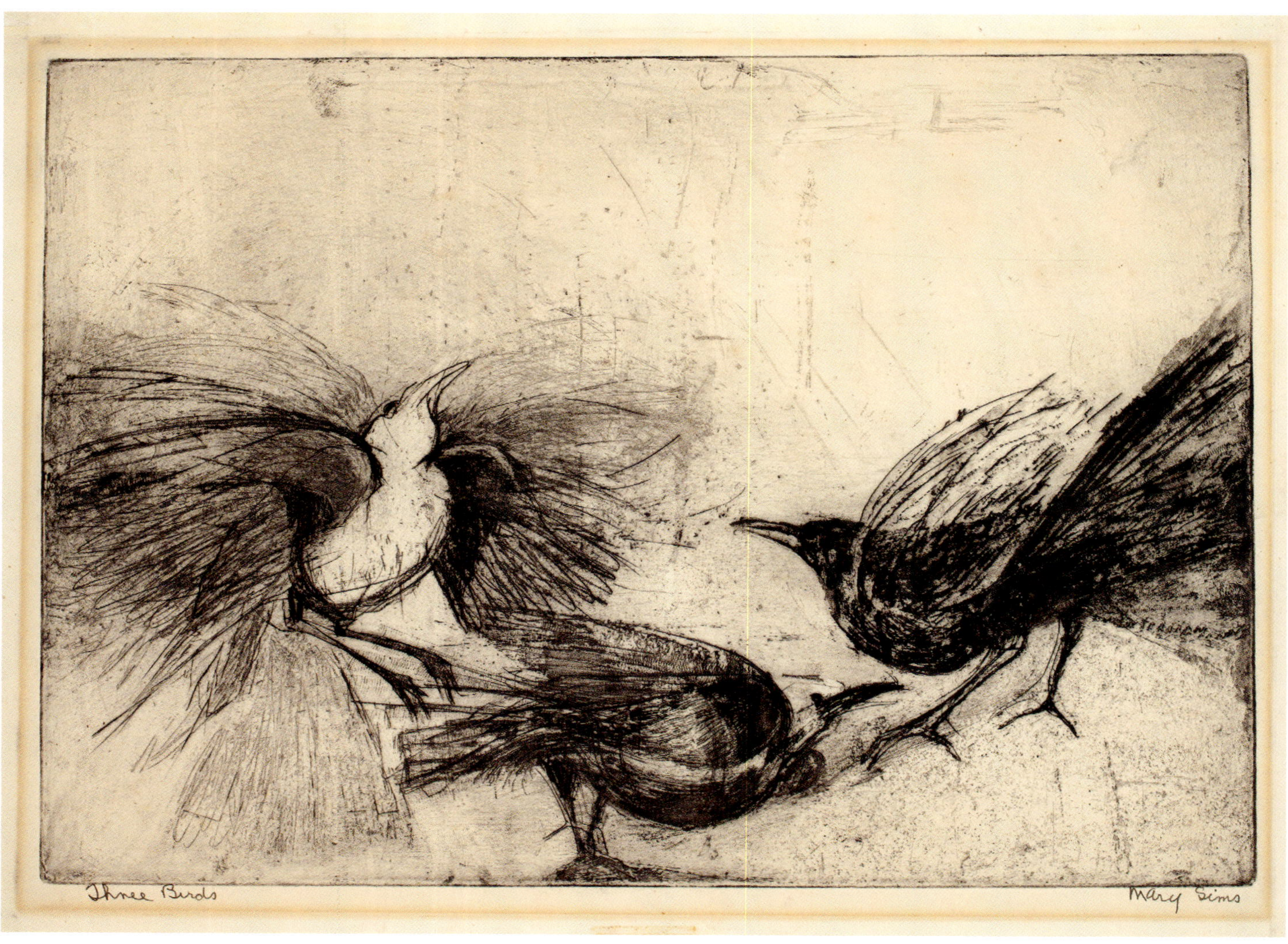

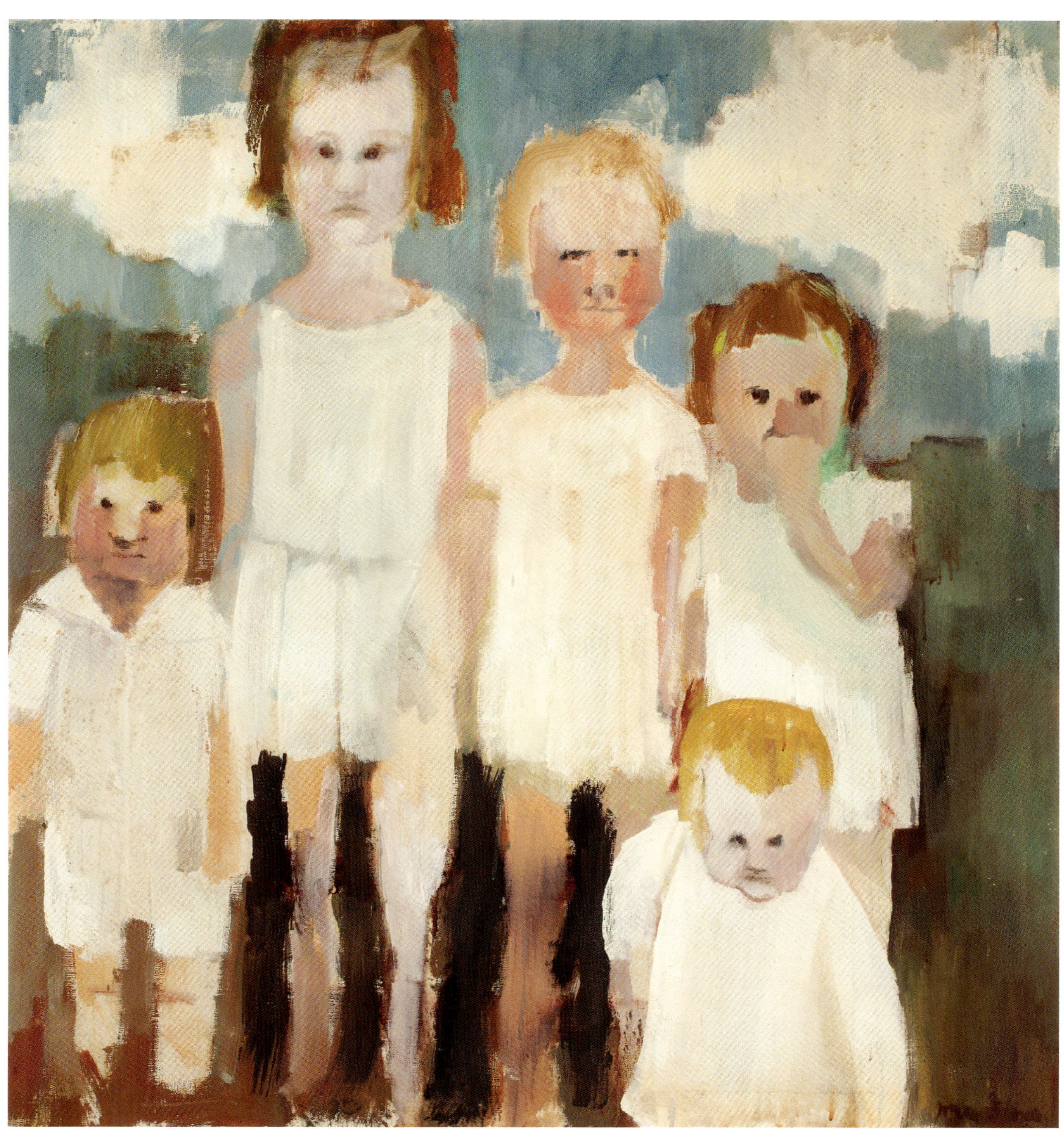

Cat. 2
Untitled (Five Children), 1960
Oil on canvas
42 × 40 in.
Estate of Mary Sims

Alice and Inky, ca. 1960s
Etching
18 ¾ × 16 ⅞ in.
Private collection

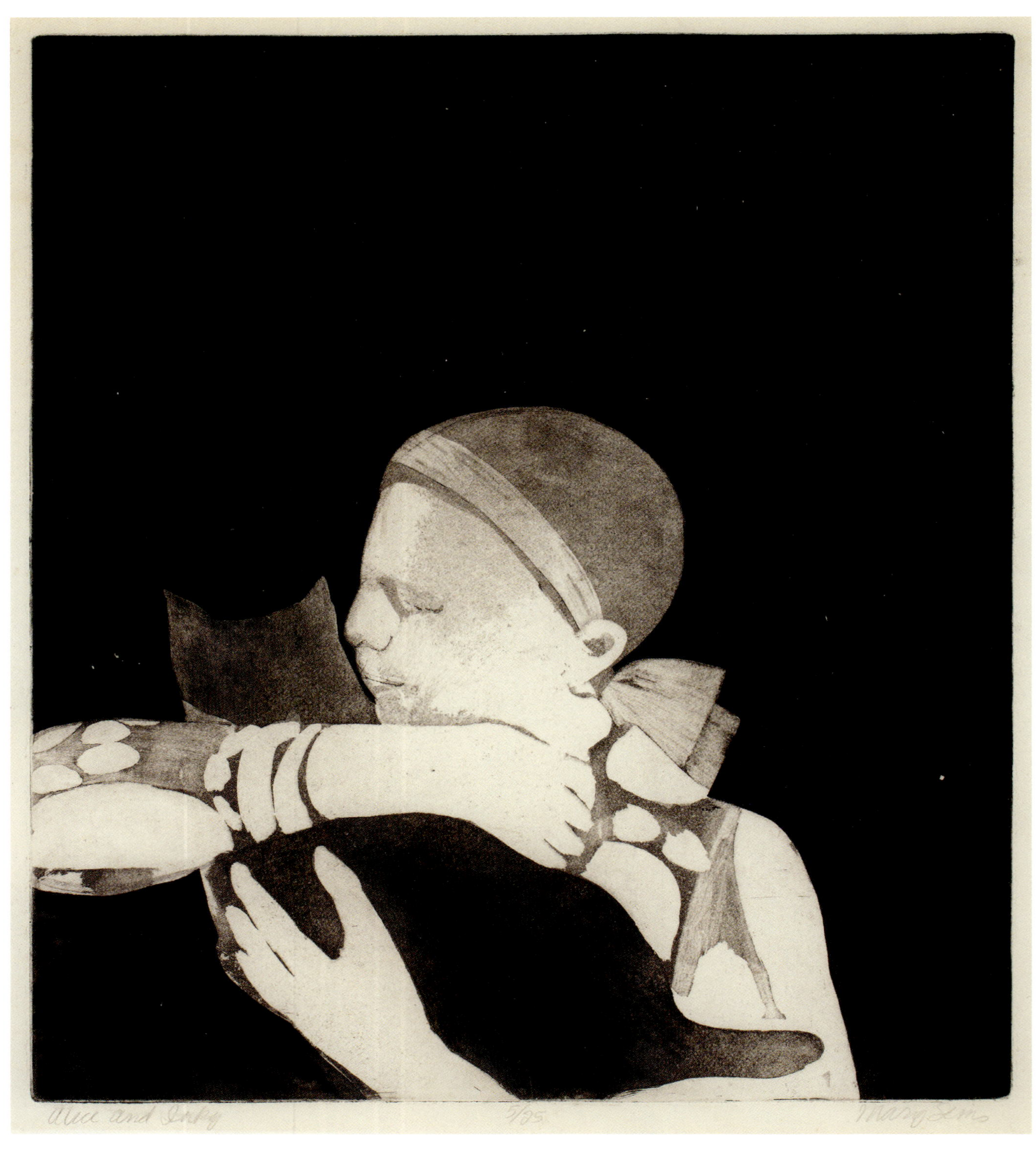

Cat. 4
*Untitled (Portrait of Robert
Mezey)*, ca. 1961
Oil on canvas
39 × 31 ½ in.
Estate of Mary Sims

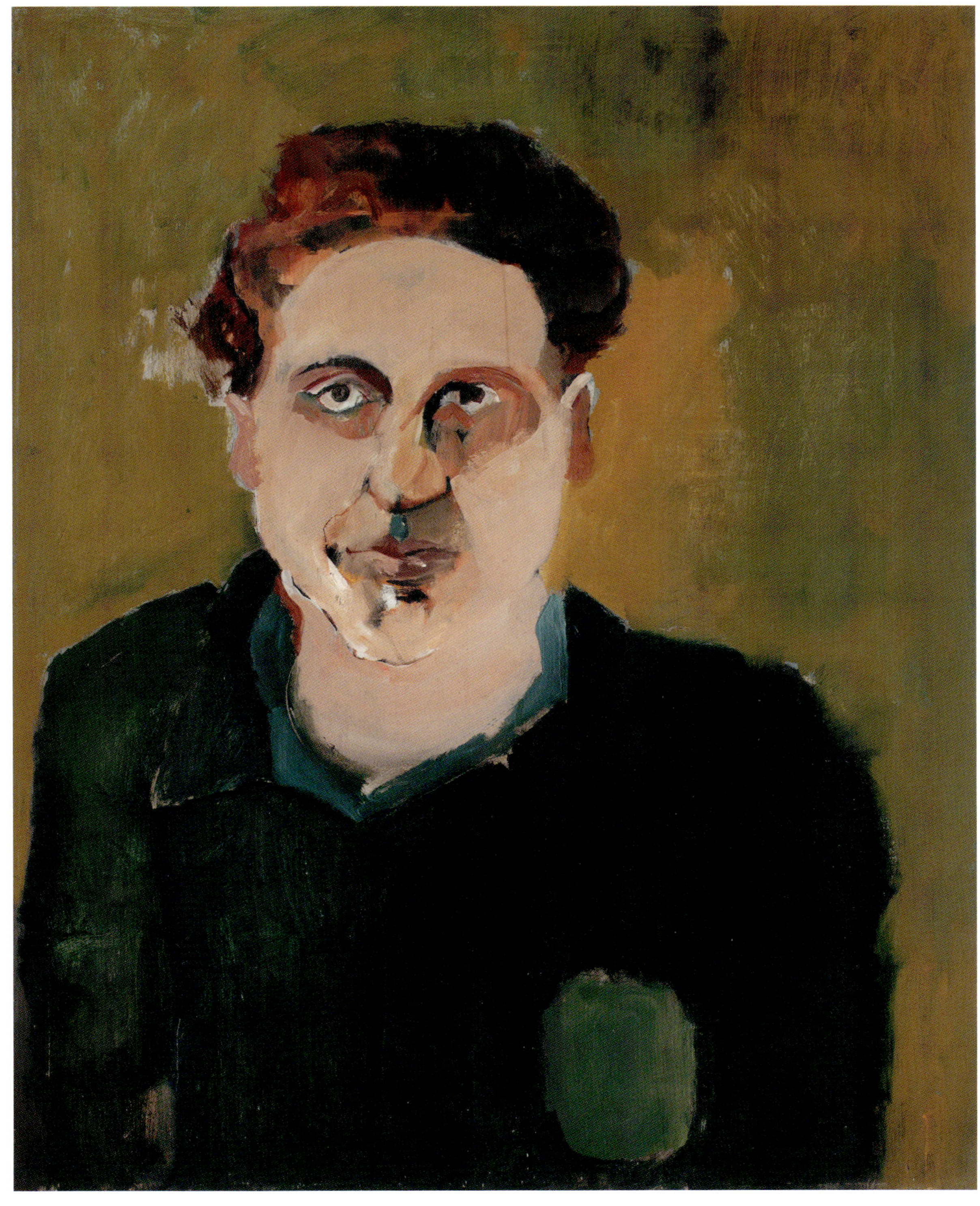

Cat. 5
A Studio Portrait, 1968
Oil on canvas
51 × 30 in.
Estate of Mary Sims

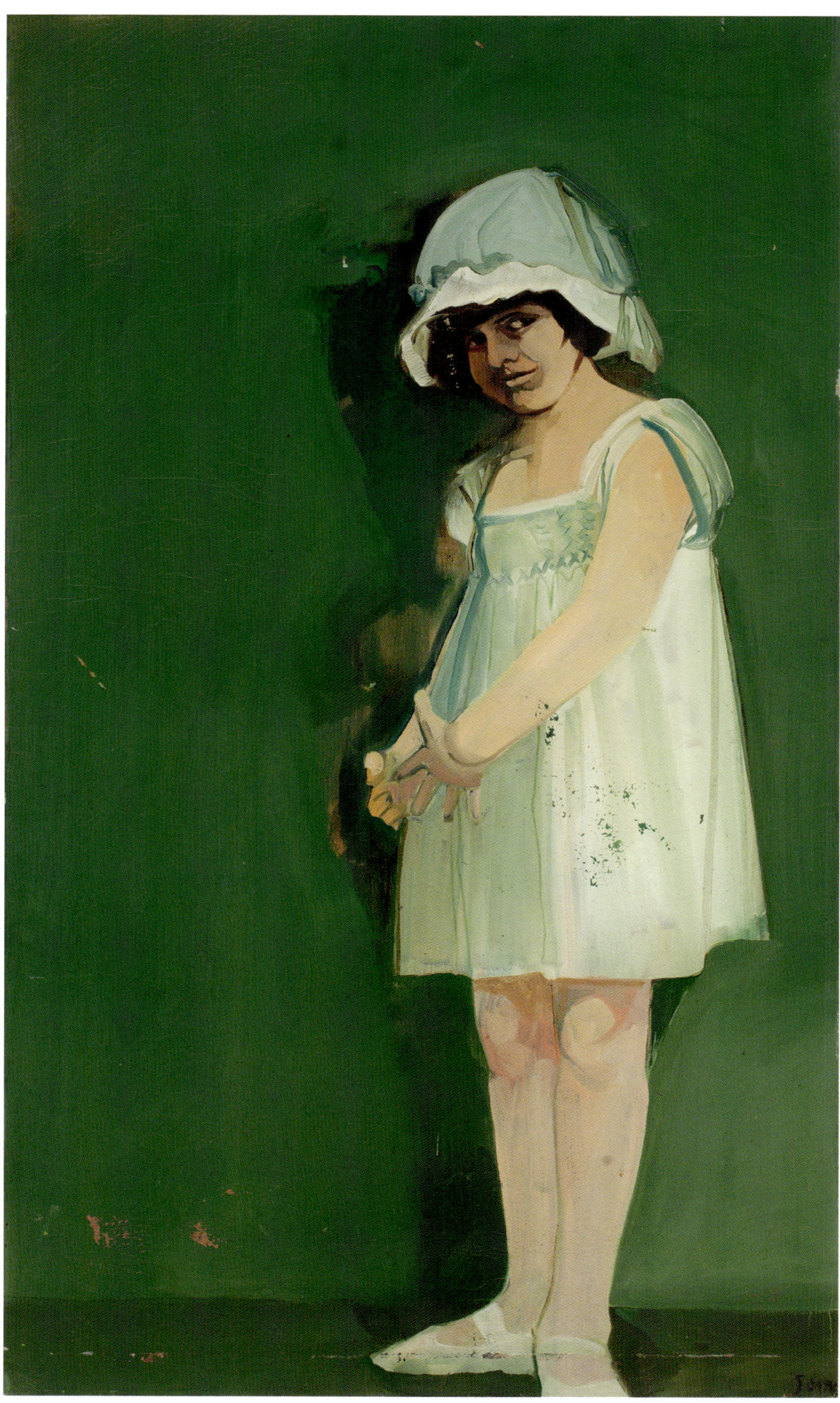

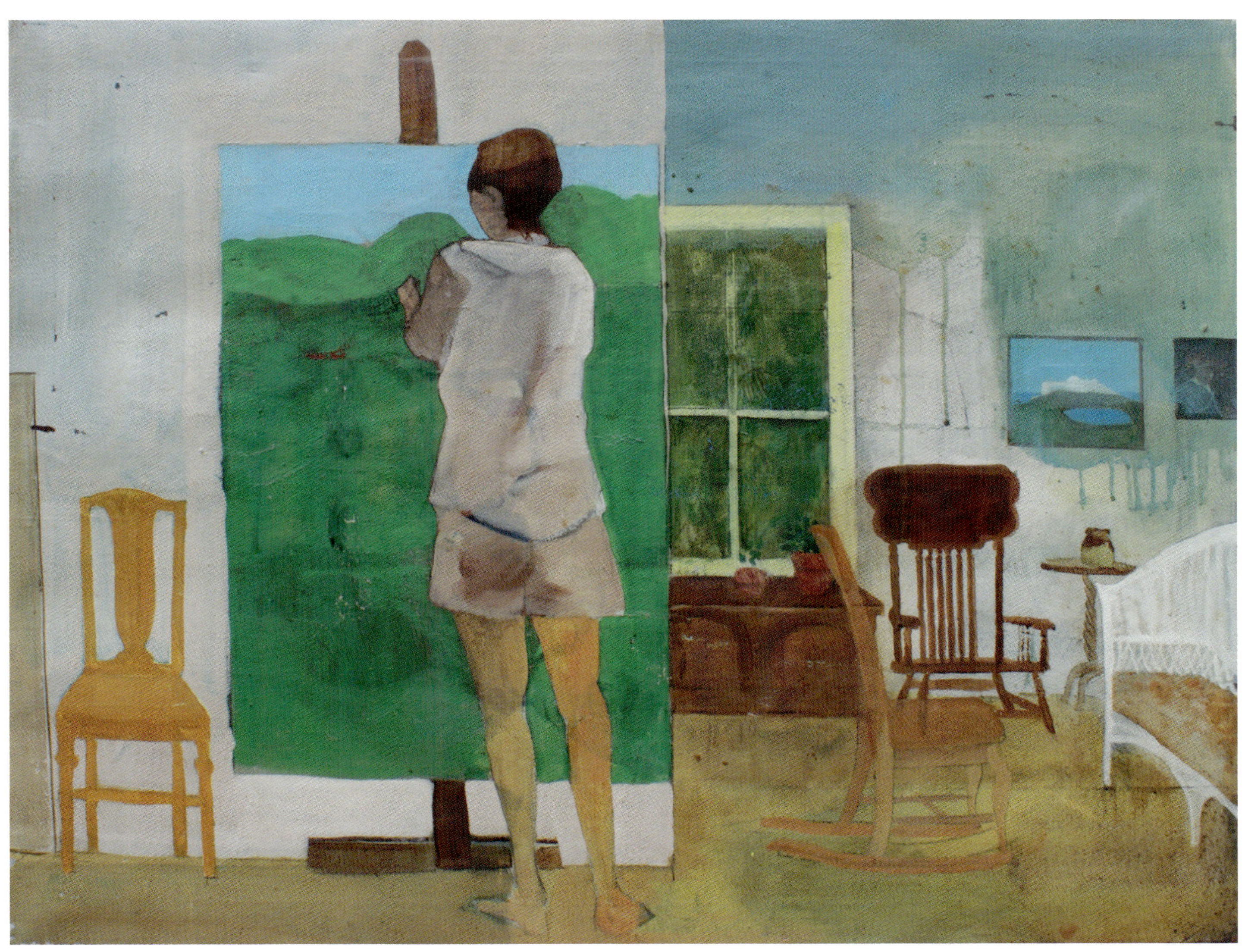

Cat. 7
For Cynthia, 1969
Acrylic on canvas
72 × 54 in.
Collection of Cynthia Bringle

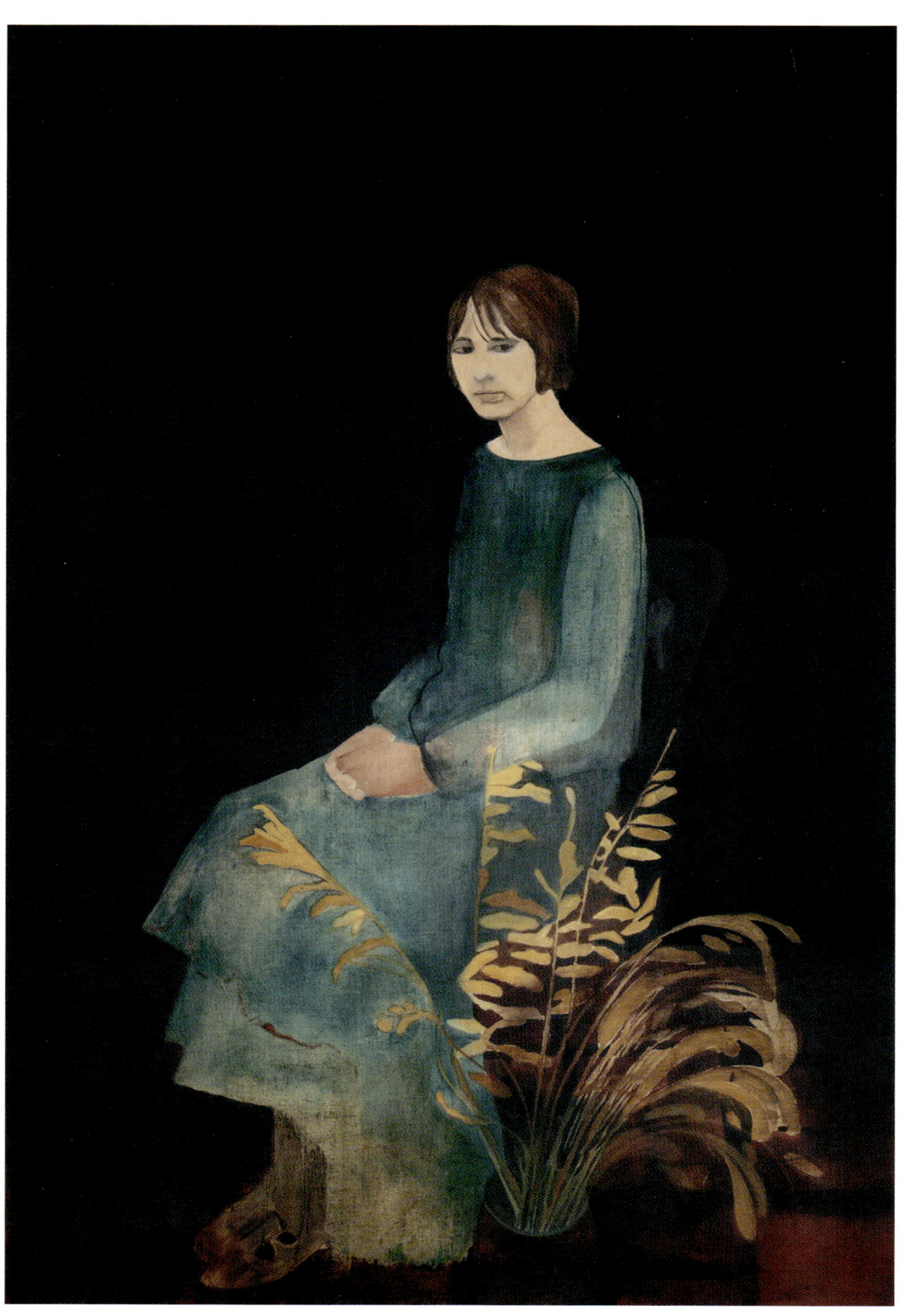

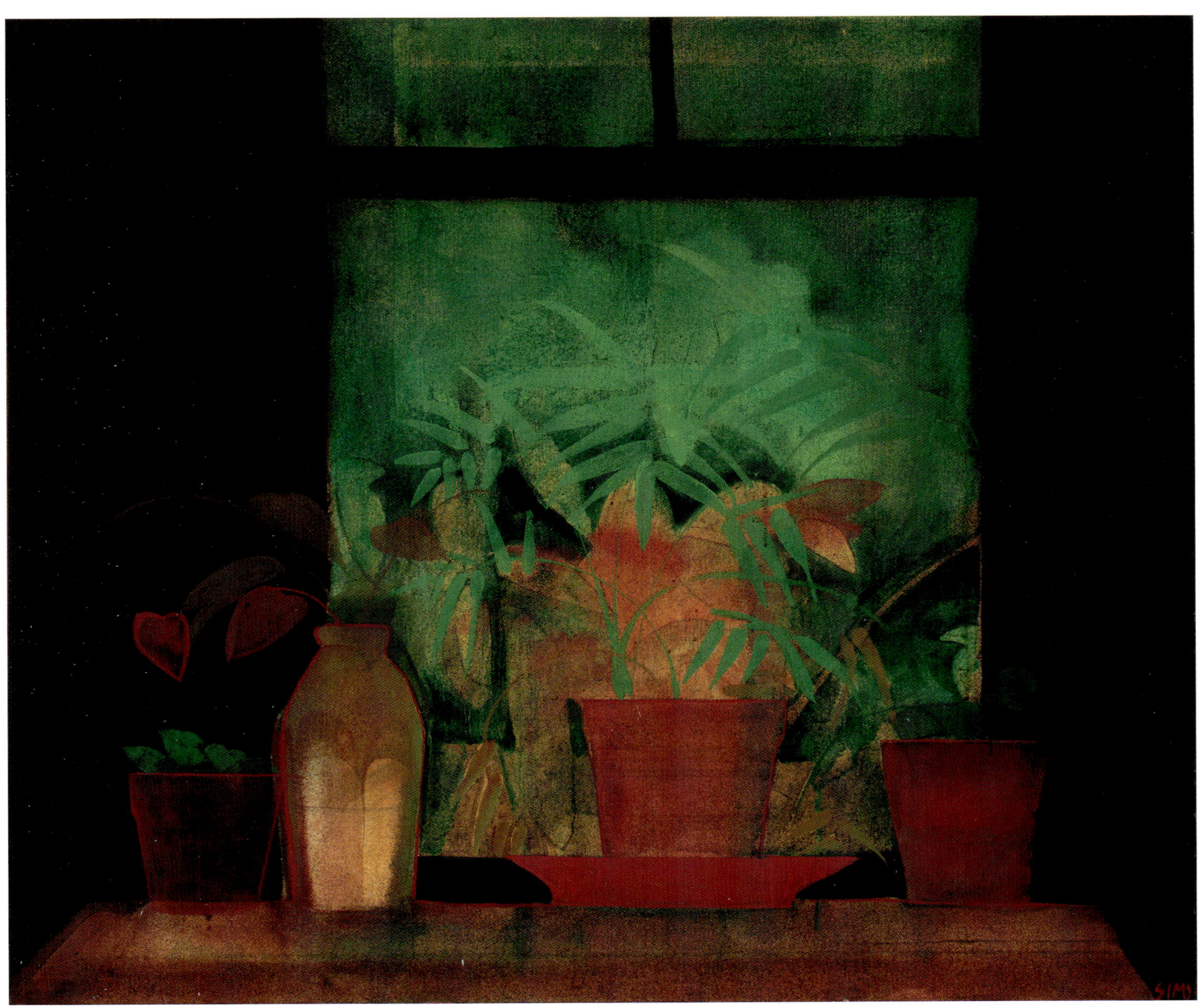

Cat. 9
The Beggared Outcast, 1970
Acrylic and graphite on canvas
60 × 49 in.
Private collection

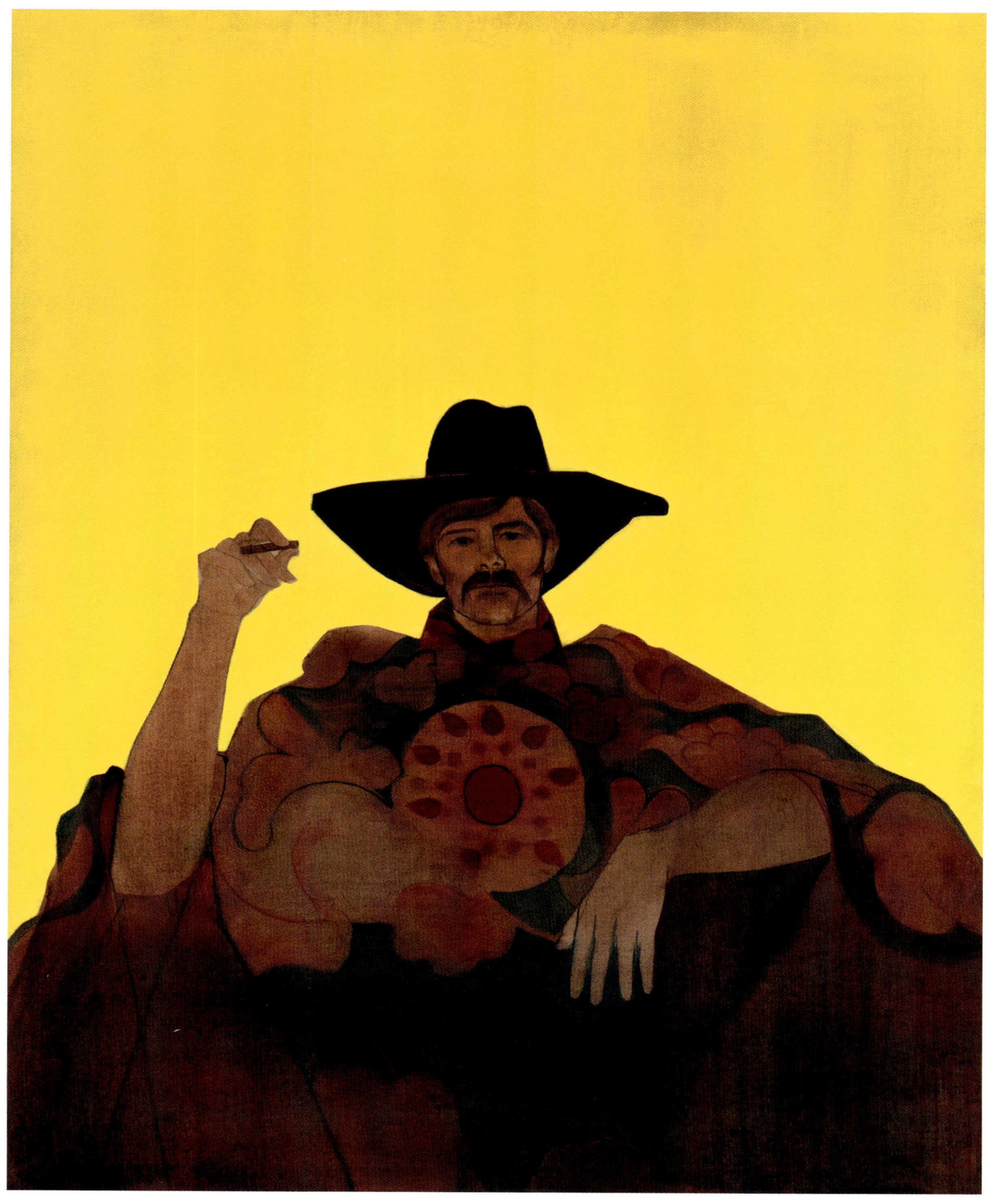

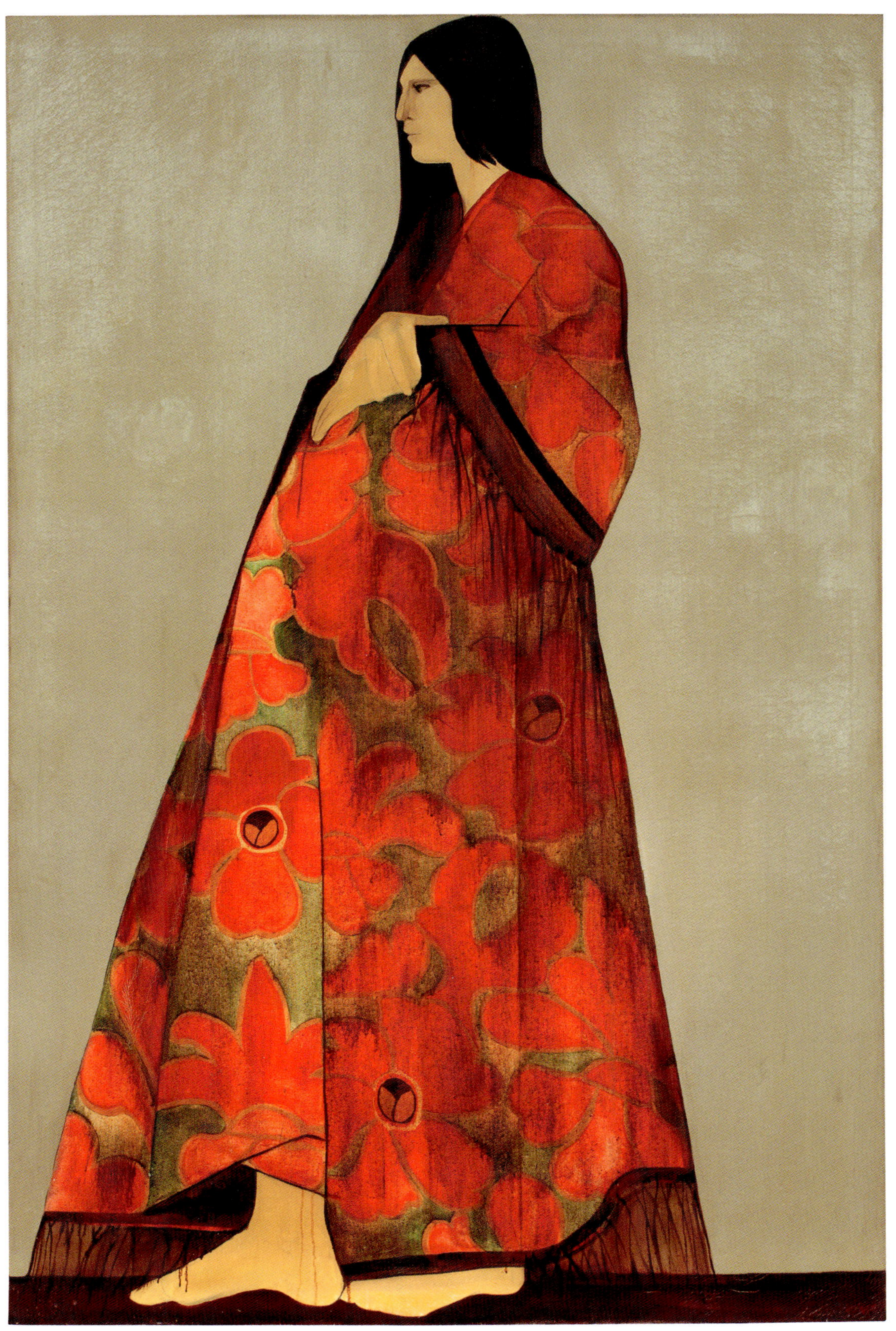

Cat. 10
Emma and Me, 1970
Acrylic and graphite on canvas
65 × 42 in.
Collection of Katharine
Stanwood Menke

Miss November, 1970
Acrylic and
graphite on canvas
74 × 48 in.
Collection of Lance Oliver

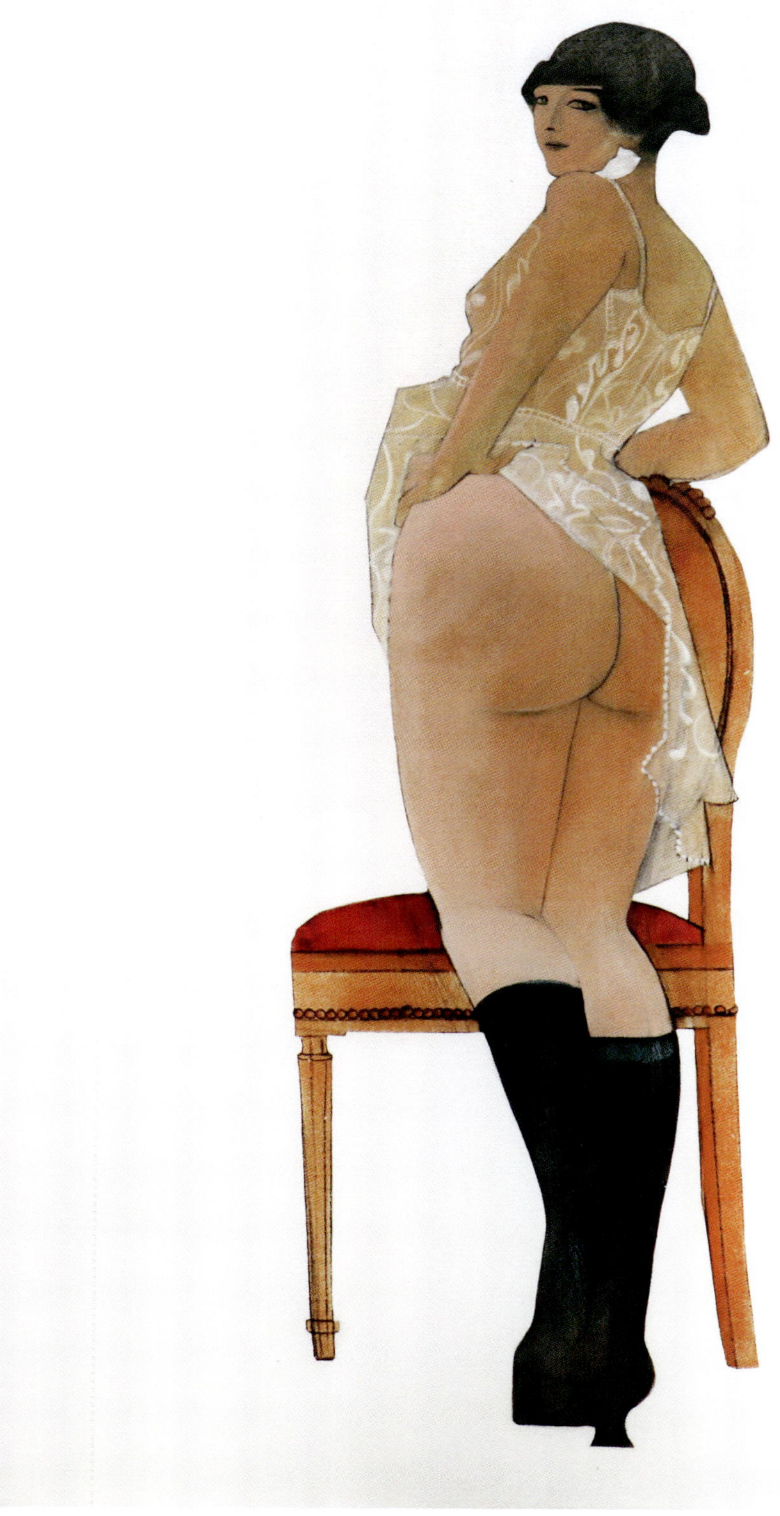

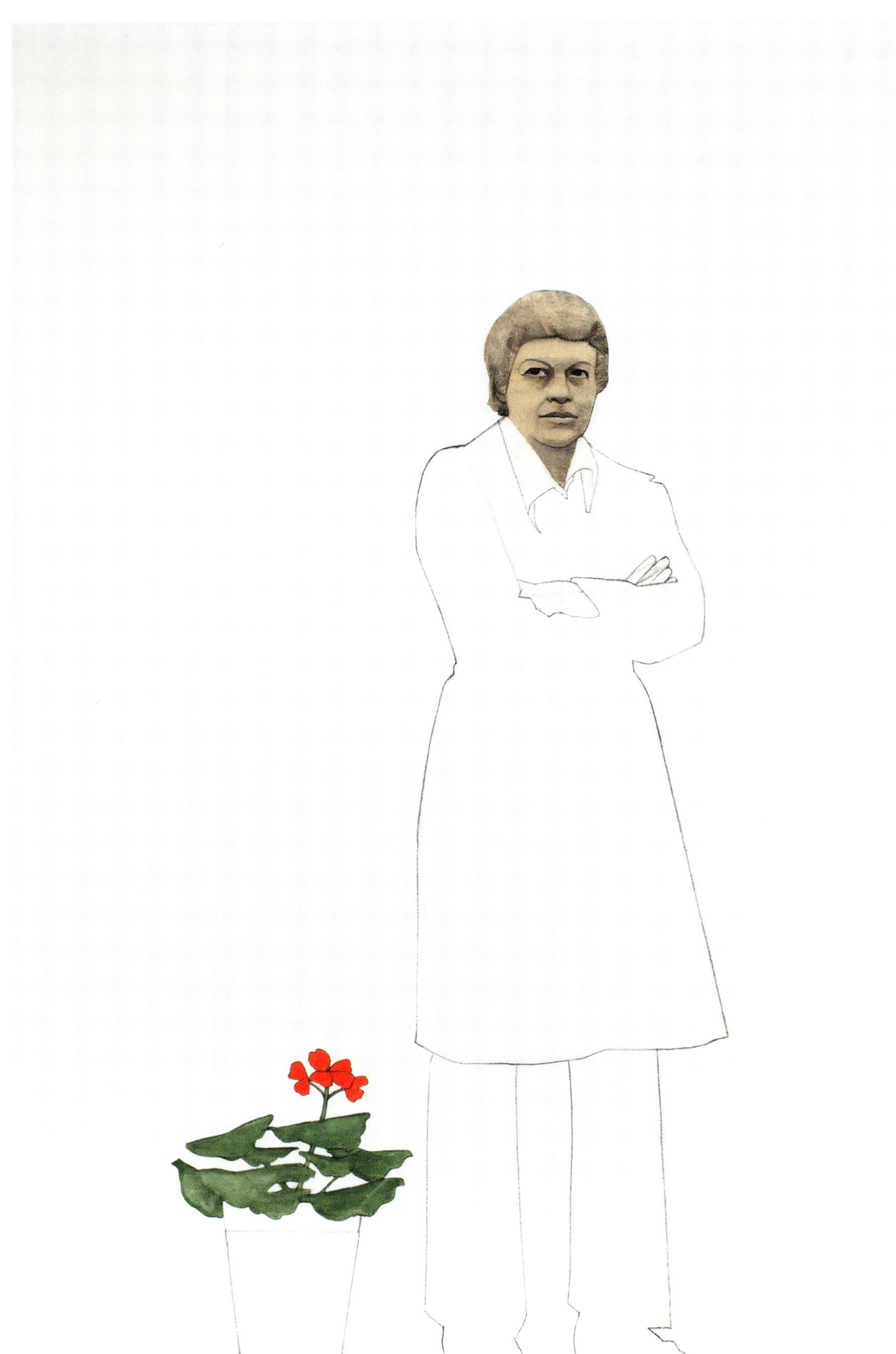

Cat. 13
All Dressed Up, Nowhere to Go, 1972
Acrylic and graphite on canvas
60 × 34 in.
Collection of Katherine and
Adrian Blackney

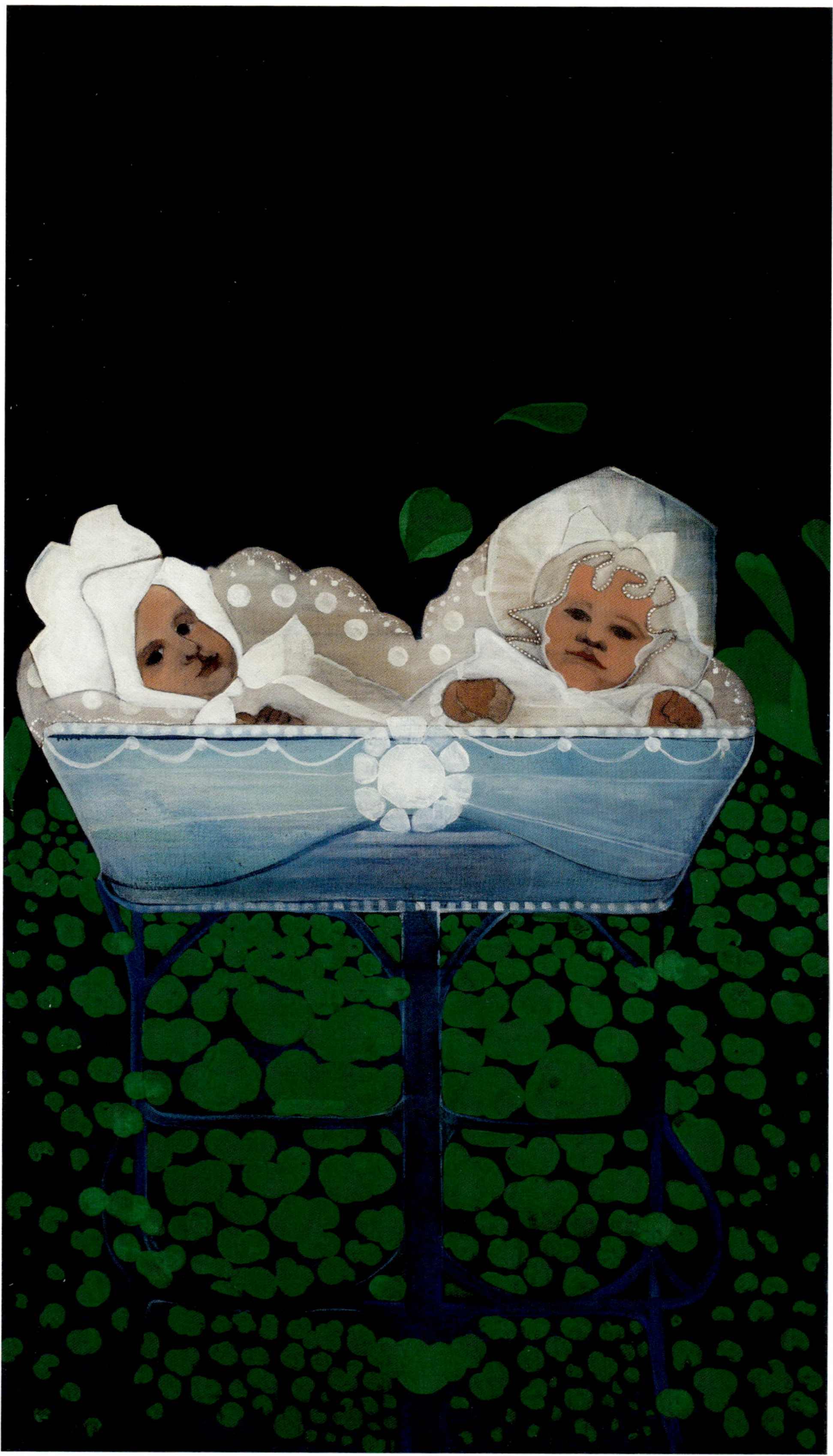

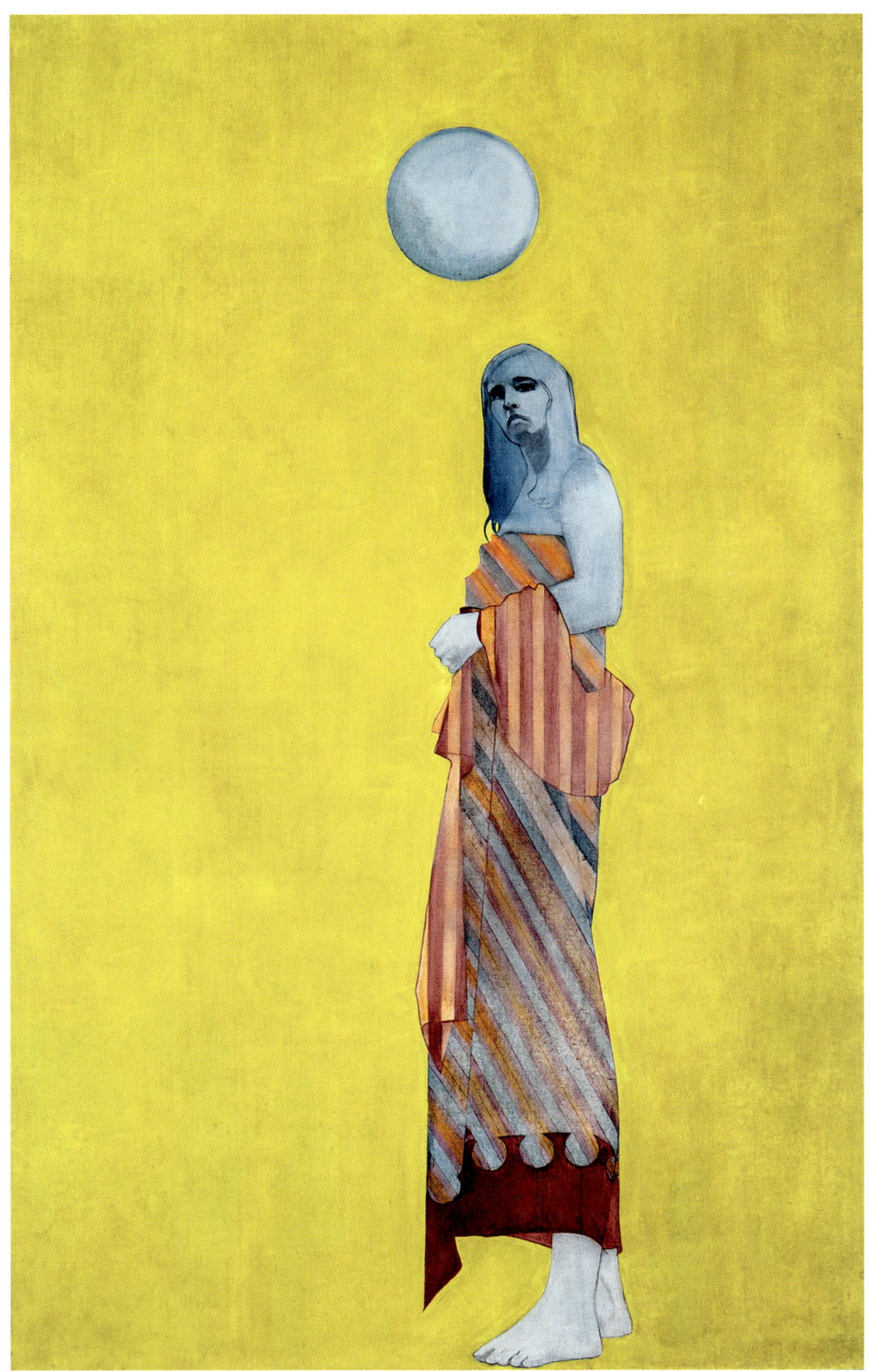

Cat. 14
Queen of the Moon, 1972
Acrylic and graphite on canvas
84 × 48 in.
Collection of Audrey
Taylor Gonzalez

Snow White and Rose Red, 1972
Acrylic and graphite on canvas
60 × 54 in.
Collection of Meg Menzies

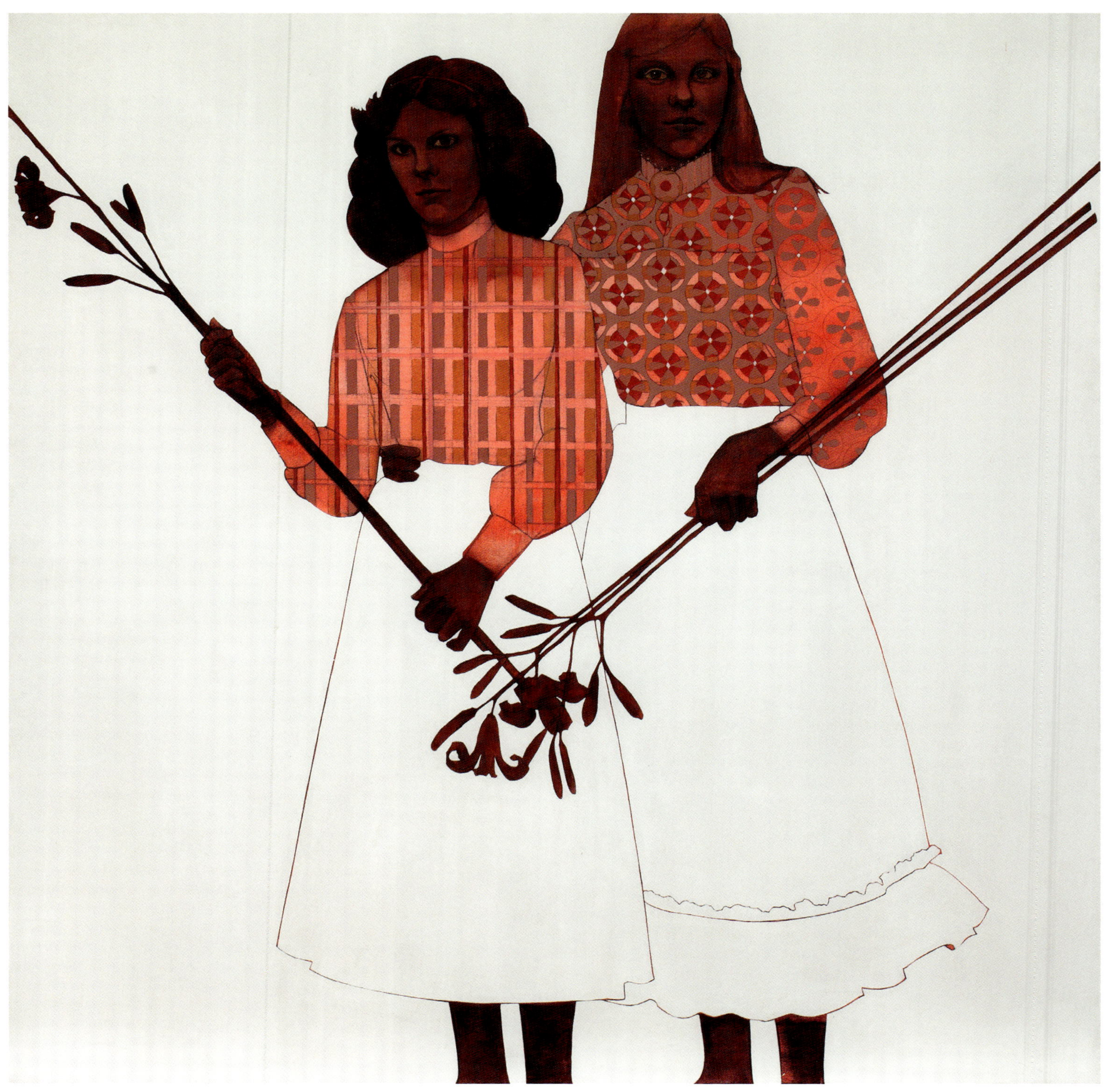

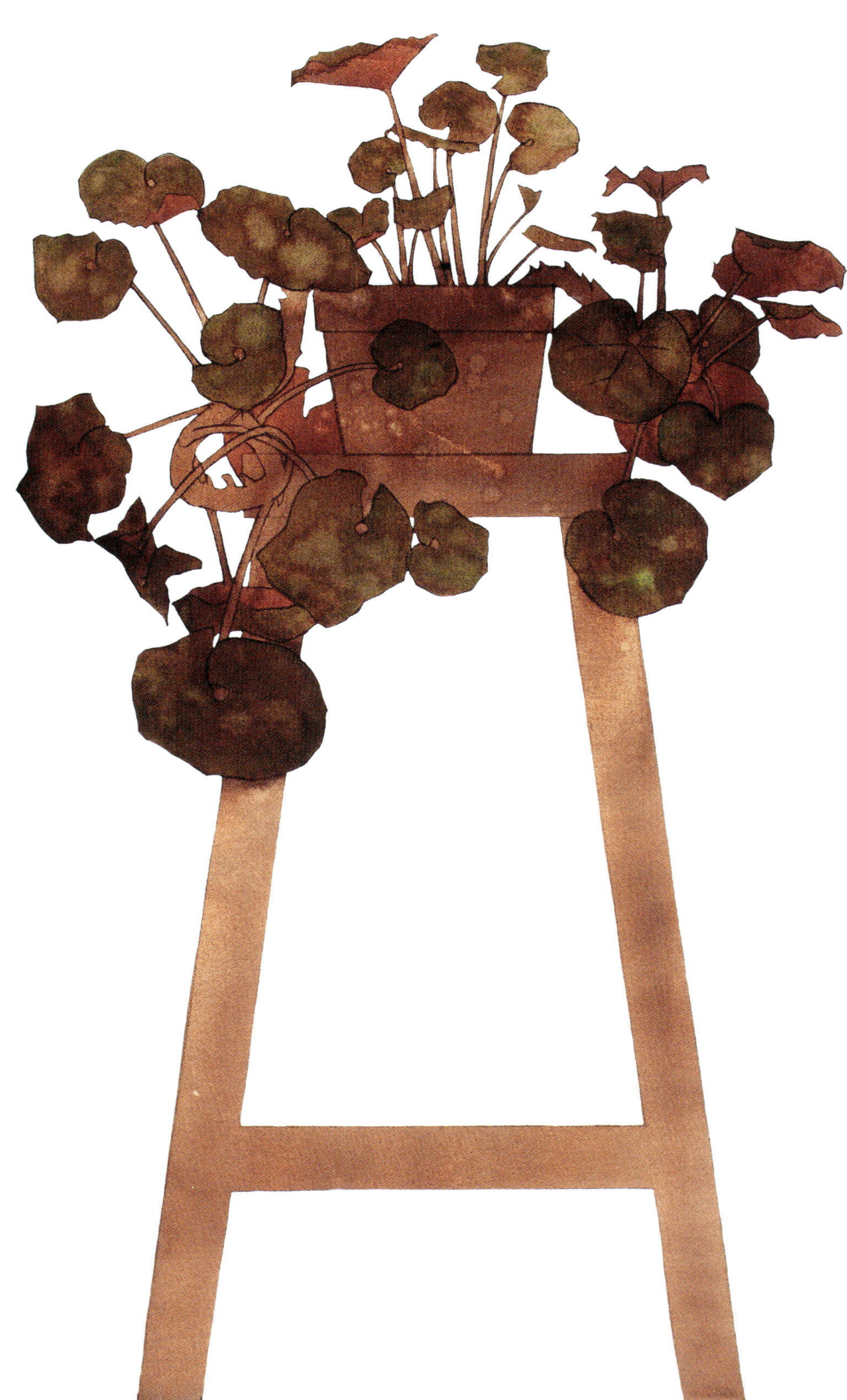

Cat. 16
Flowerstand, ca. 1972
Acrylic and graphite on canvas
48 × 28 in.
Collection of Beth and
David Skudder

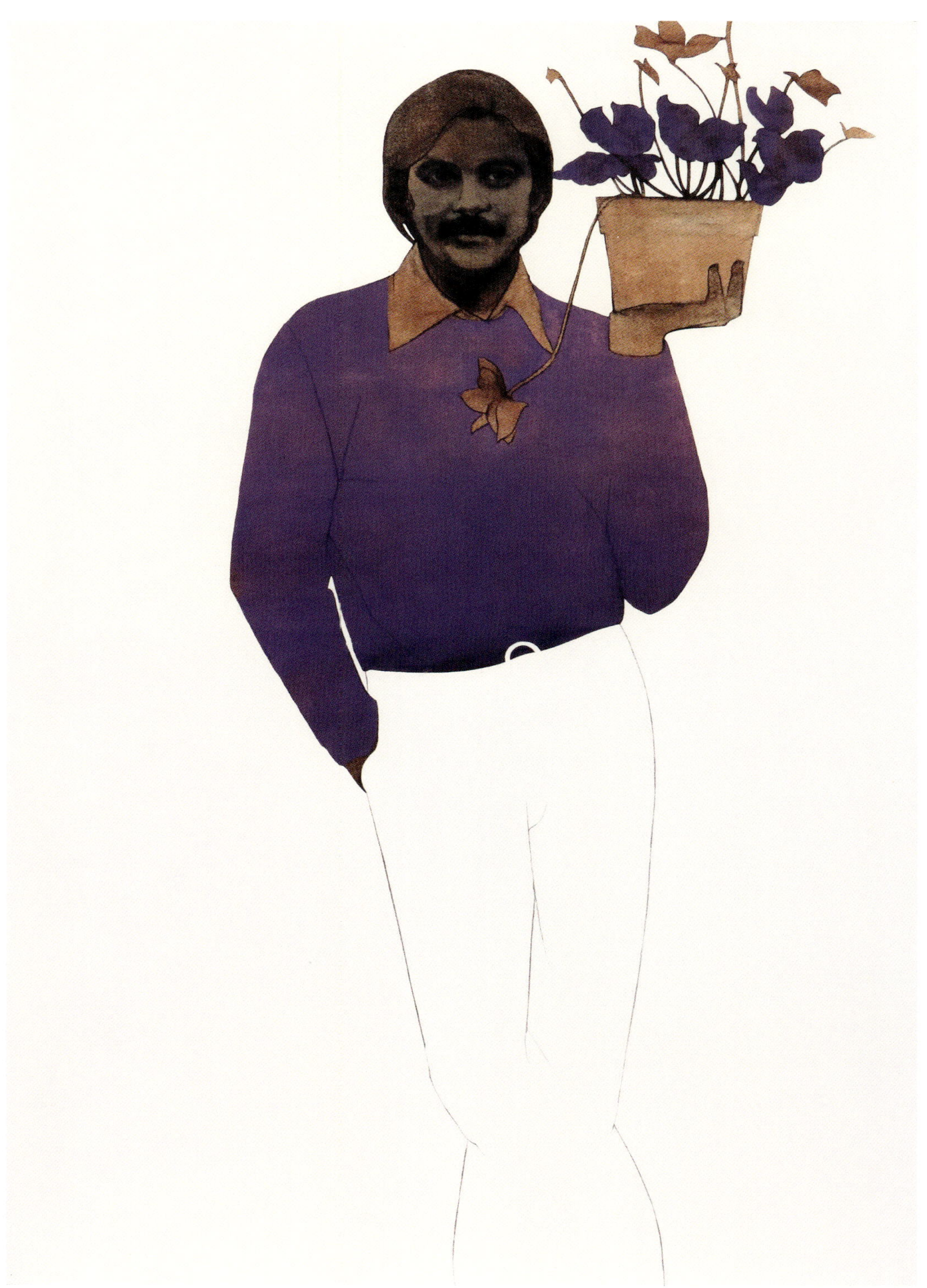

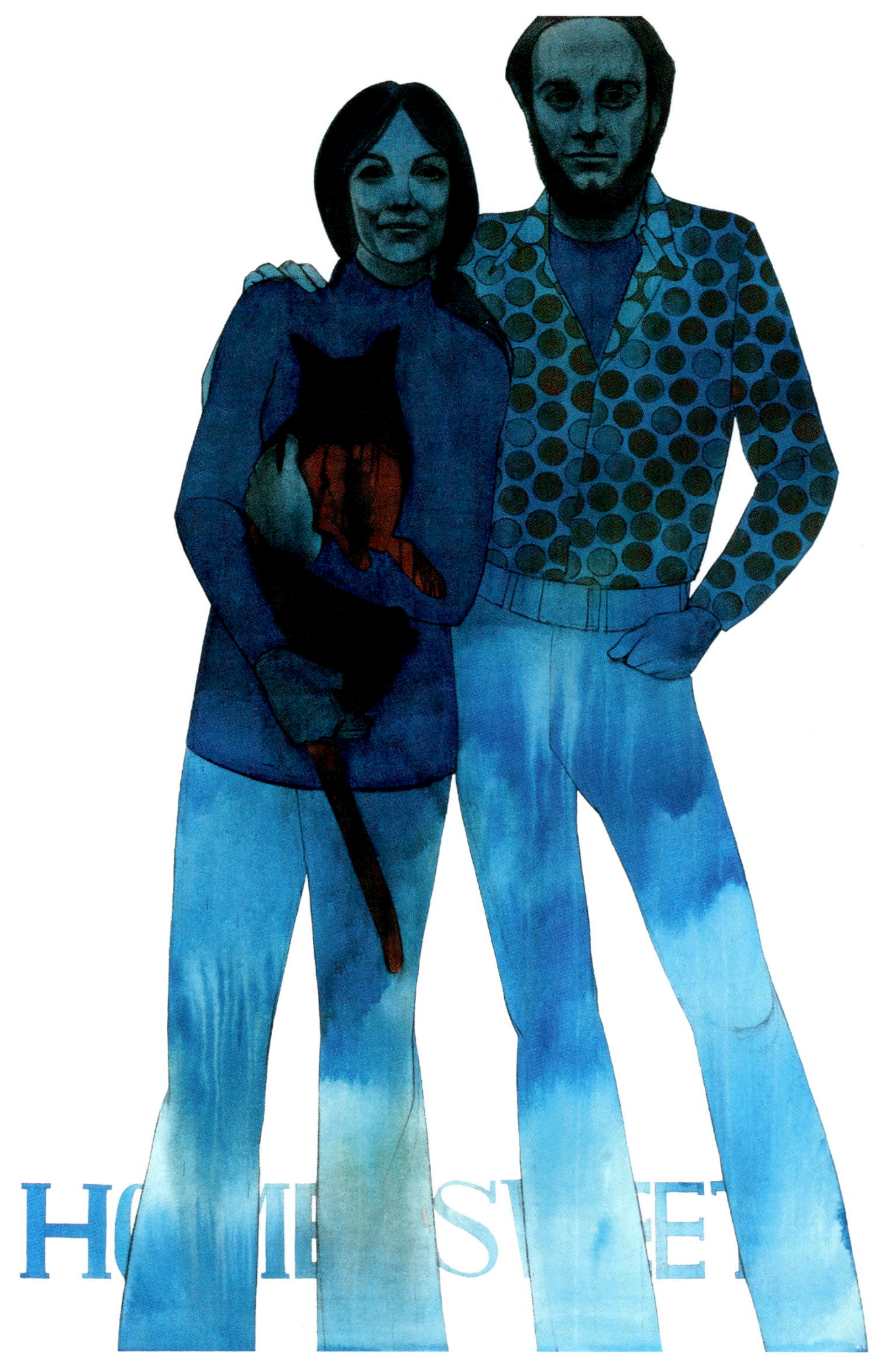

Cat. 18
Mutual Consent (Portrait of Jessie and Dolph Smith), ca. 1972
Acrylic and graphite on canvas
72 × 48 in.
Collection of Dolph Smith

Untitled (Woman with Branches), ca. 1972
Acrylic and graphite on canvas
72 × 60 in.
Collection of Robert Donovan Smith

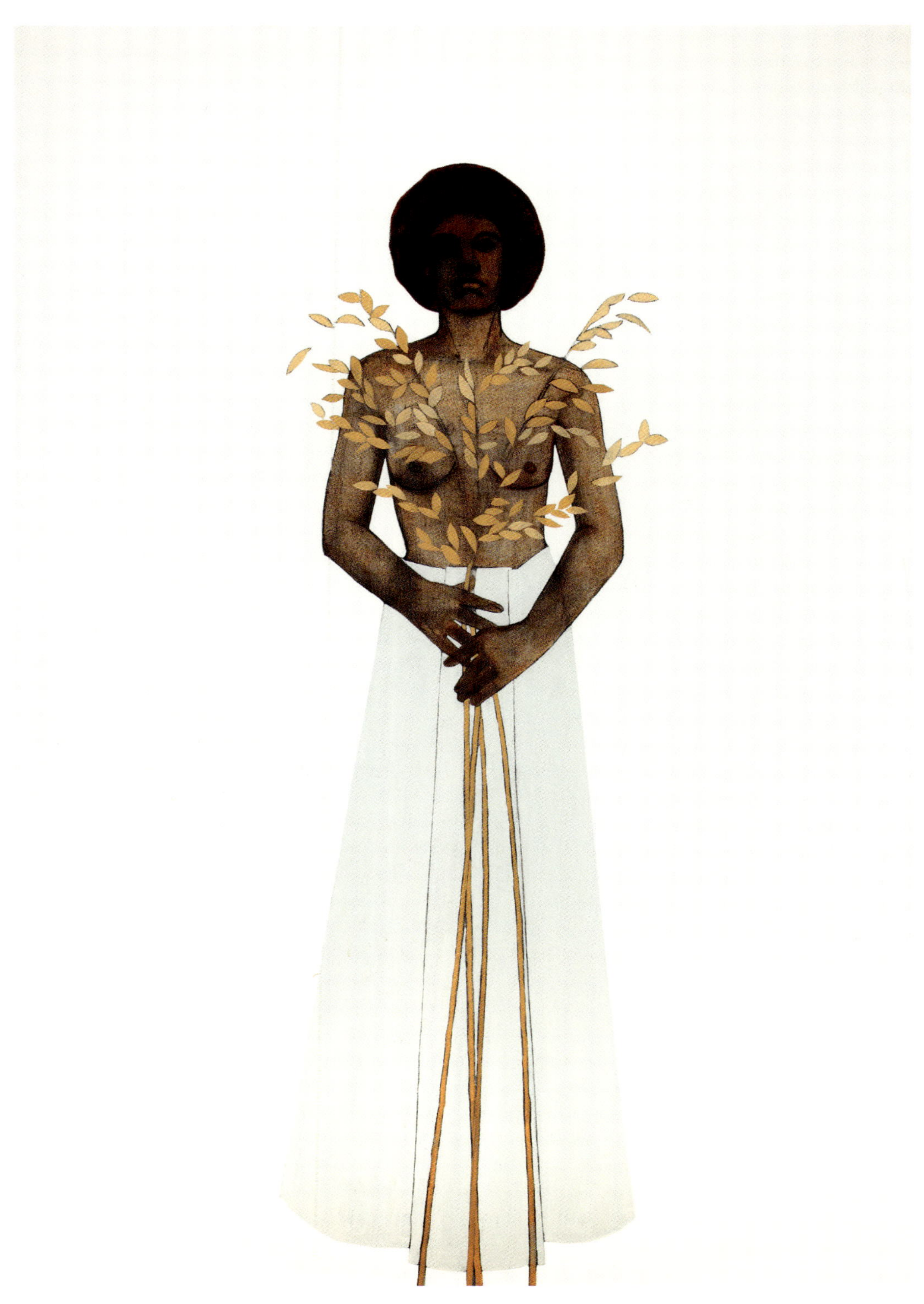

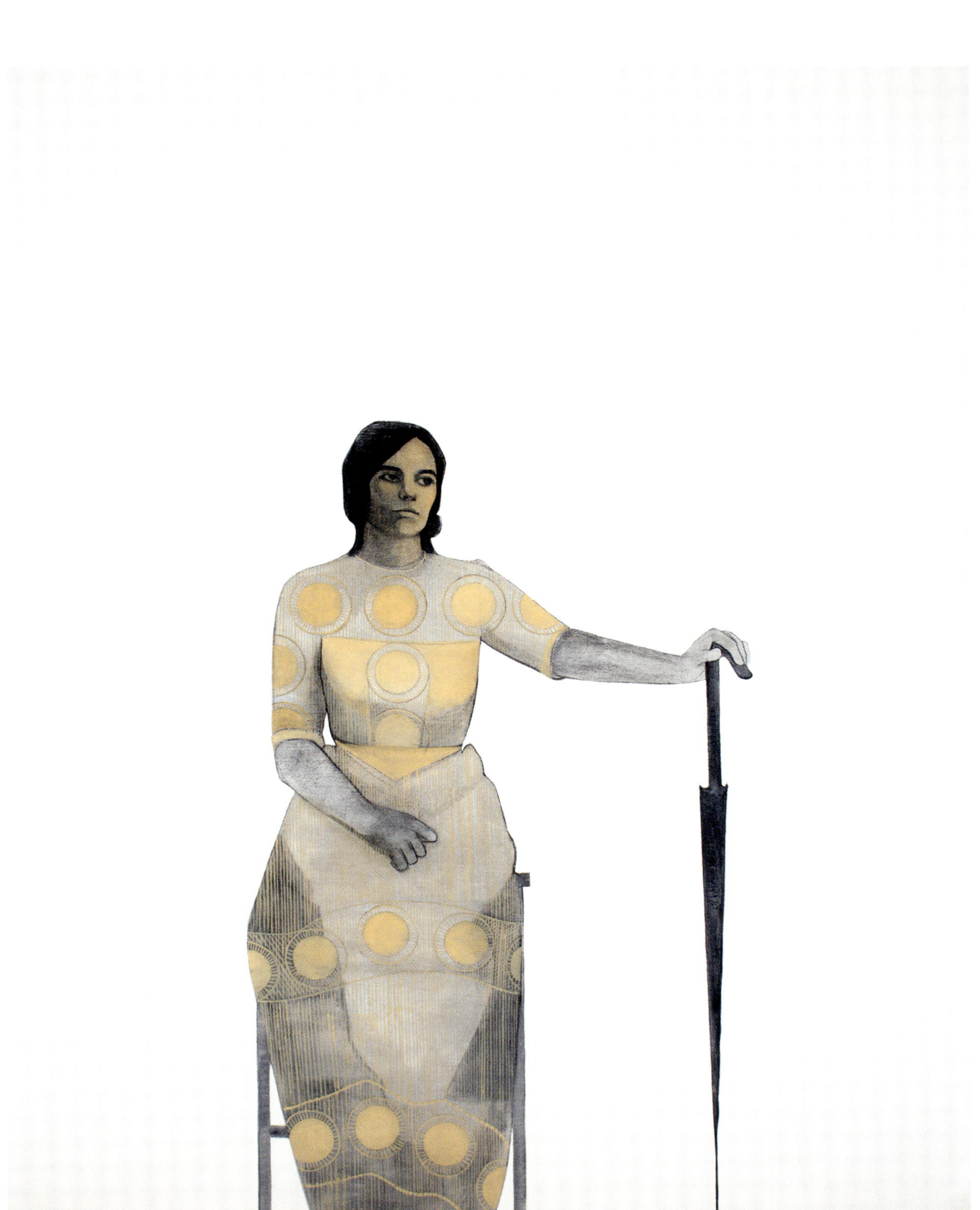

Cat. 20
Brier, ca. 1973
Acrylic and graphite on canvas
72 × 60 in.
Collection of Brier Smith Turner

Cat. 21

Untitled (Man on a Park Bench), 1975
Acrylic and graphite on canvas
72 × 57 ¼ in.
David Lusk Gallery, Memphis and
Nashville, Tennessee

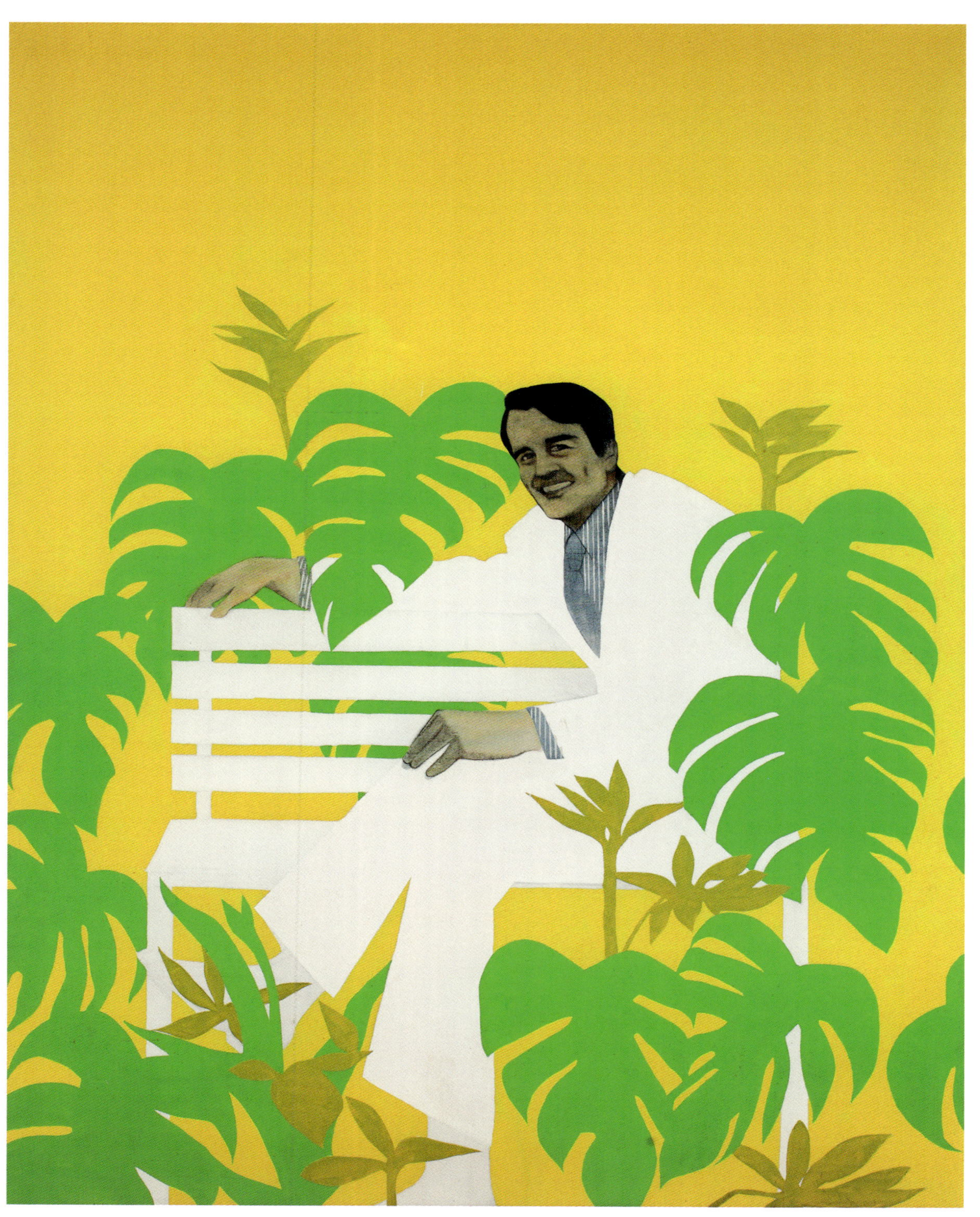

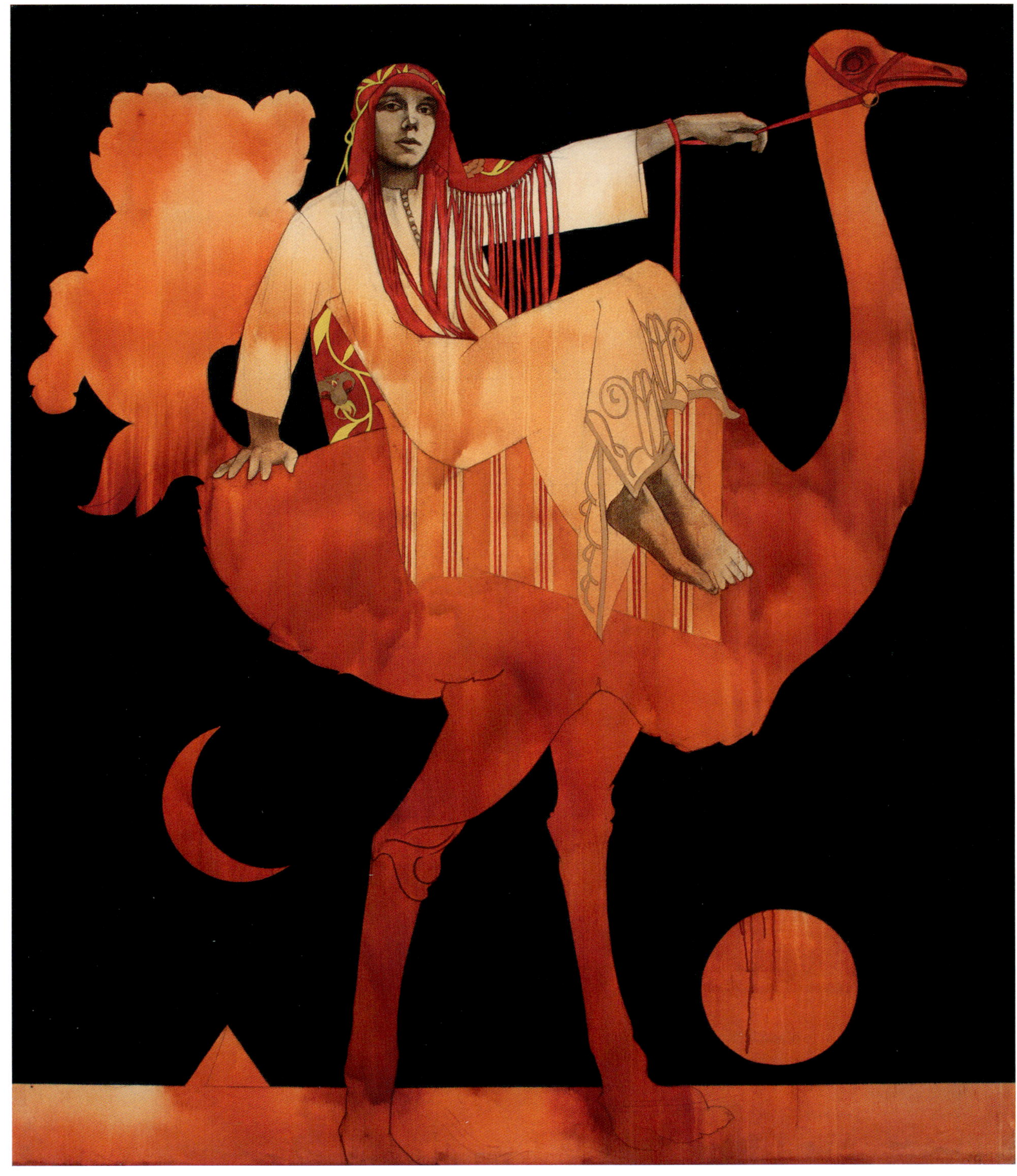

Cat. 22
Drop Dead Chic, 1976
Acrylic and graphite on canvas
90 × 78 in.
Collection of Jim Herbst

Cat. 23
The Blue Cat (Janet's Rose Garden), 1976
Acrylic and graphite on canvas
60 × 60 in.
St. Mary's Episcopal School, Memphis,
Tennessee

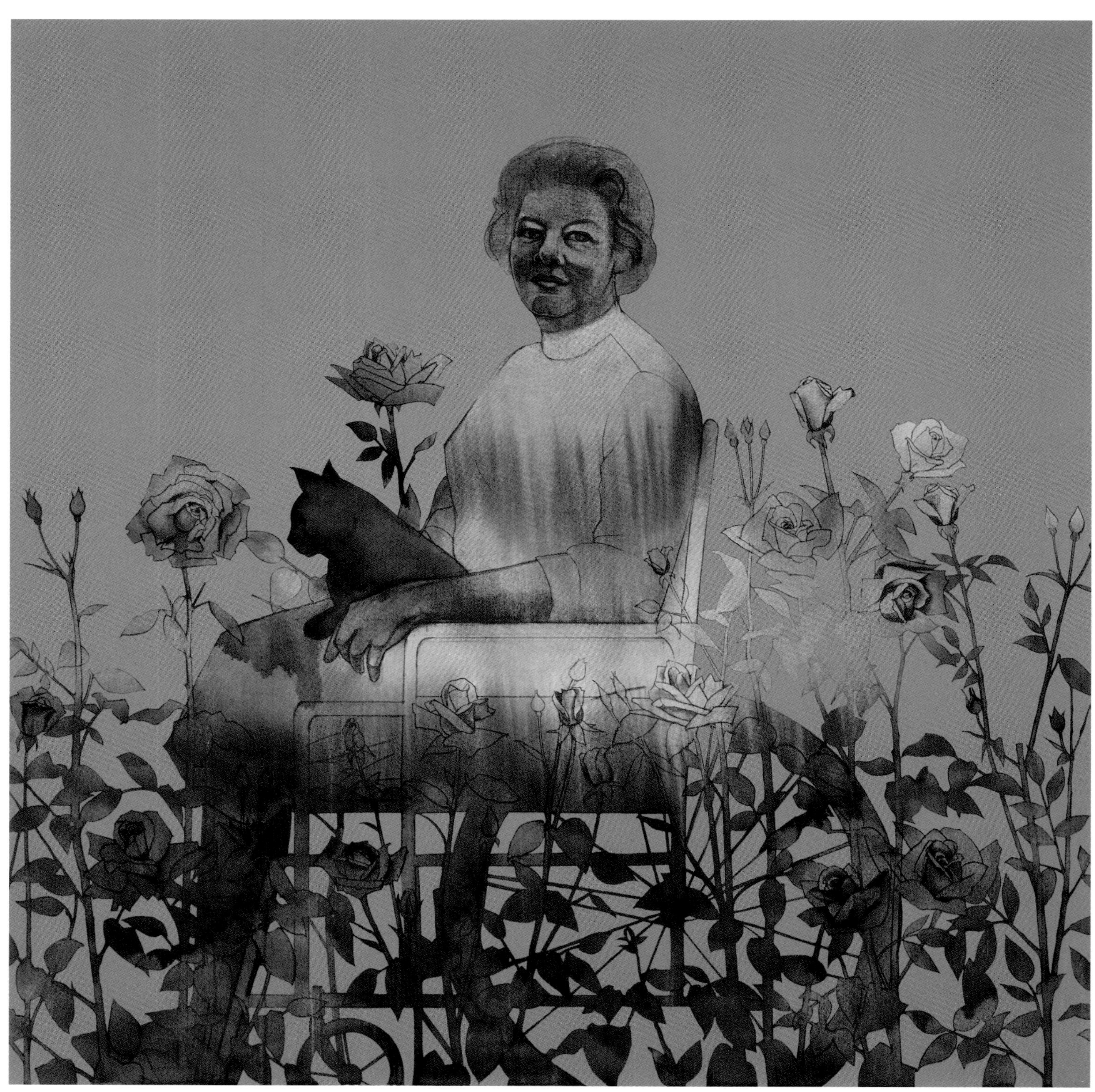

Cat. 24
Portrait of Elise, 1976
Acrylic and graphite on canvas
60 × 60 in.
Collection of JJ and Jay Keras

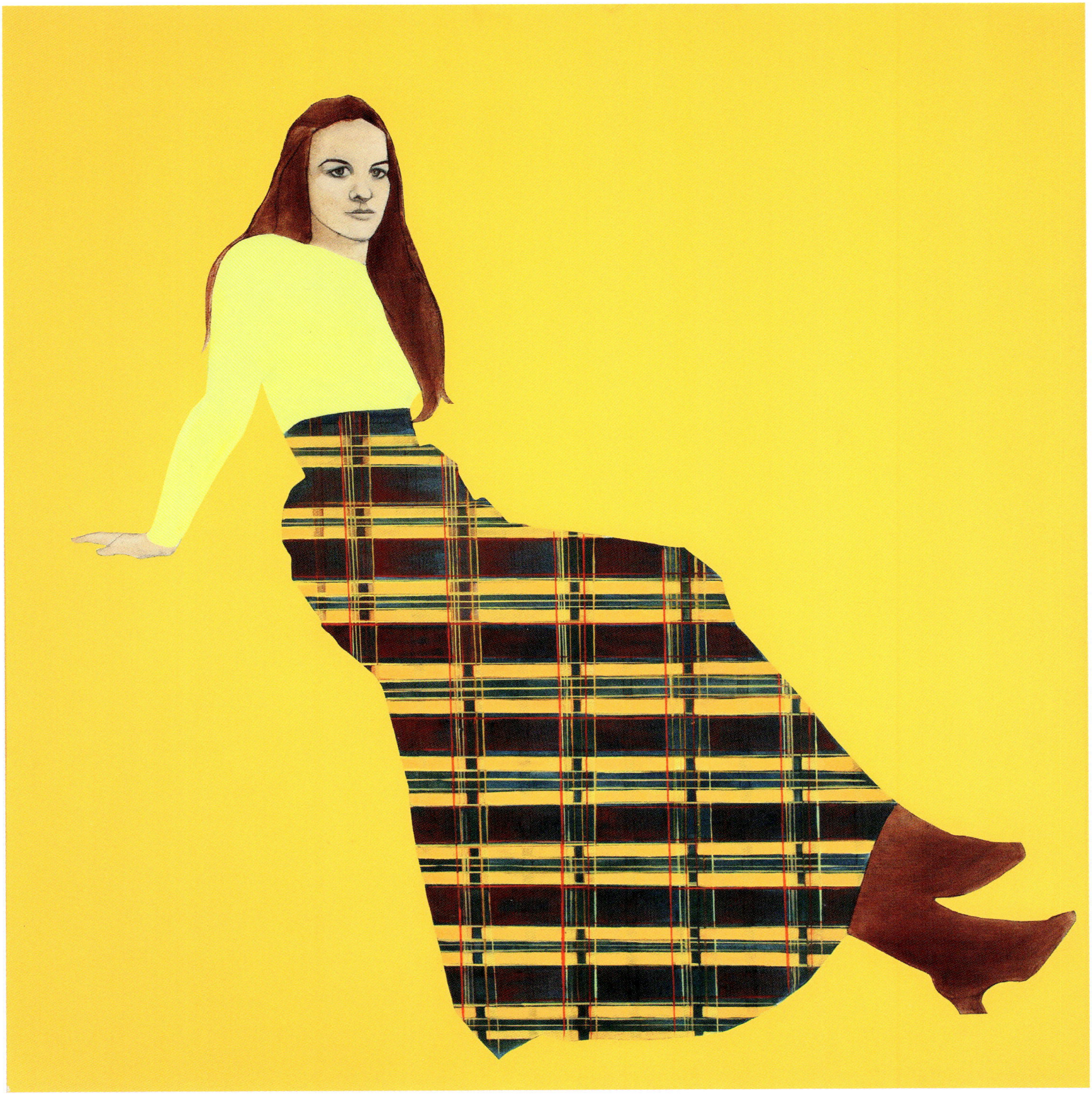

Virgin Guadalupe, 1976
Acrylic and graphite on canvas
54 × 32 in.
St. Mary's Episcopal School,
Memphis, Tennessee

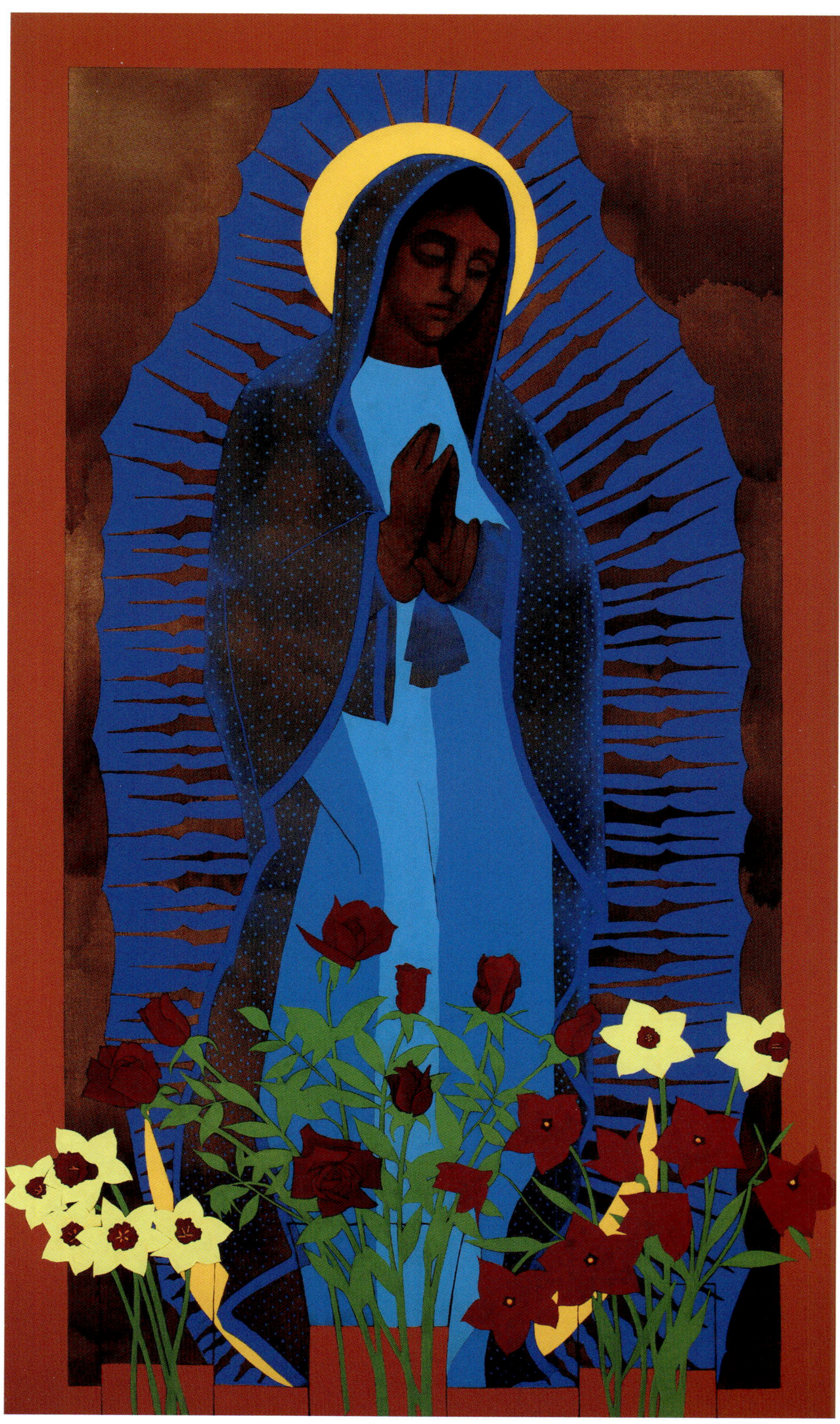

Cat. 26
Dr. Feelgood, 1977
Acrylic and graphite on canvas
82 × 58 in.
Collection of Roger Ross and
Trae Winston

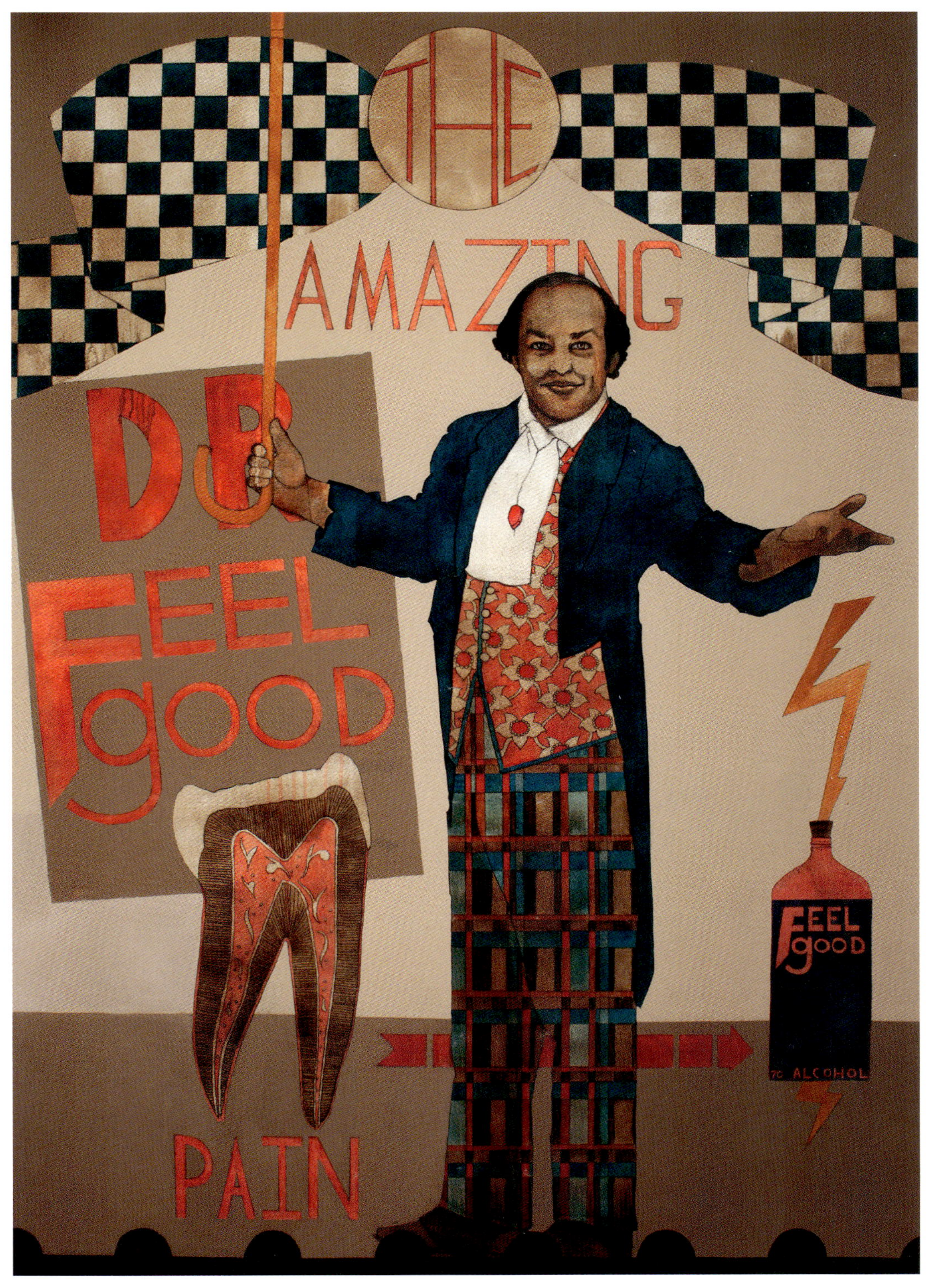
THE
AMAZING
DR
FEEL
good
PAIN
FEEL
good
70 ALCOHOL

Untitled (3 Parrots), 1977
Acrylic and graphite on canvas
40 × 40 in.
Collection of Maggie and Milton Lovell

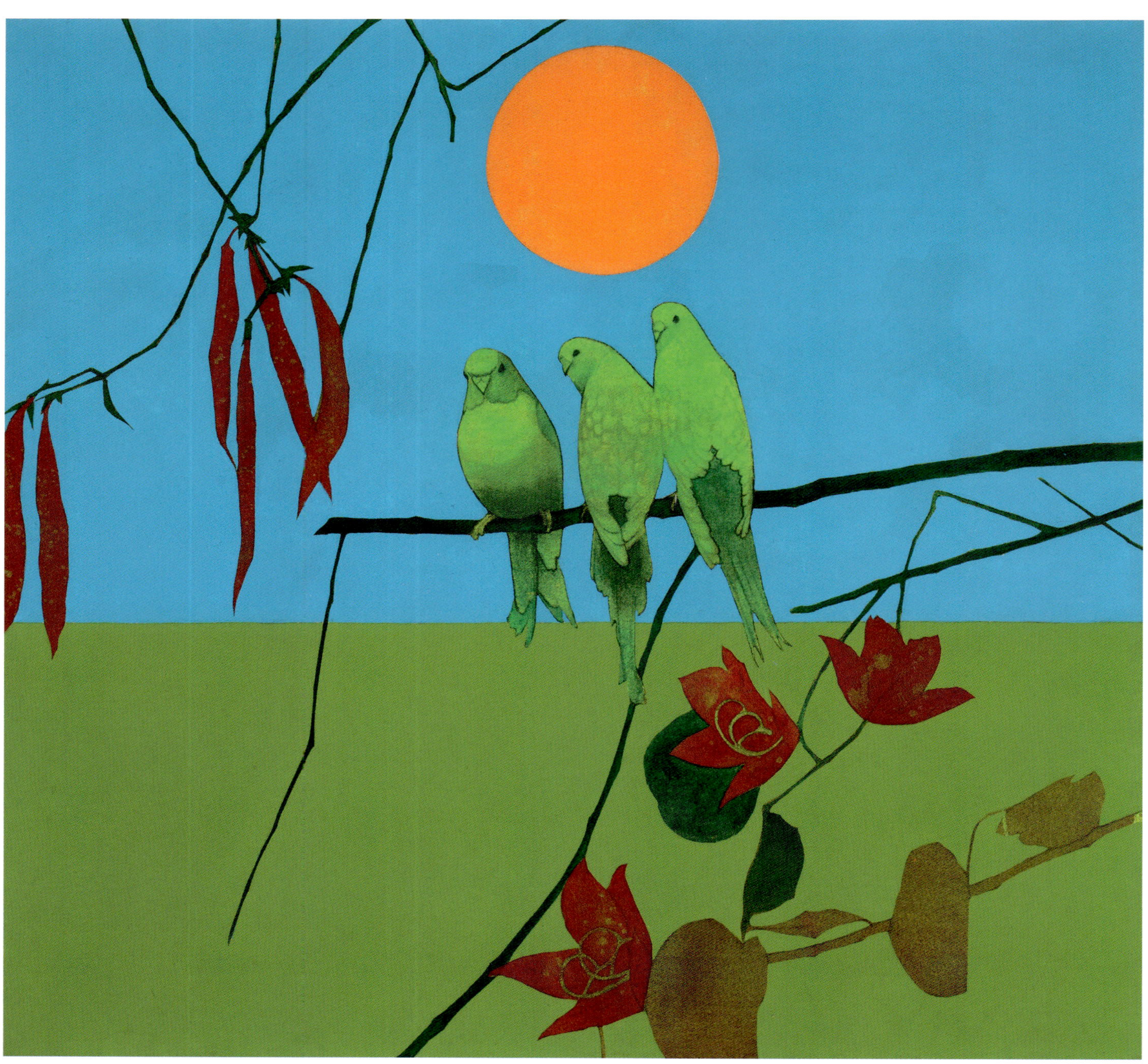

ONE WAY

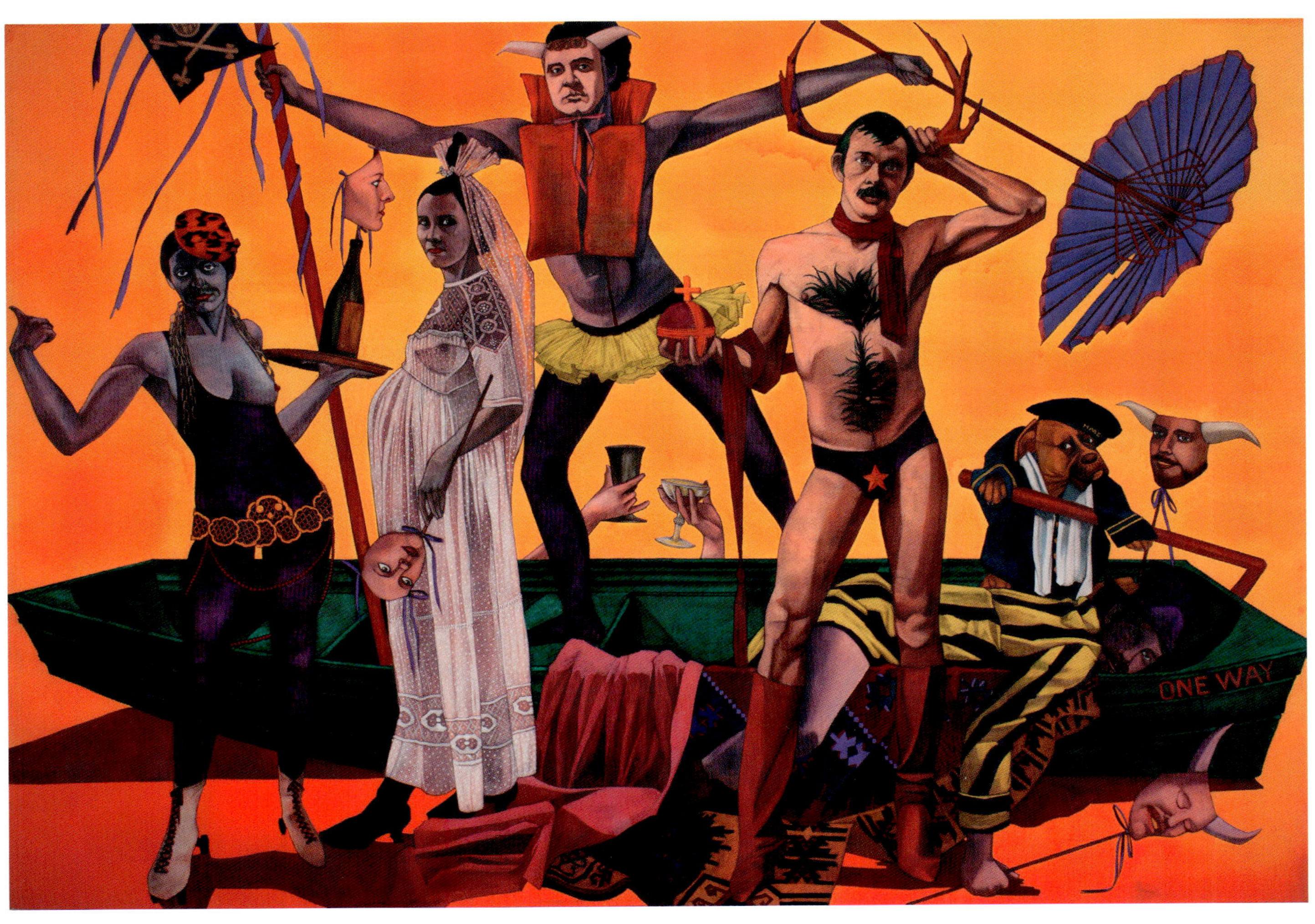

A Bride for Hosea, 1978
Acrylic and graphite on canvas
96 × 132 in.
Private collection

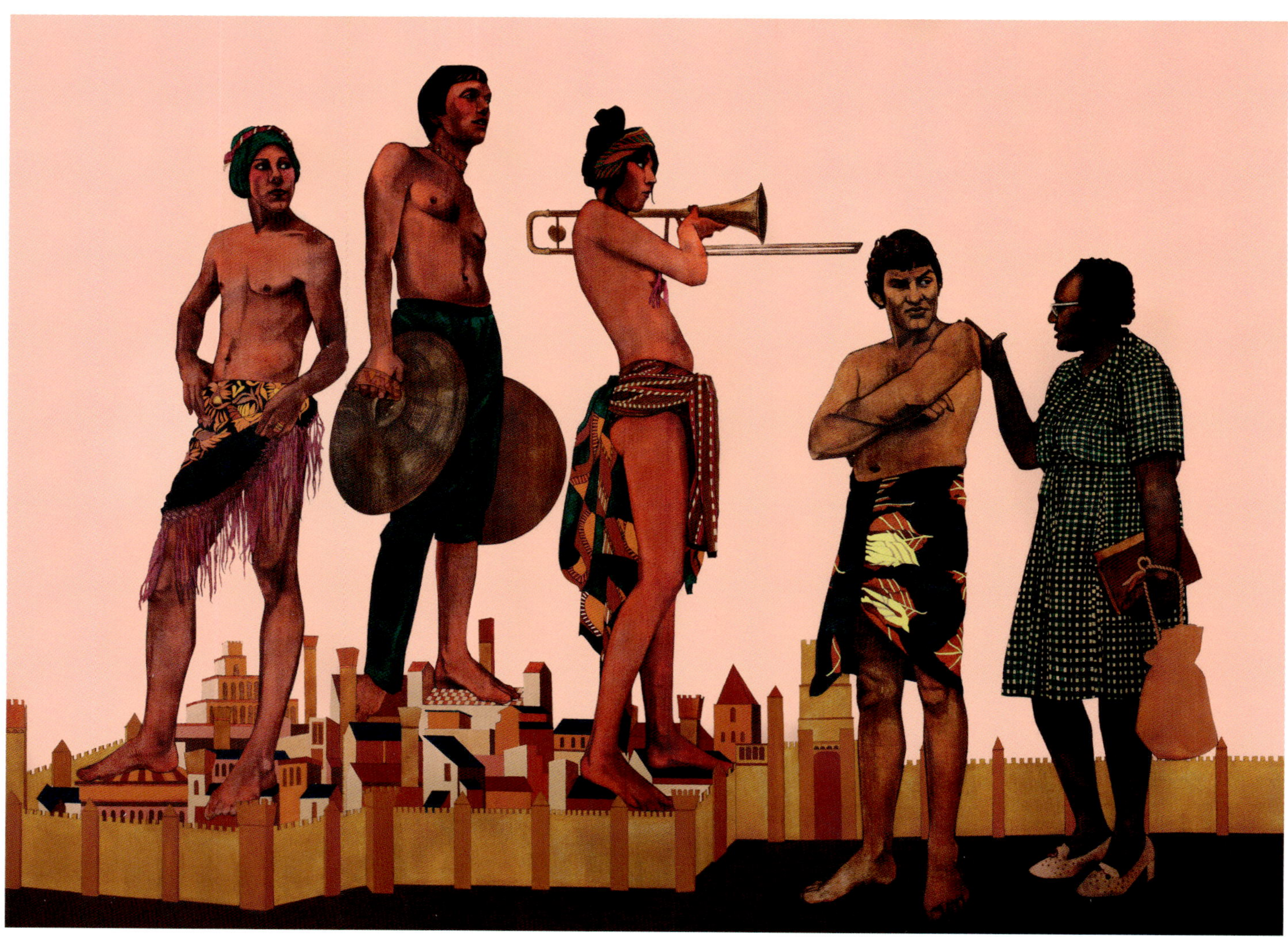

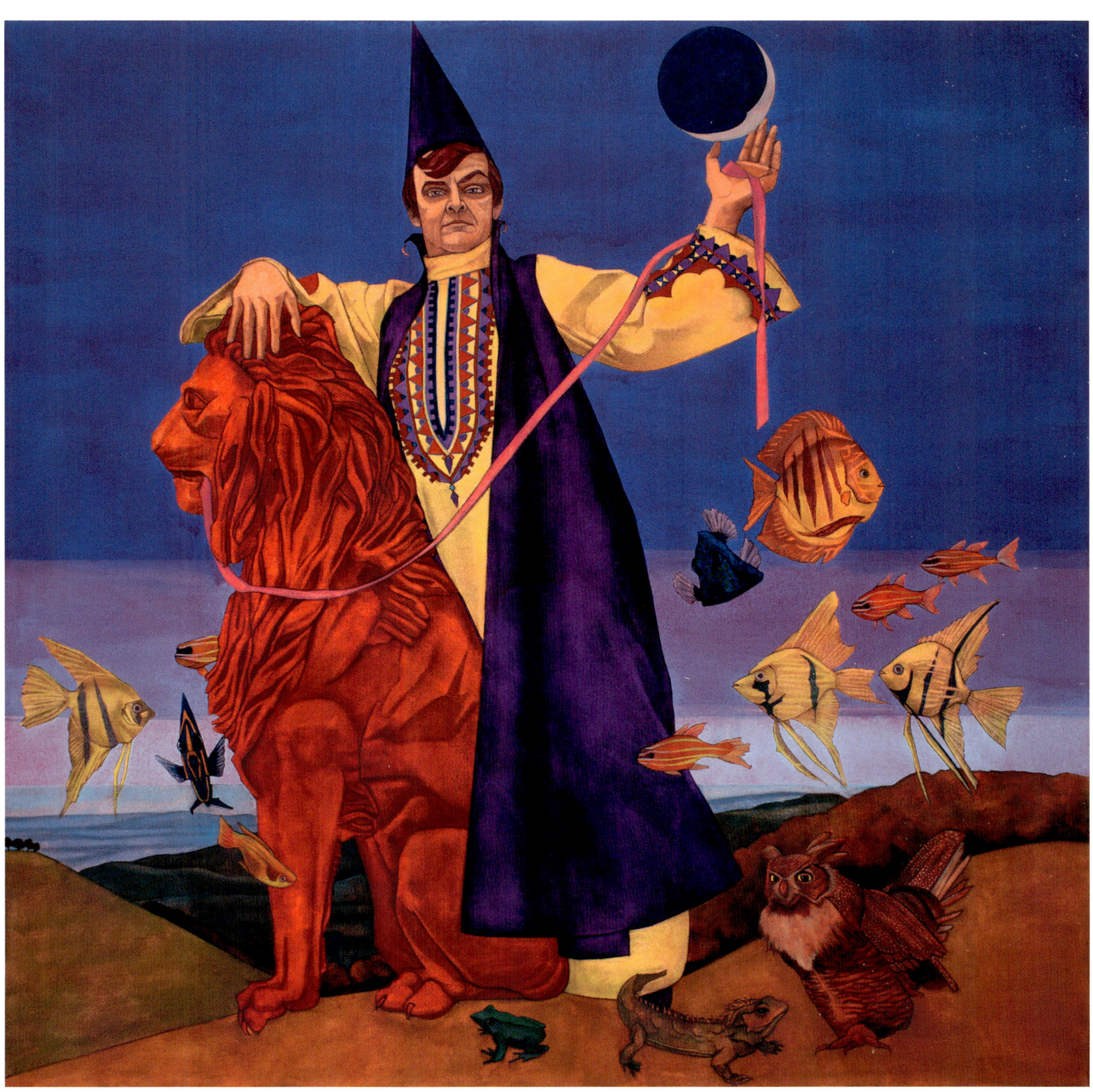

Cat. 30
Merlin, 1978
Acrylic and graphite on canvas
72 × 60 in.
Collection of Rodgers Menzies

Cat. 31
Untitled (Flamingo), 1978
Acrylic and graphite on canvas
42 ½ × 42 ⅝ in.
Collection of Neville and
Warfield Williams

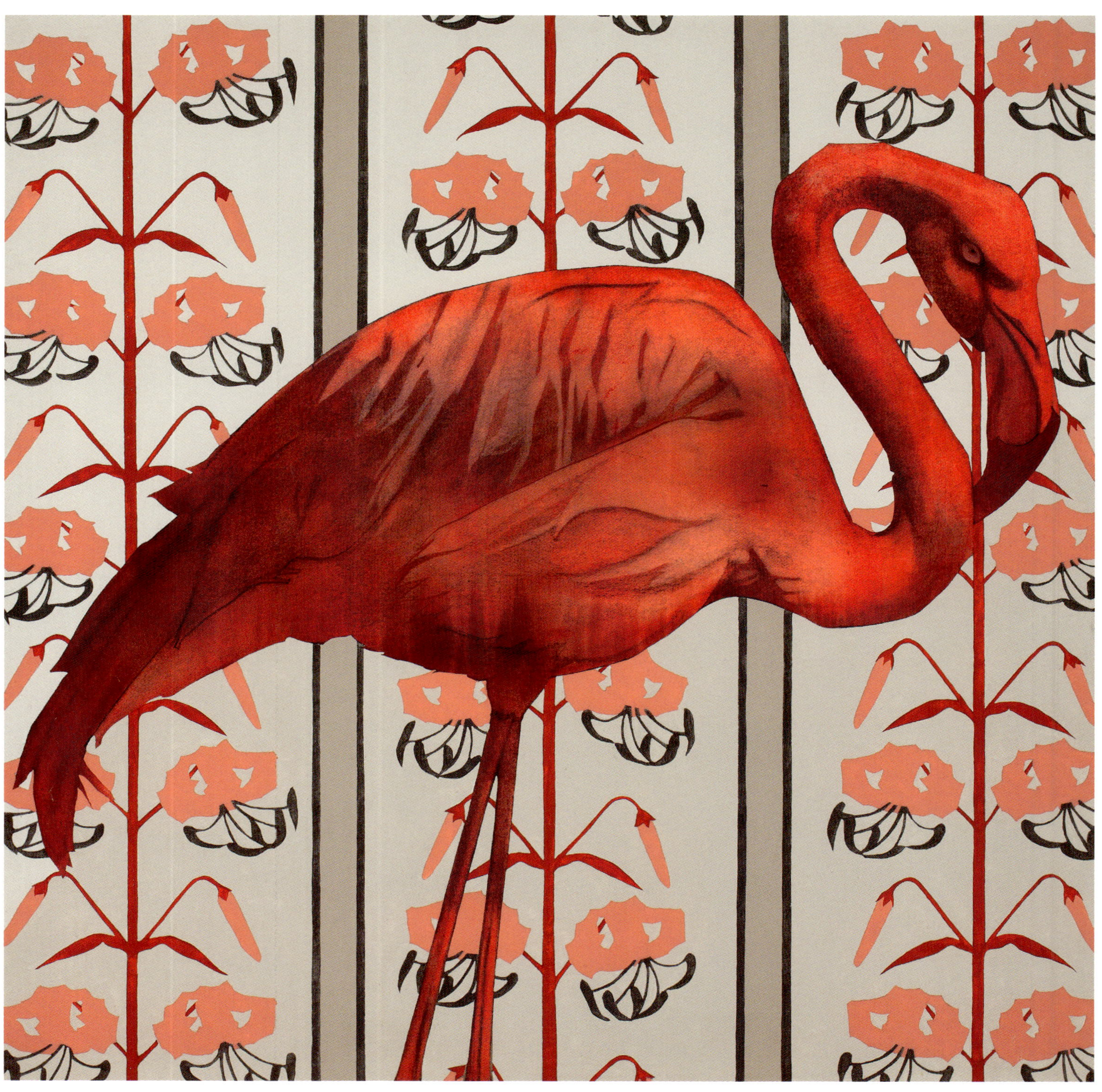

Cat. 32
Untitled (Lake Leatherwood), 1978
Acrylic and graphite on canvas
60 × 60 in.
Collection of Katherine and
Adrian Blackney

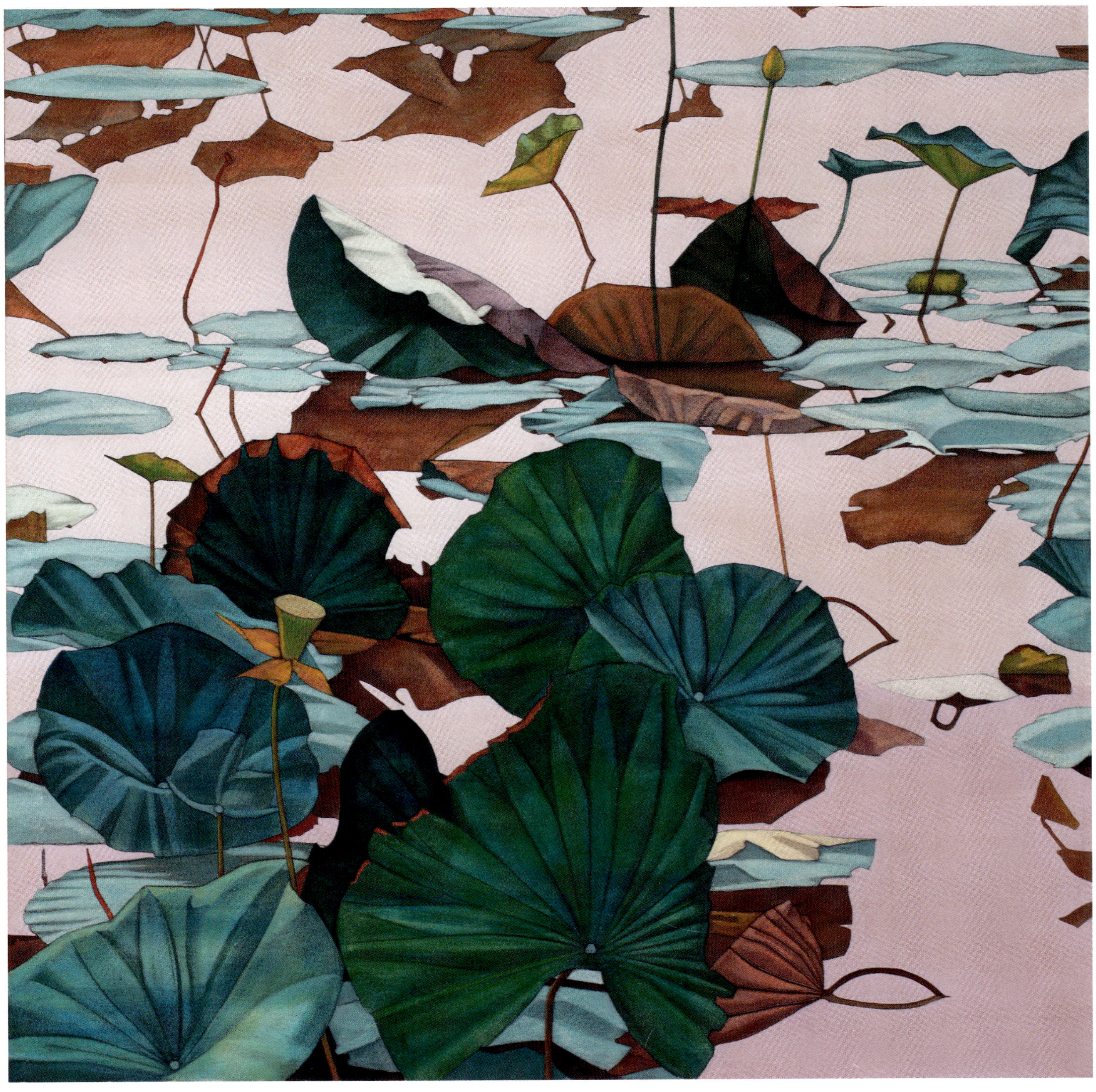

Cat. 33
Mexican Petunias, ca. 1978
Acrylic on canvas
42 × 36 in.
Collection of Katherine and Stephen Bush

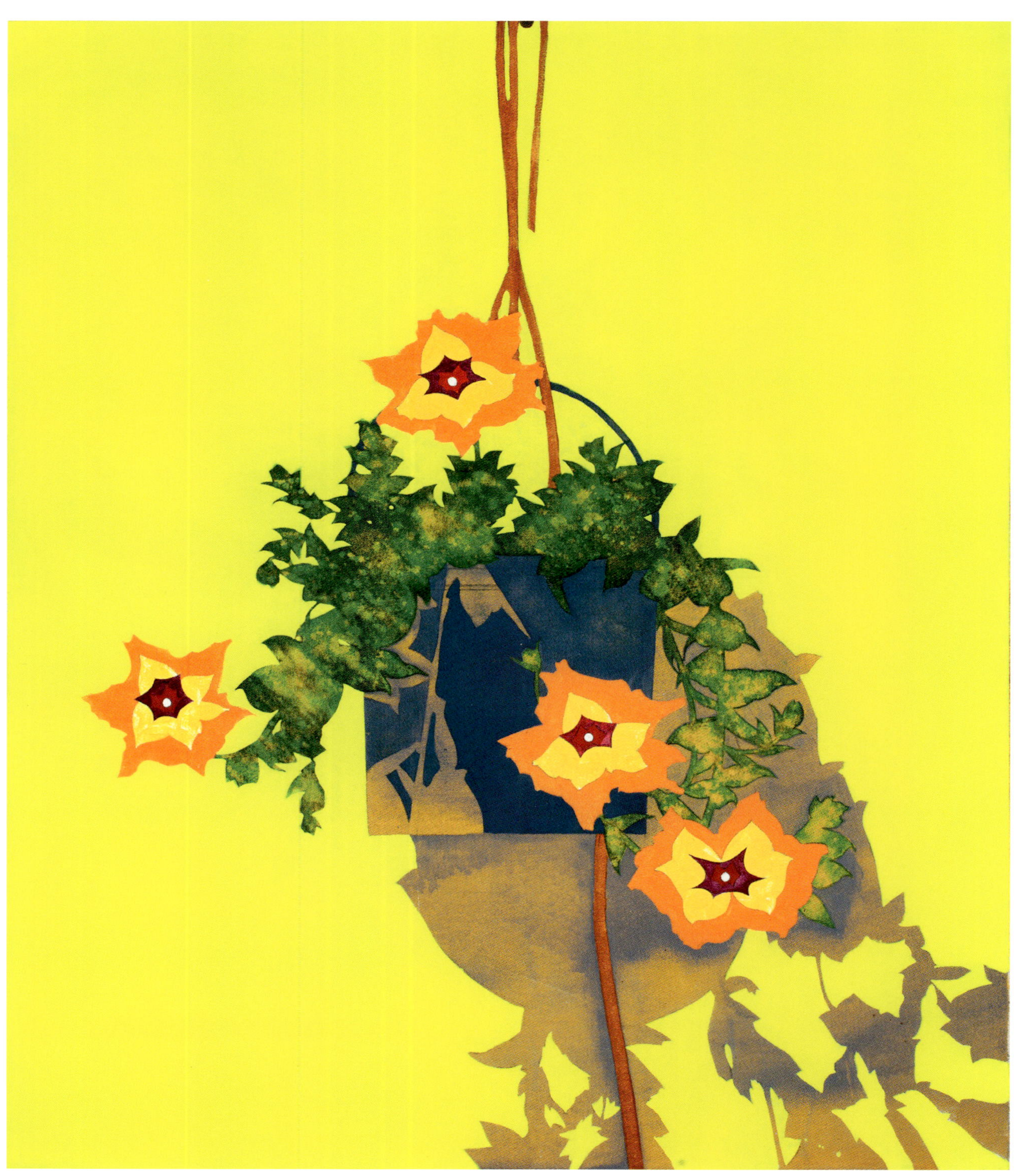

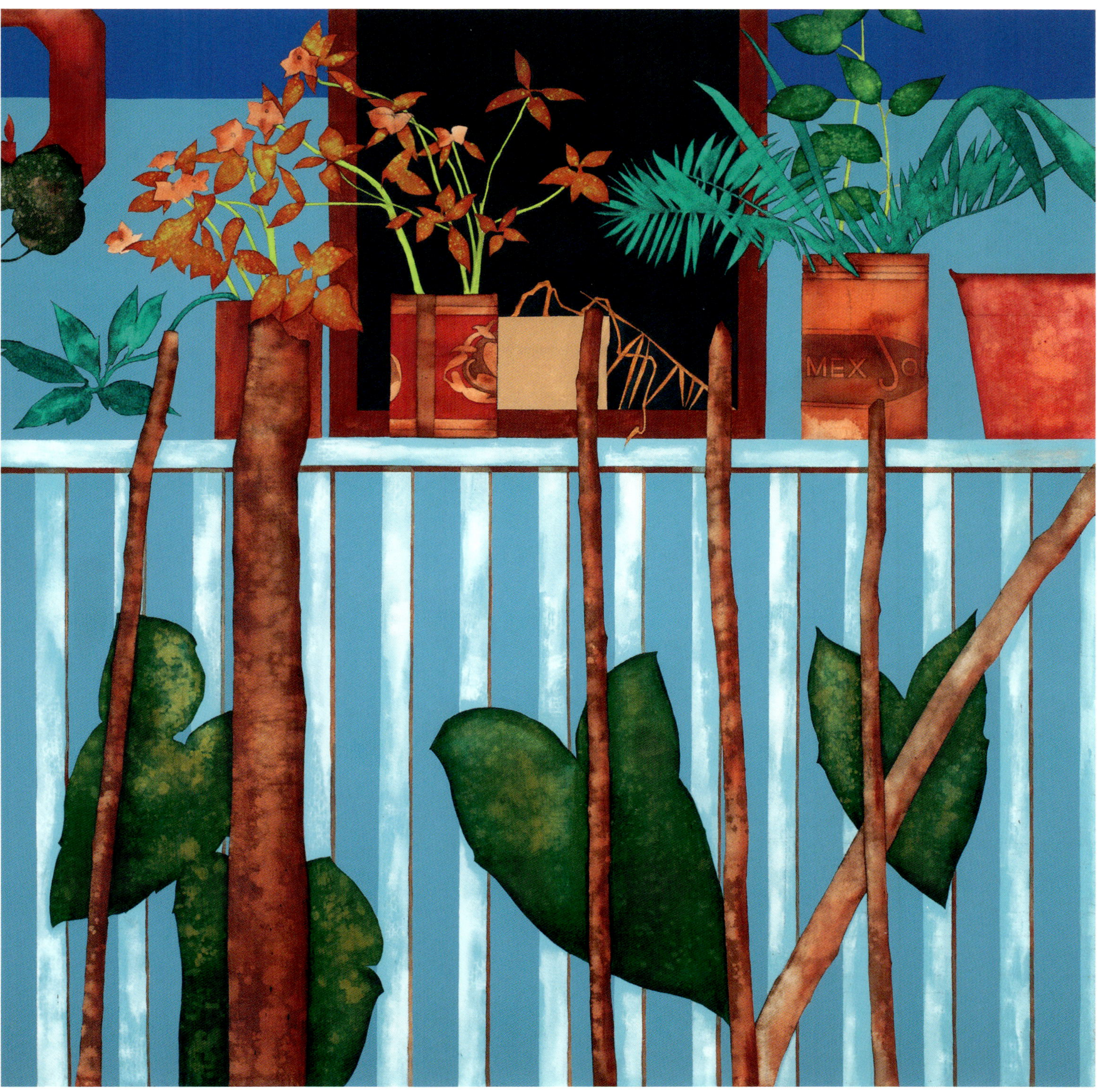

Cat. 34
Porch Flowers, ca. 1978
Acrylic and graphite on canvas
60 × 60 in.
Collection of Carissa Hussong
and David Lusk

Cat. 35
Untitled (Blue Wall, Red Flowers), ca. 1978
Acrylic and graphite on canvas
53 ¾ × 42 in.
Collection of Holly and Paul T. Combs

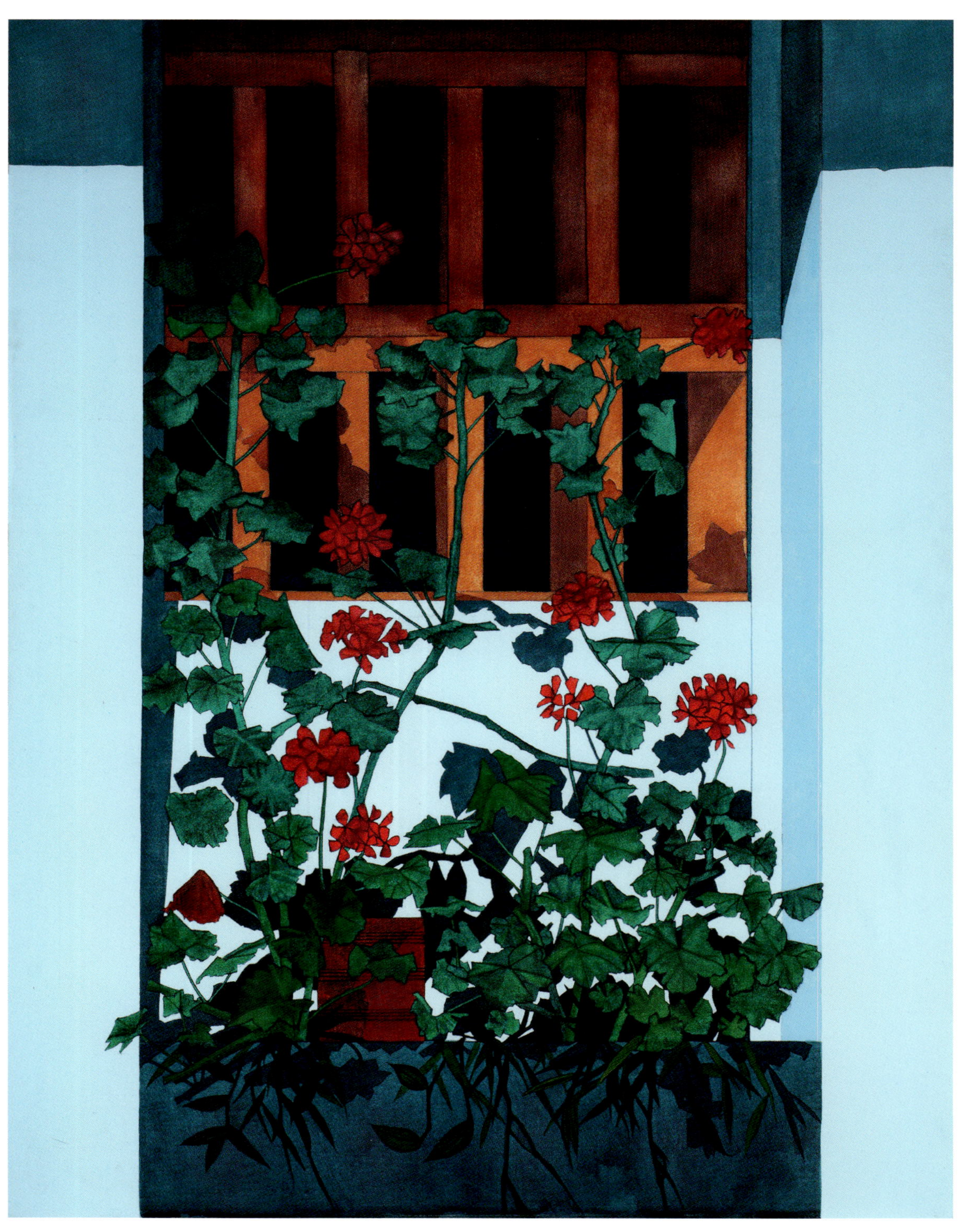

Untitled (Lake Leatherwood), ca. 1978
Acrylic and graphite on canvas
60 × 75 in.
Private collection

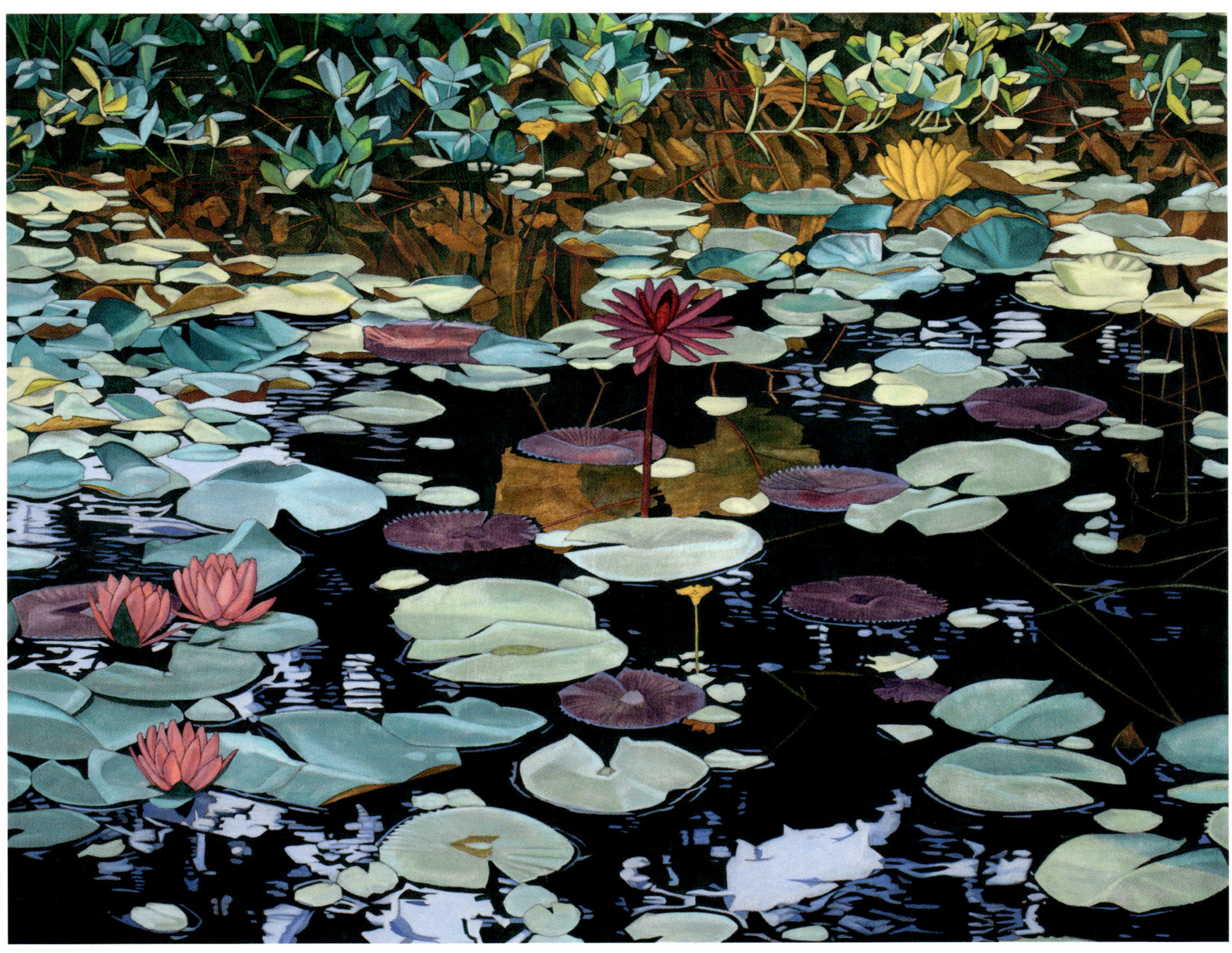

Untitled (Lake Leatherwood), ca. 1980
Acrylic and graphite on canvas
96 × 96 in.
Private collection

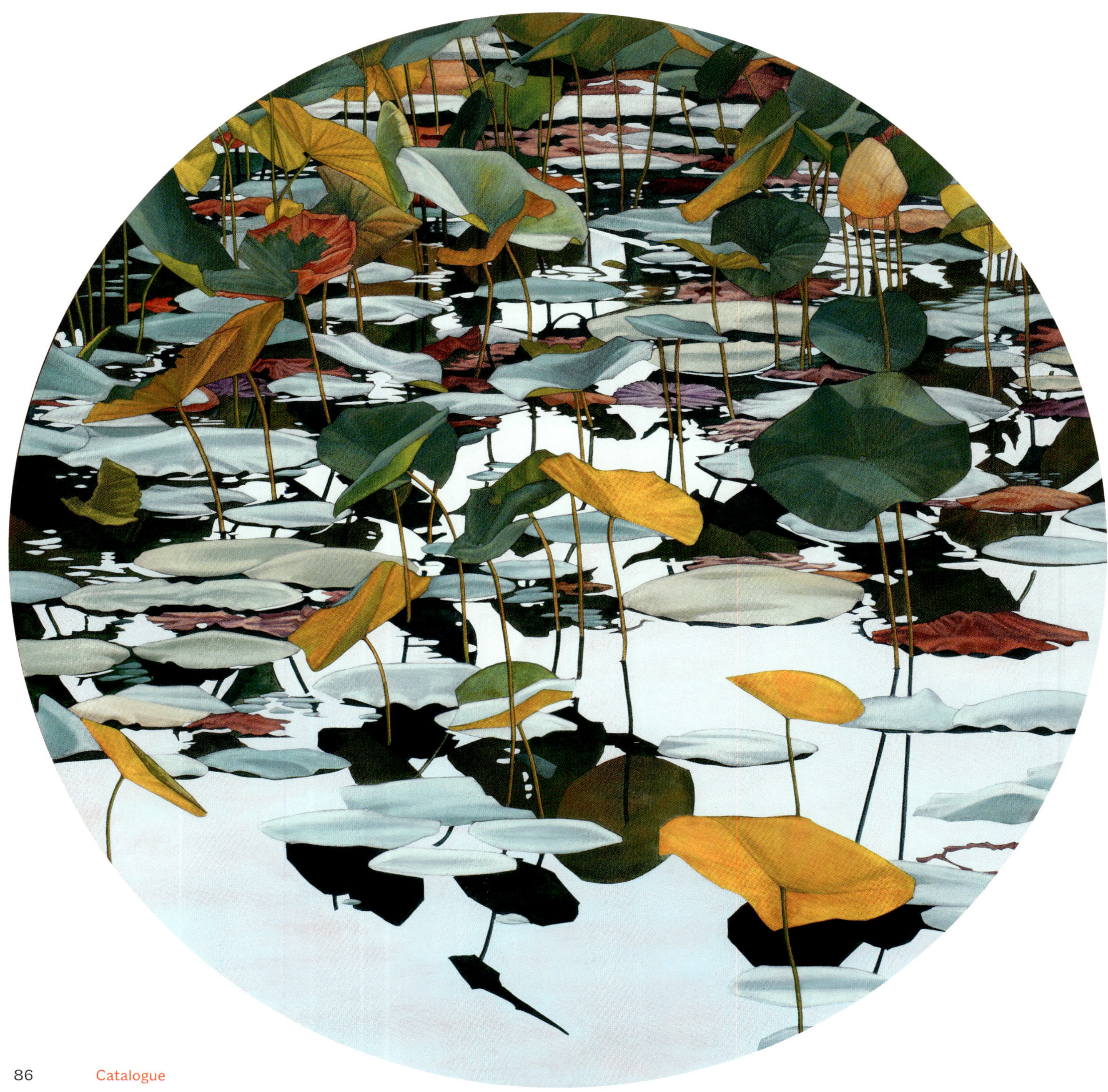

Cat. 38
Salute to Egypt, 1981
Acrylic on canvas
55 × 43 in.
Memphis in May International
Festival Collection,
Memphis, Tennessee

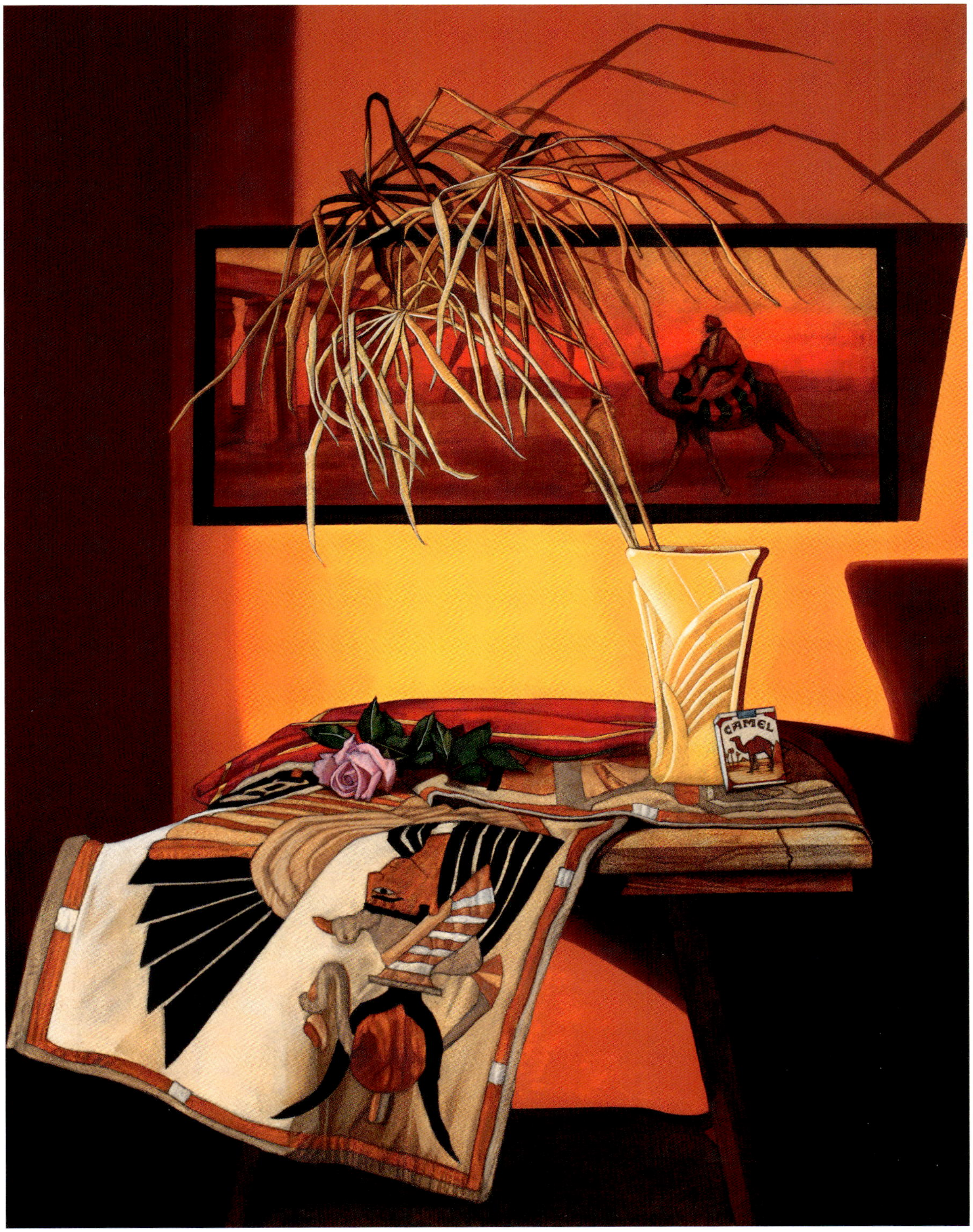

Cat. 39
Leda and the Cake, 1982
Acrylic on canvas
60 × 72 in.
Private collection

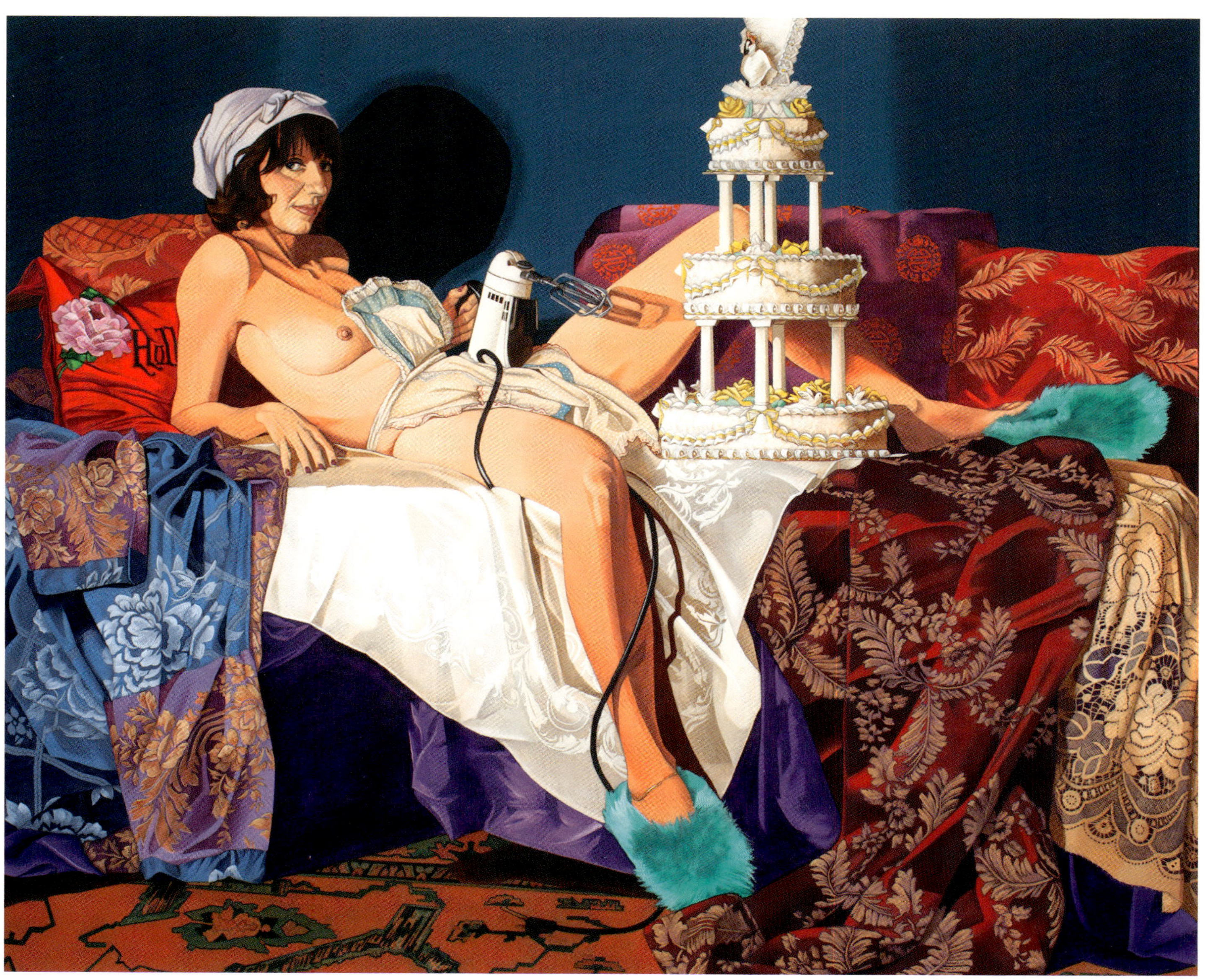

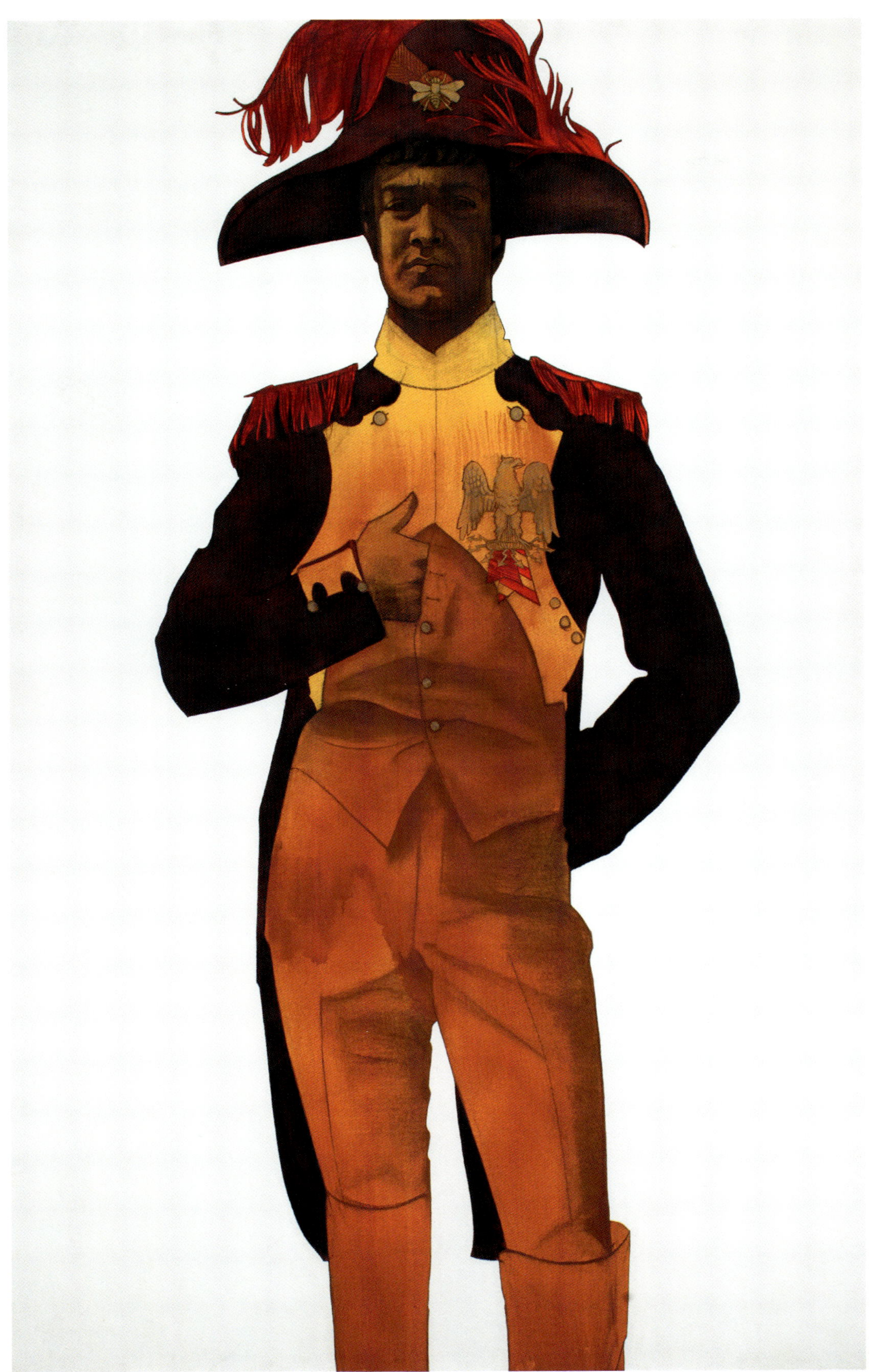

Cat. 40
Untitled (Napoleon), 1982
Acrylic and graphite on canvas
72 × 48 in.
Collection of Dianne and
Myron Mall

Cat. 41
Mama, ca. 1982
Charcoal on canvas
64 × 56 in.
Mississippi Museum of Art, Jackson,
Gift of Larry and Nina Riley, courtesy
David Lusk Gallery, Memphis,
Tennessee, 2003.002

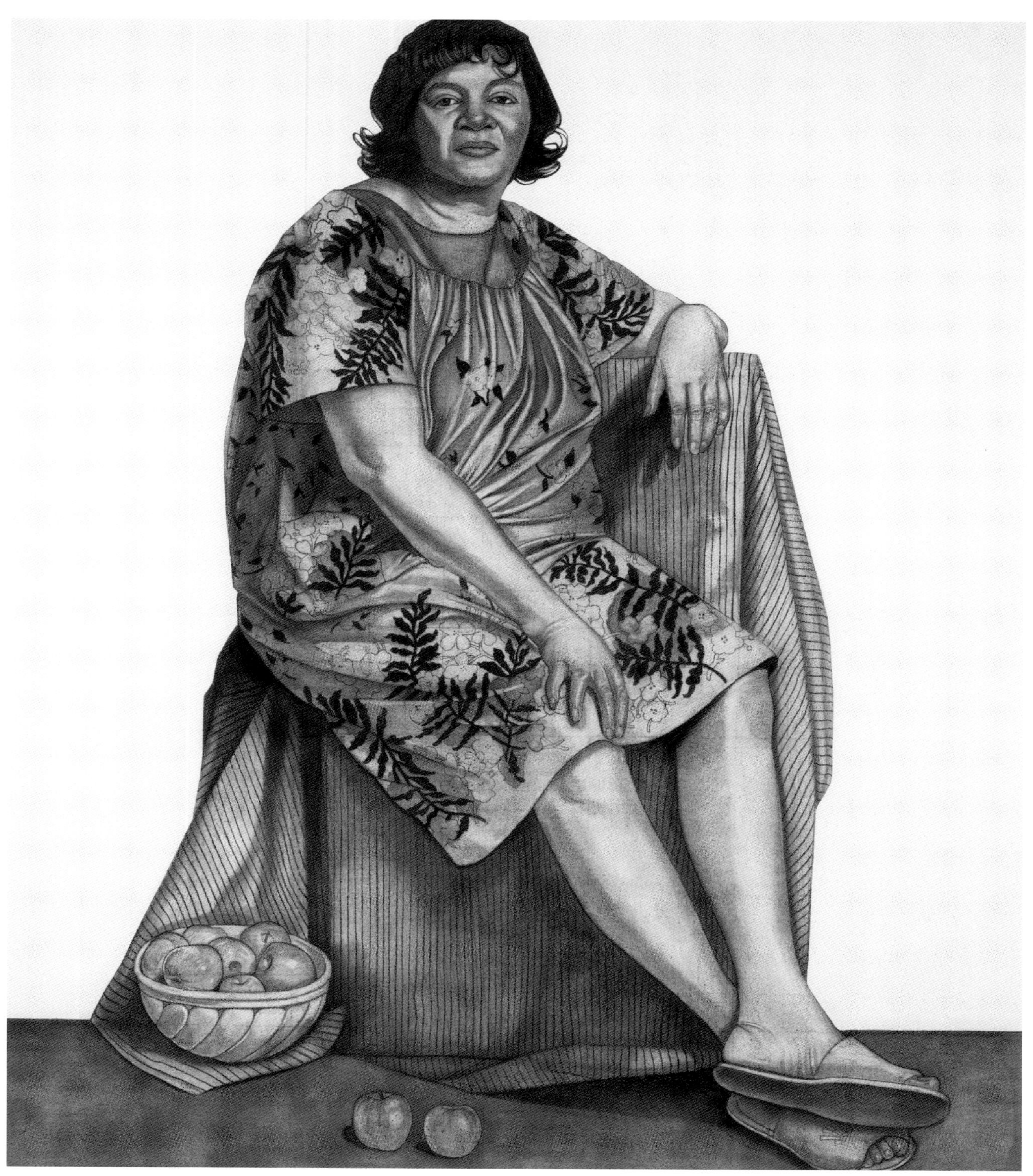

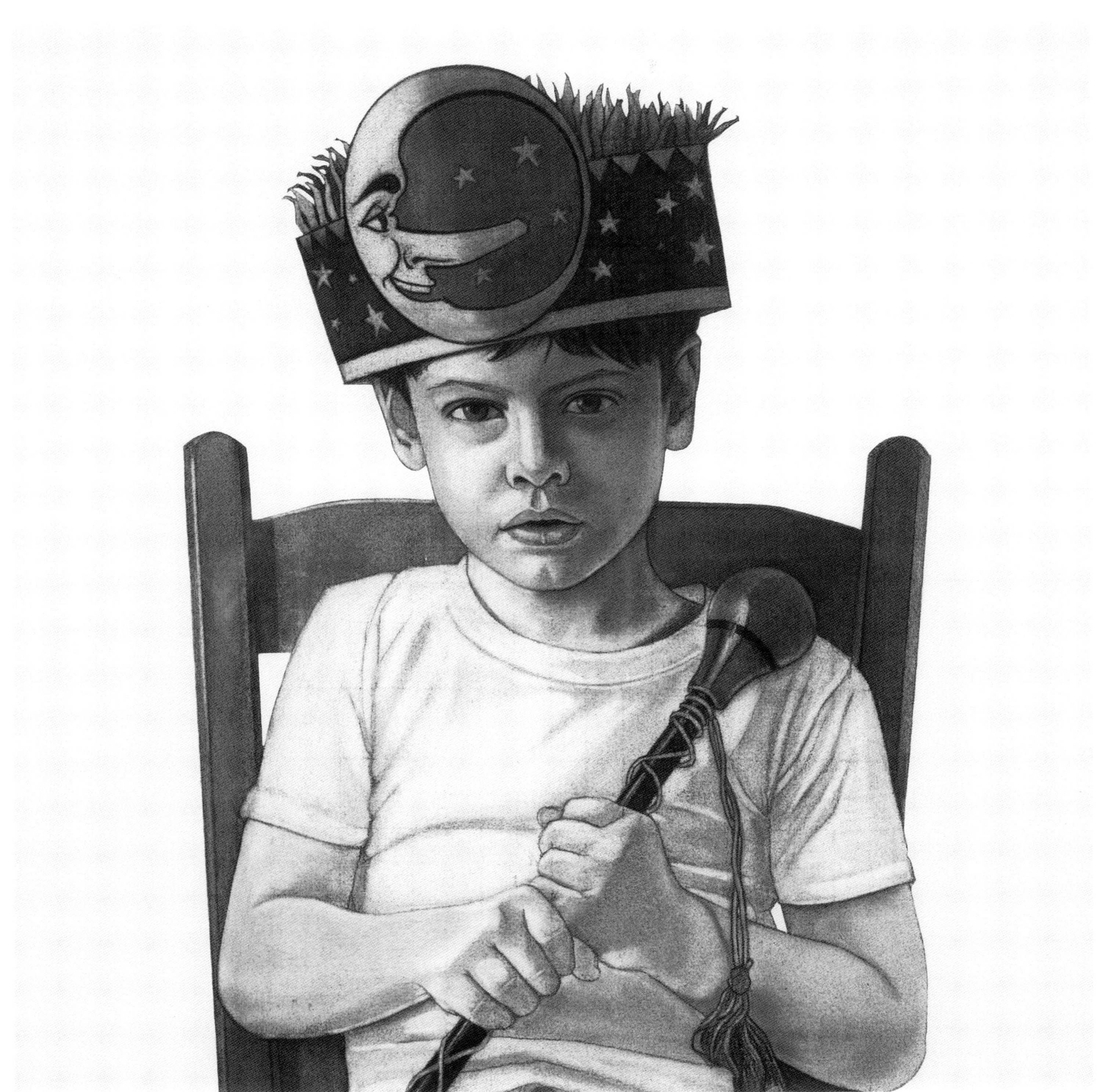

Cat. 42
Let the Wild Rumpus Begin, 1983
Graphite on canvas
24 × 20 in.
Collection of Carissa Hussong
and David Lusk

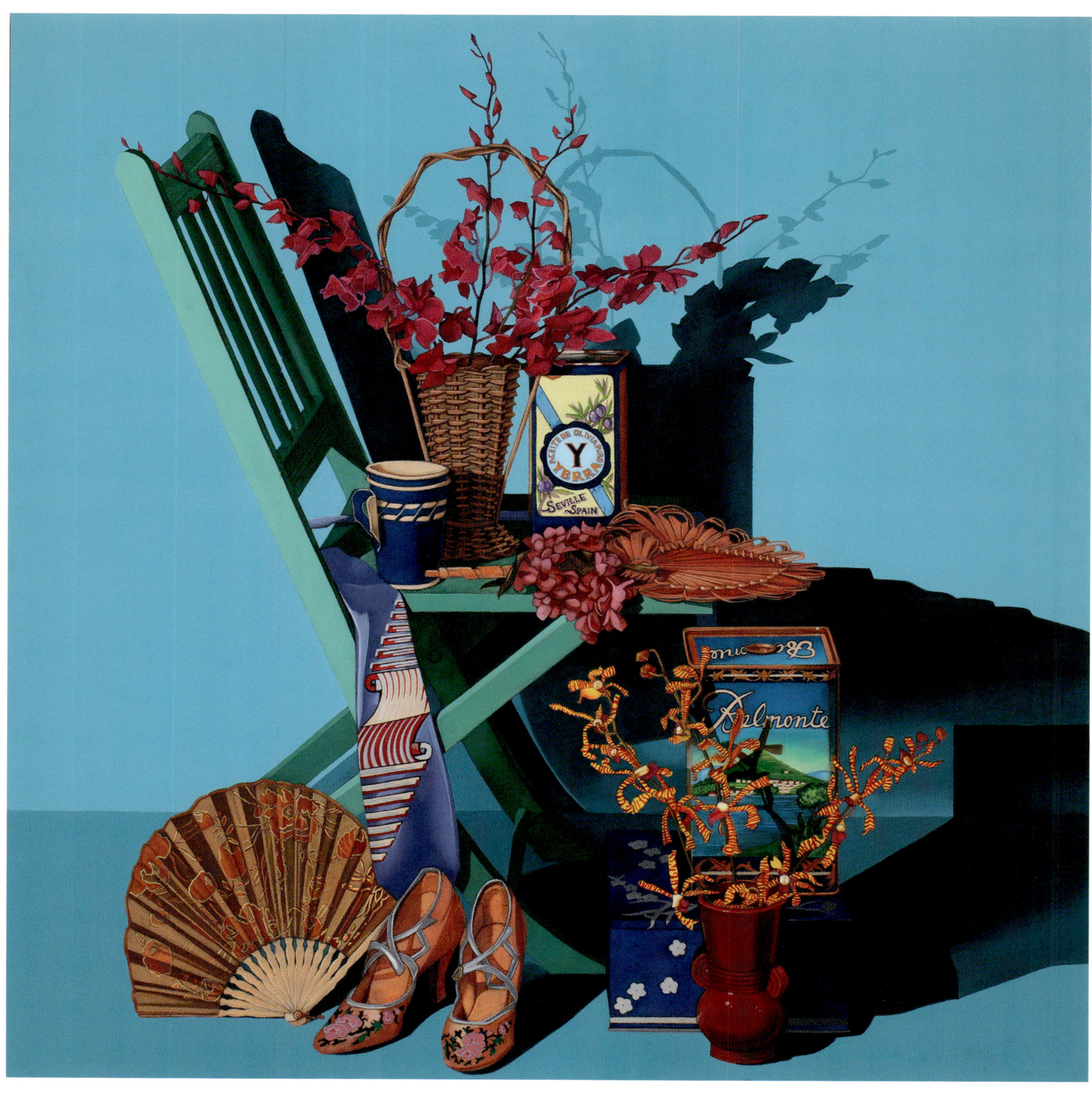

Cat. 43
Olive Oil and Orchids, 1983
Acrylic on canvas
50 ¼ × 50 ¾ in.
Collection of Grace Megel and Sarkis Kish

Cat. 44
Old Glory, 1985
Acrylic on canvas
20 × 16 in.
Courtesy of David Lusk Gallery,
Memphis and Nashville, Tennessee

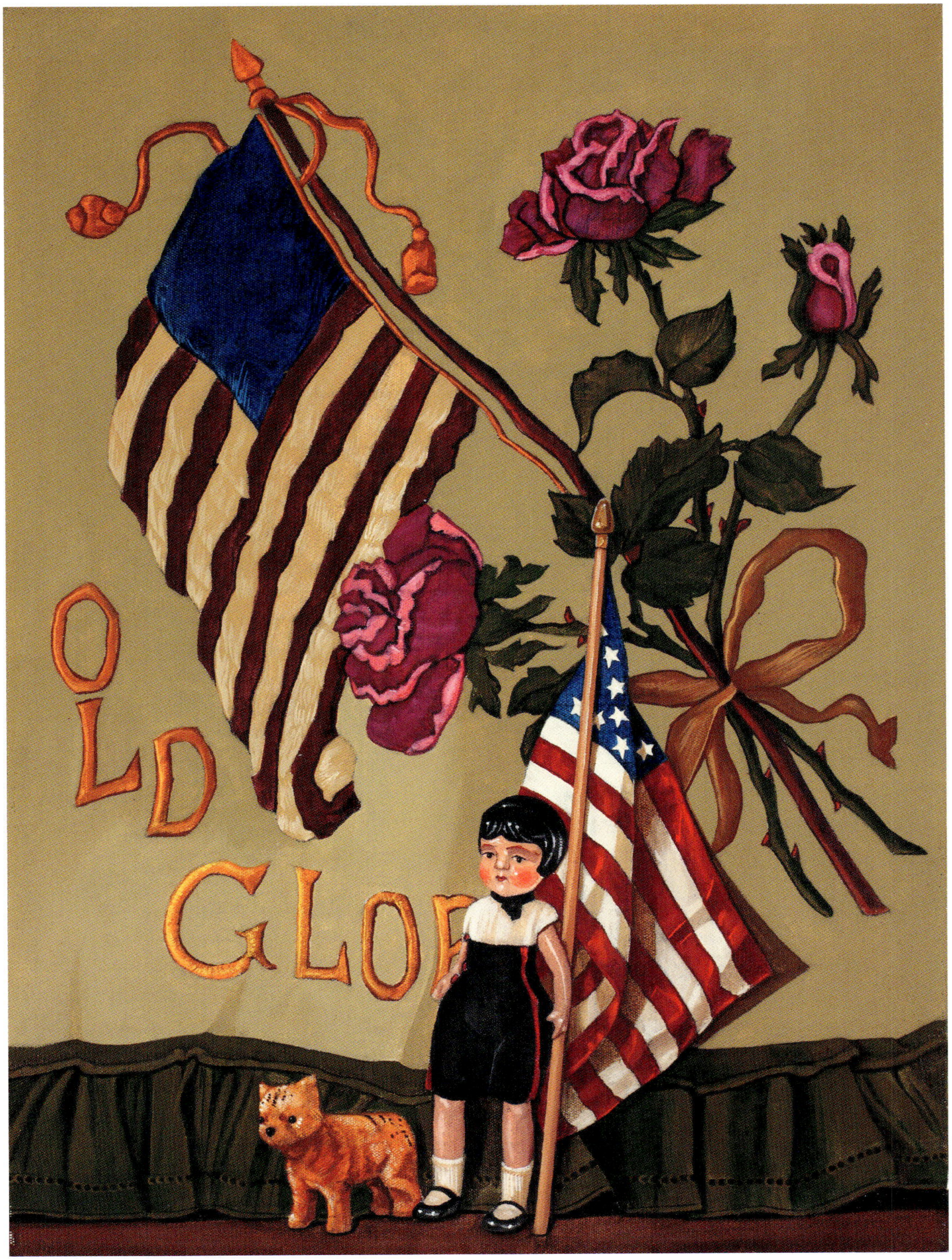

Cat. 45
Easter Parade, ca. 1985
Acrylic on canvas
48 × 48 ⅛ in.
Collection of Carey and Brad Snider

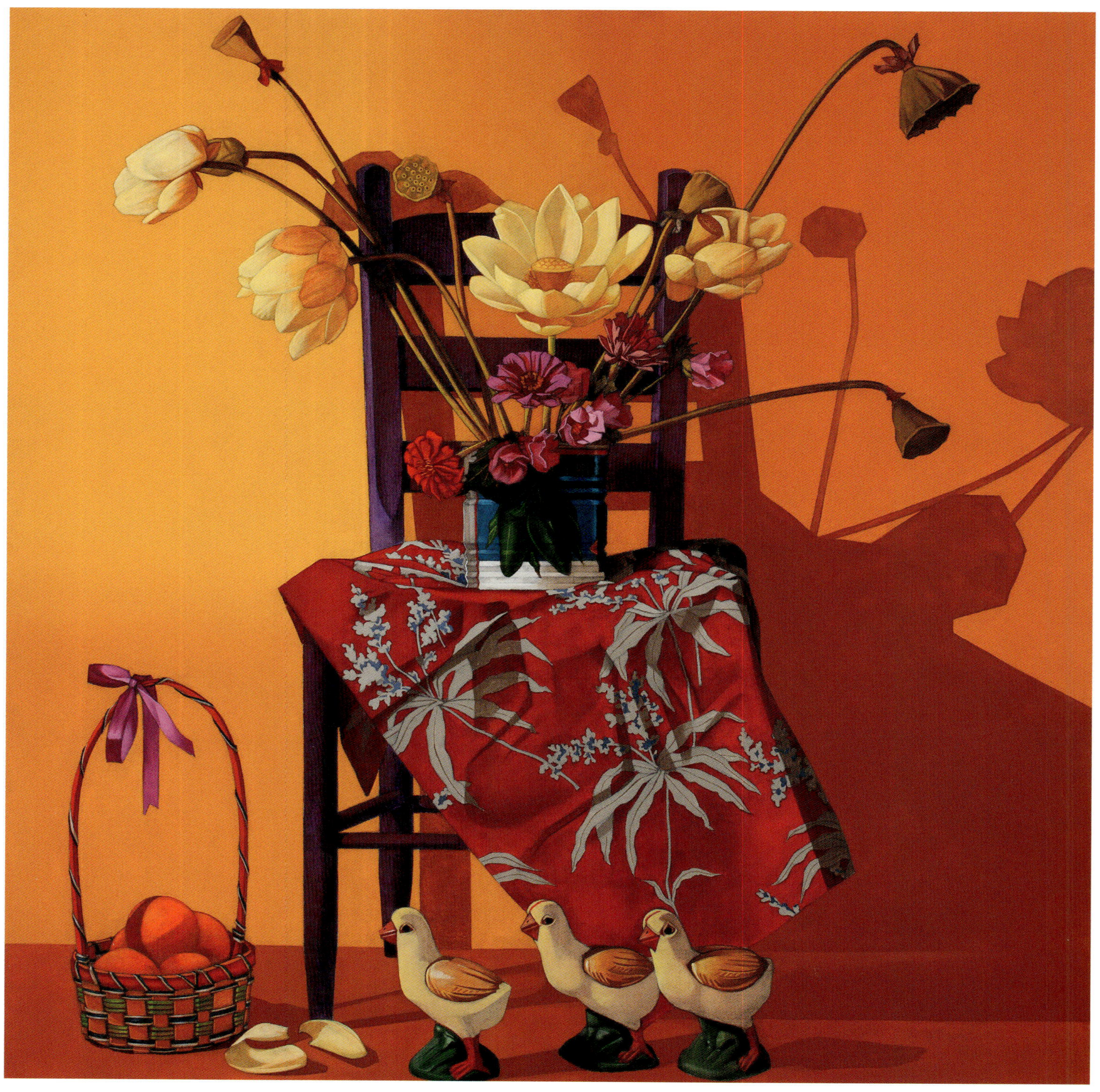

Cat. 46
Orchid Gut Bomb (Nothing Succeeds Like Excess), ca. 1985
Acrylic on canvas
50 ⅛ × 40 ¾ in.
Collection of Meg and Scott Crosby

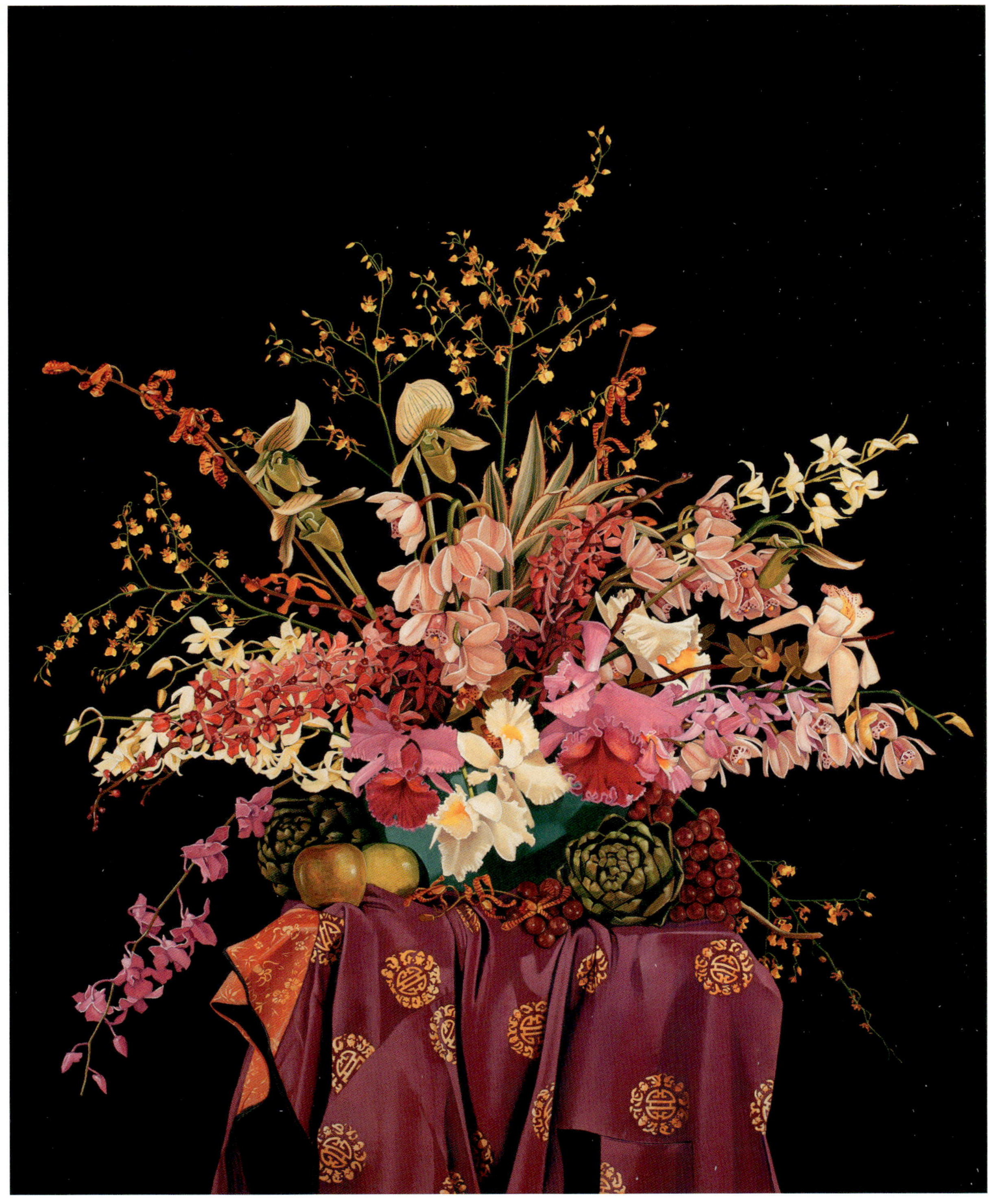

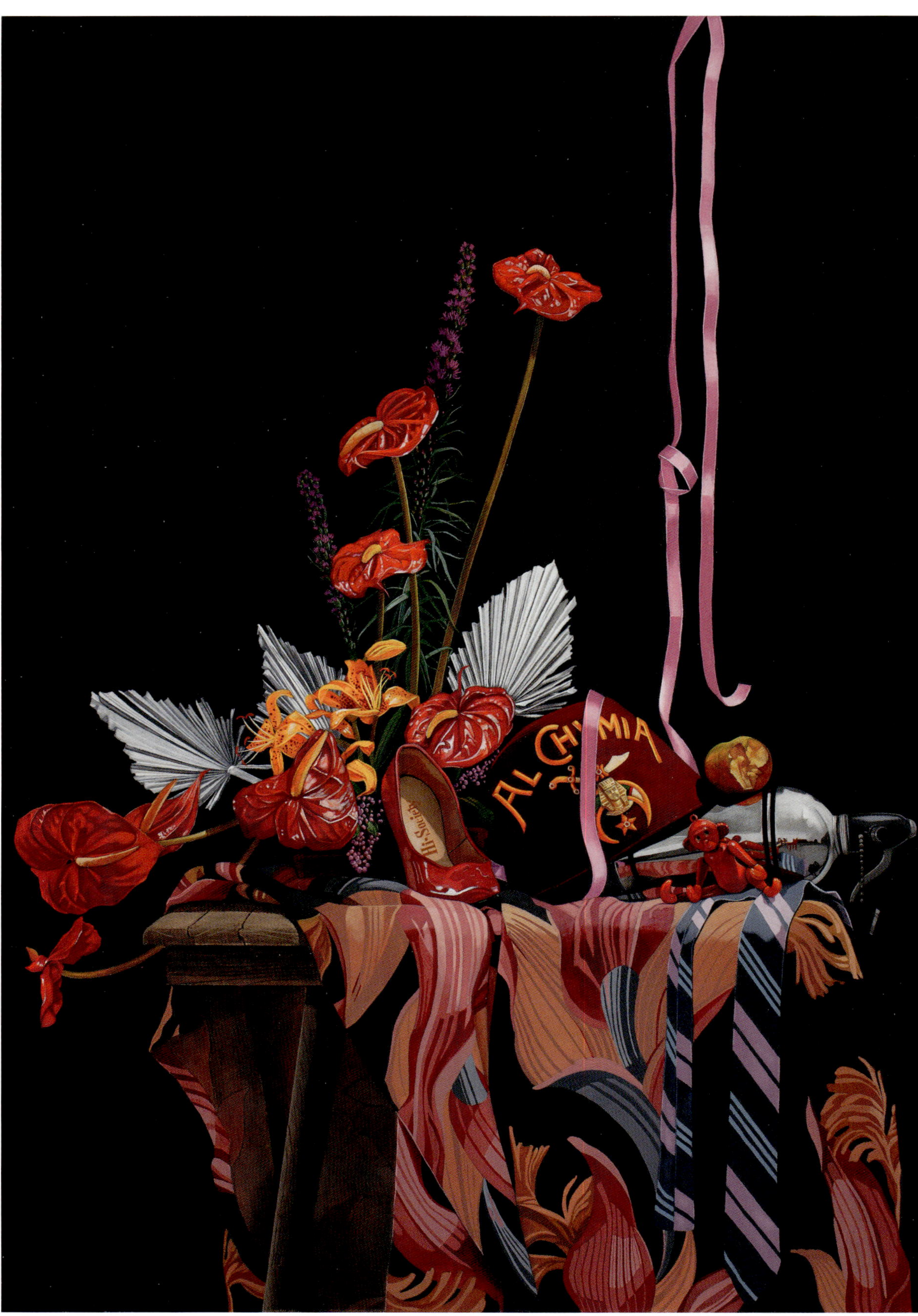

Cat. 47
Untitled, ca. 1985
Acrylic on canvas
46 ⅛ × 32 ⅛ in.
Collection of
Anne Curtis

Cat. 48
Deborah, Sweet Little Sixteen, 1987
Acrylic on canvas
66 × 60 in.
Collection of Gail Kreunen

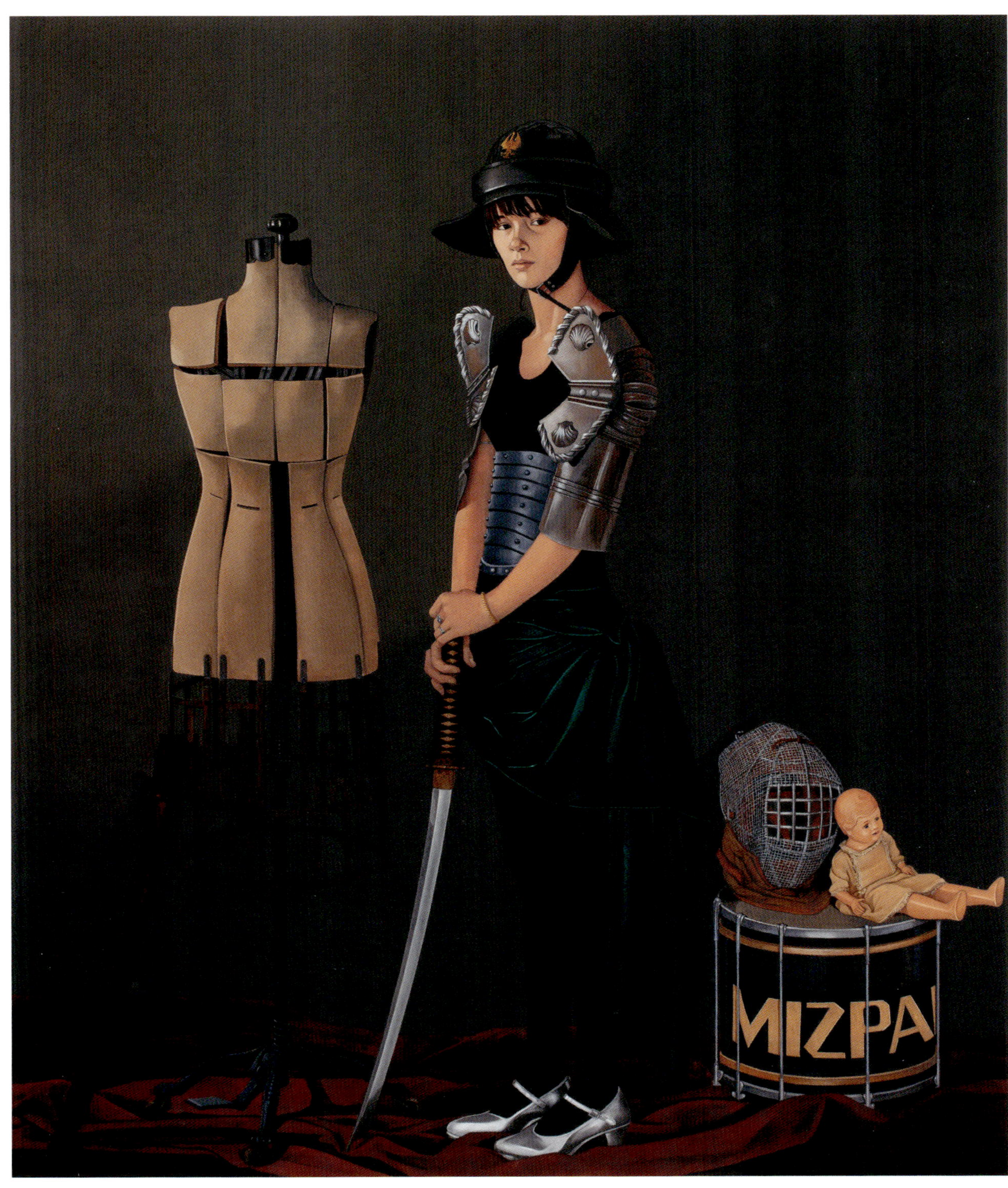
MIZPA

Another Birthday Alone, 1988
Acrylic on canvas
25 × 21 ¾ in.
Courtesy of David Lusk Gallery, Memphis
and Nashville, Tennessee

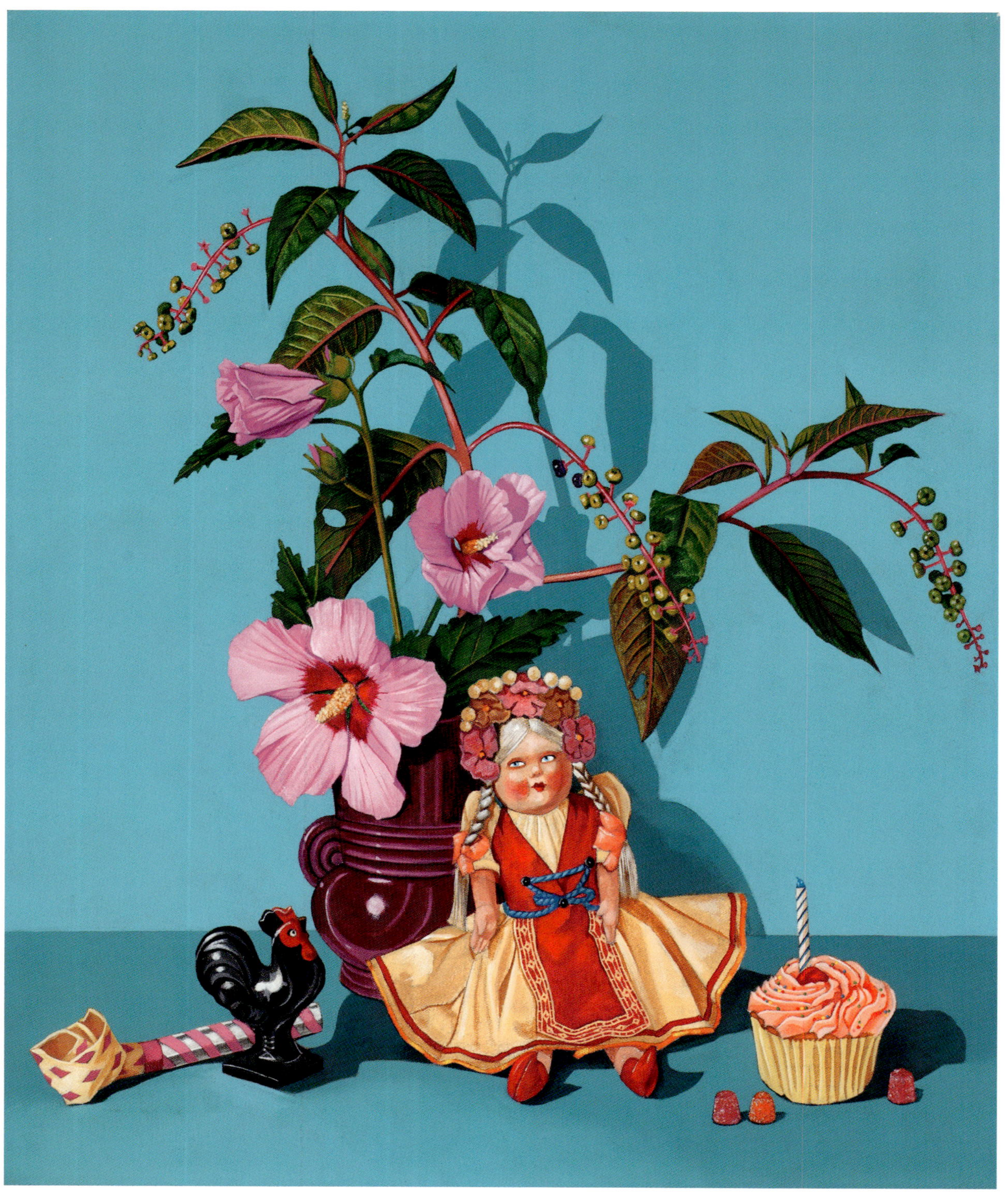

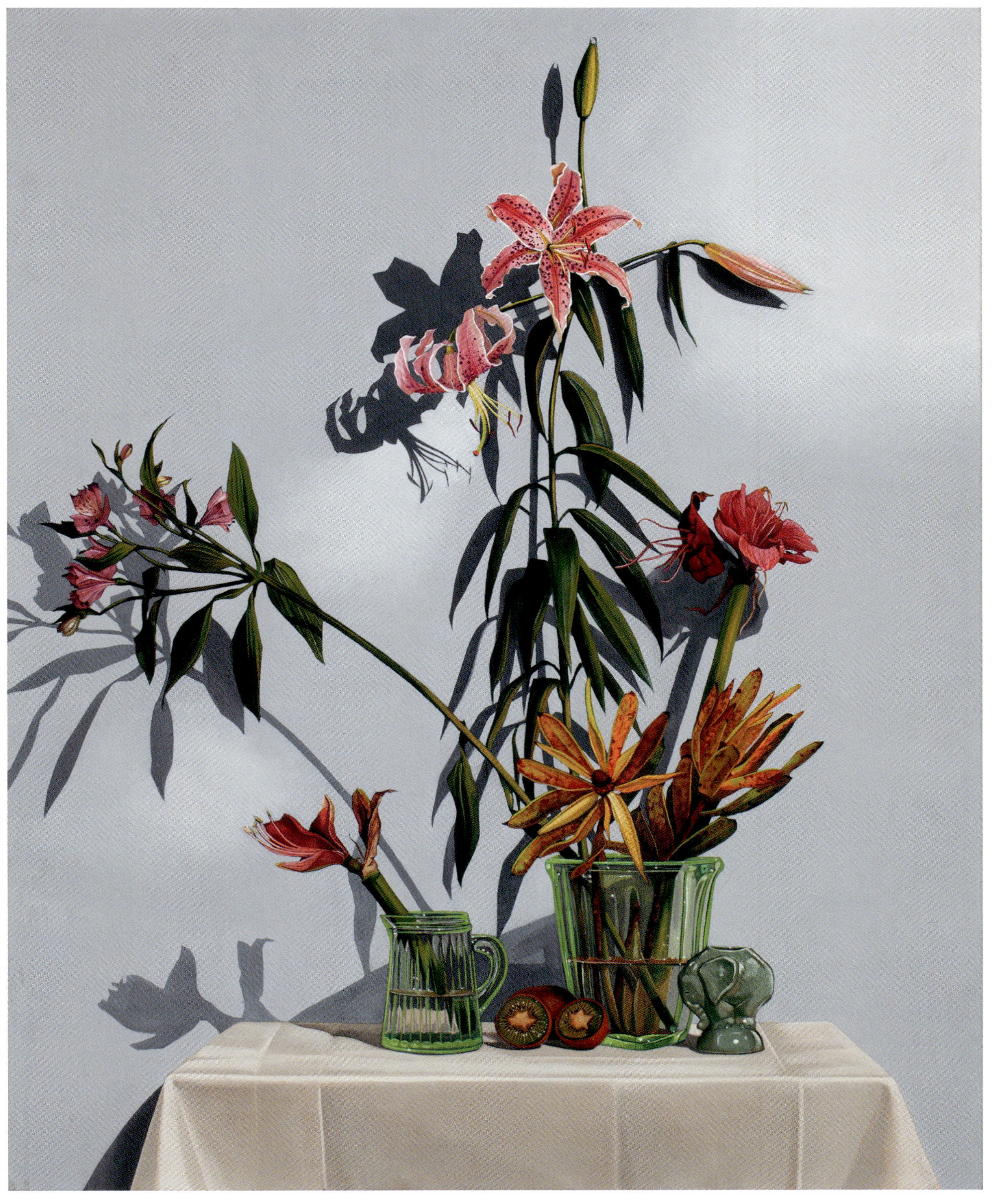

Cat. 50
Untitled, ca. 1989
Acrylic on canvas
37 ¼ × 30 ¼ in.
Collection of Gwen and Penn Owen

Spare One, 1991
Acrylic on canvas
40 × 30 in.
Collection of John Jerit

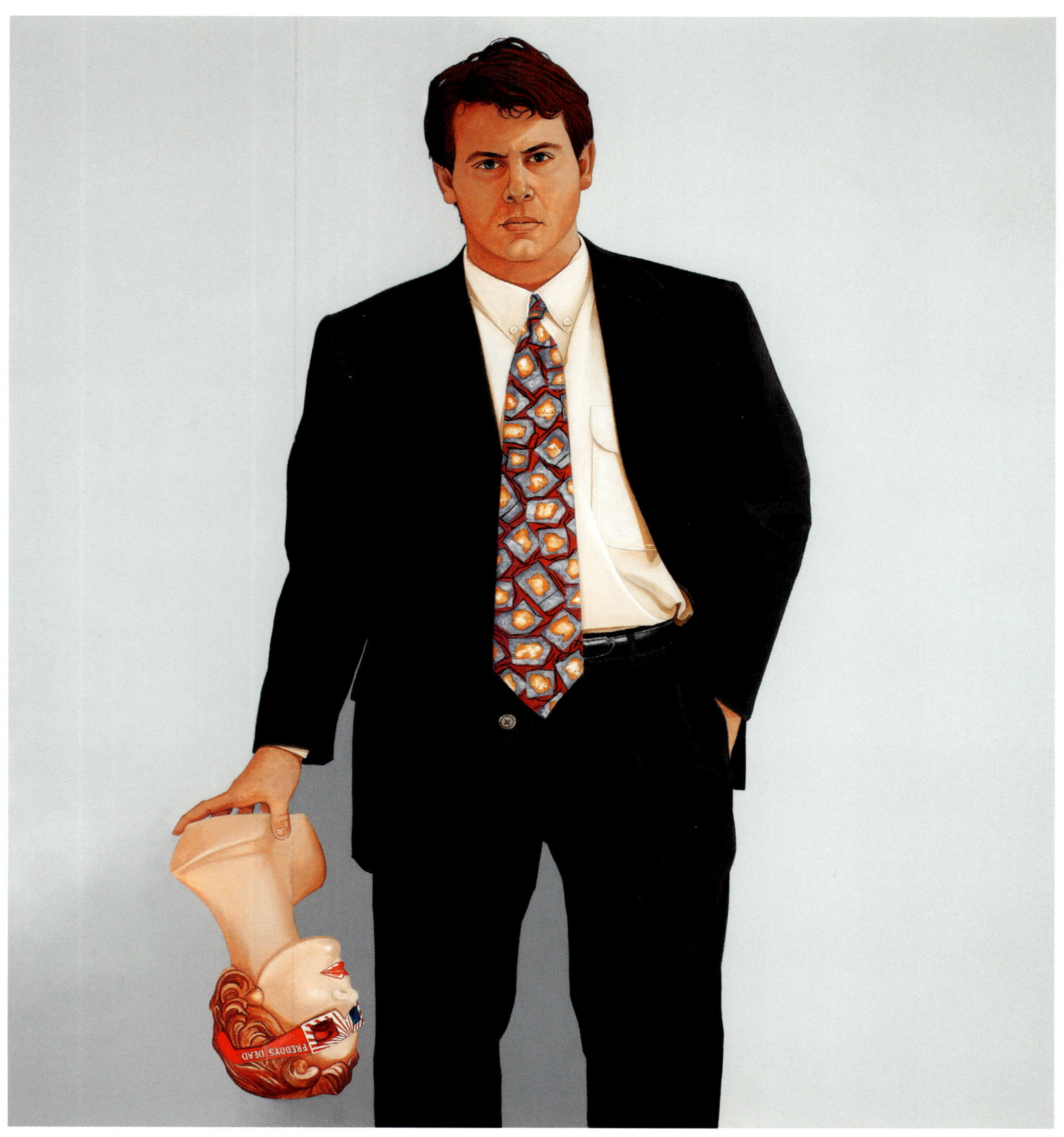

Cat. 52
Andy's Jacket, 1992
Acrylic on canvas
40 × 40 in.
First Horizon Bank, Memphis, Tennessee

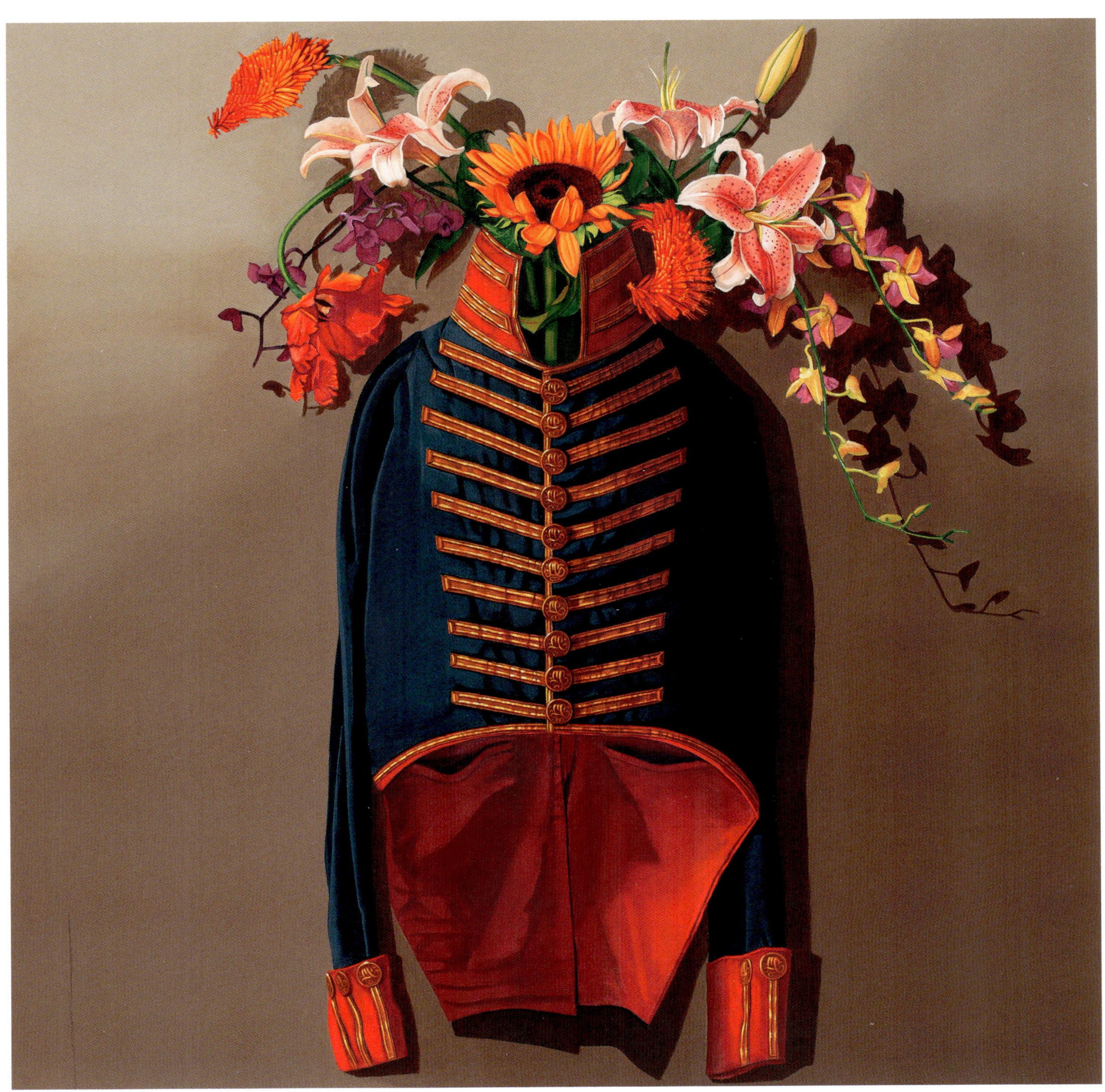

Cat. 53
Beauty and the Beast, 1993
Acrylic on canvas
25 × 26 in.
Collection of Rodgers Menzies

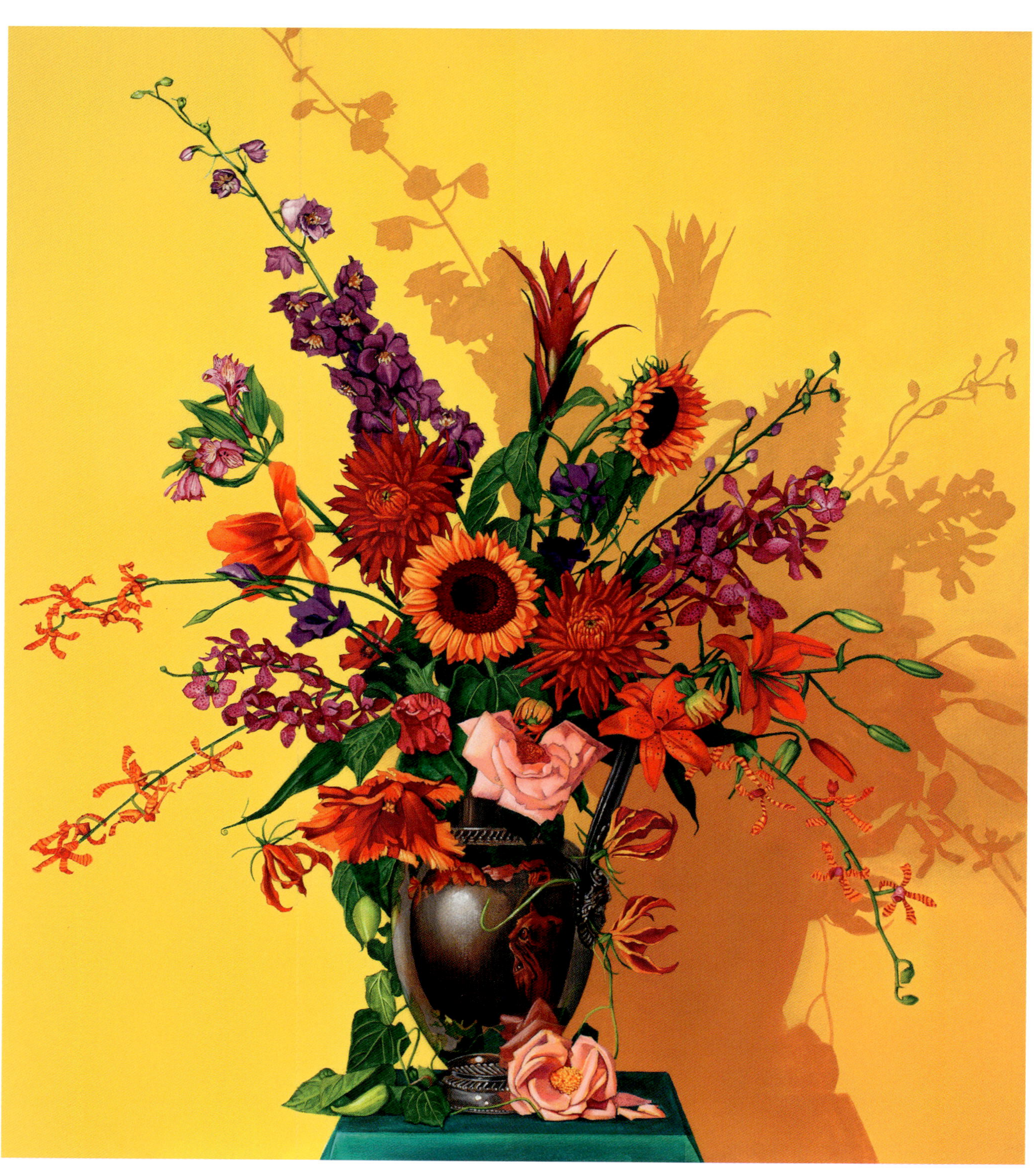

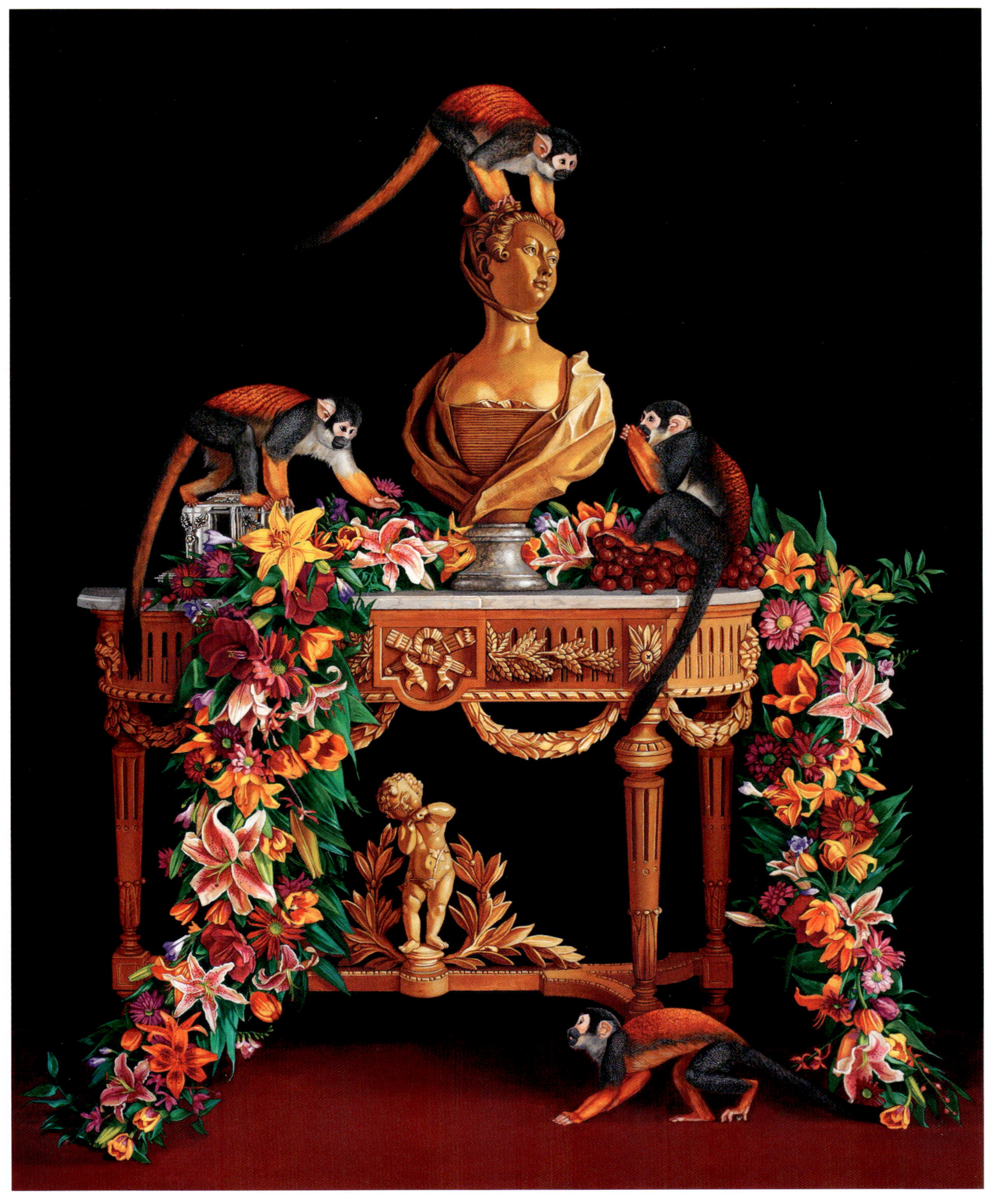

Cat. 54
Busting Out, 1995
Acrylic on canvas
60 × 53 in.
Private collection

Let the Good Times Roll, 1996
Acrylic on canvas
48 × 60 in.
Memphis in May International Festival
Collection, Memphis, Tennessee

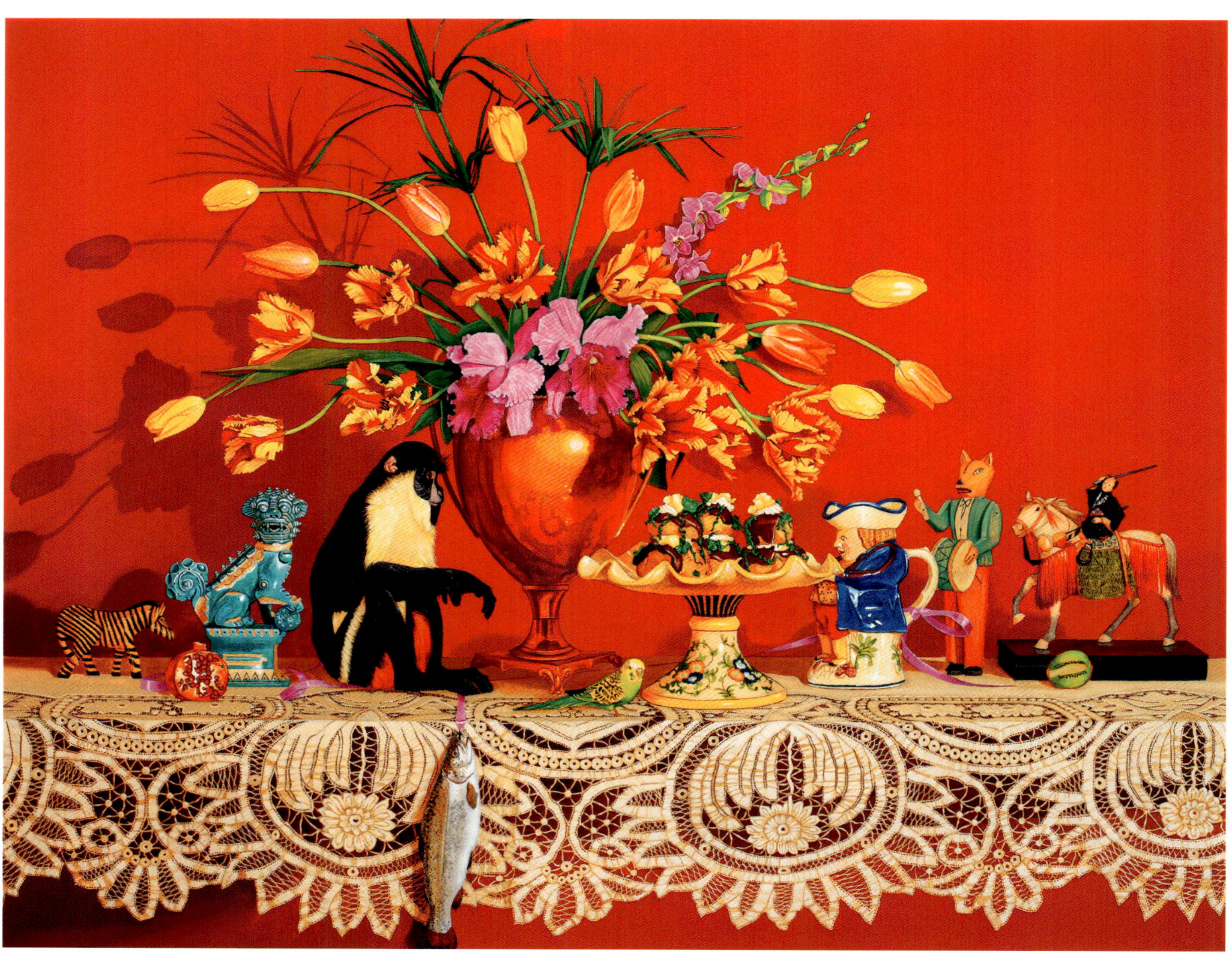

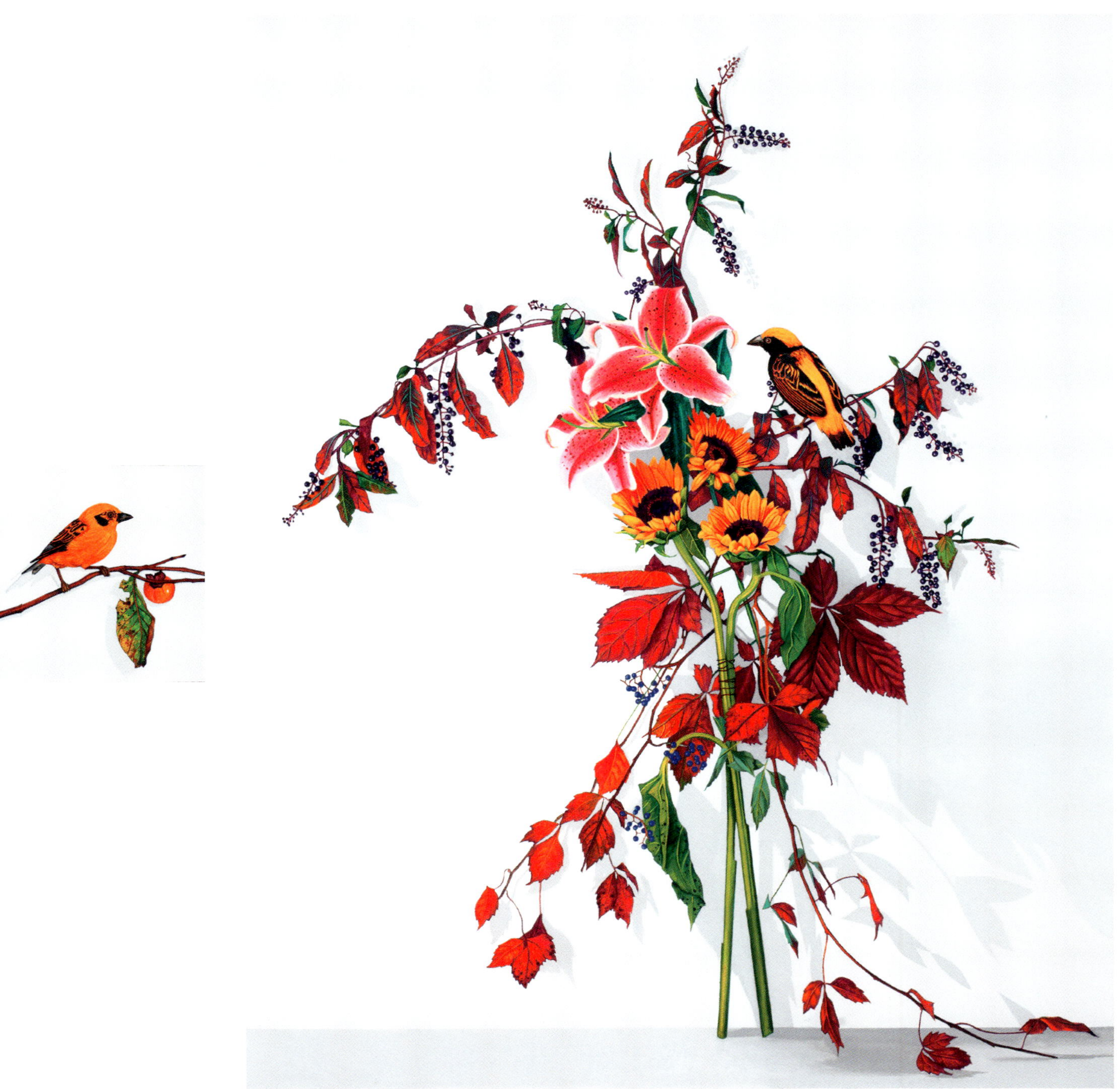

Cat. 56
A Bird on a Weed and *Sidebar*, 1996
Acrylic on canvas
10 × 10 in. (bird)
44 ⅛ × 35 ⅛ in. (flowers)
Private collection

Good Girl Kate, 1997
Acrylic on canvas
72 × 48 in.
Private collection

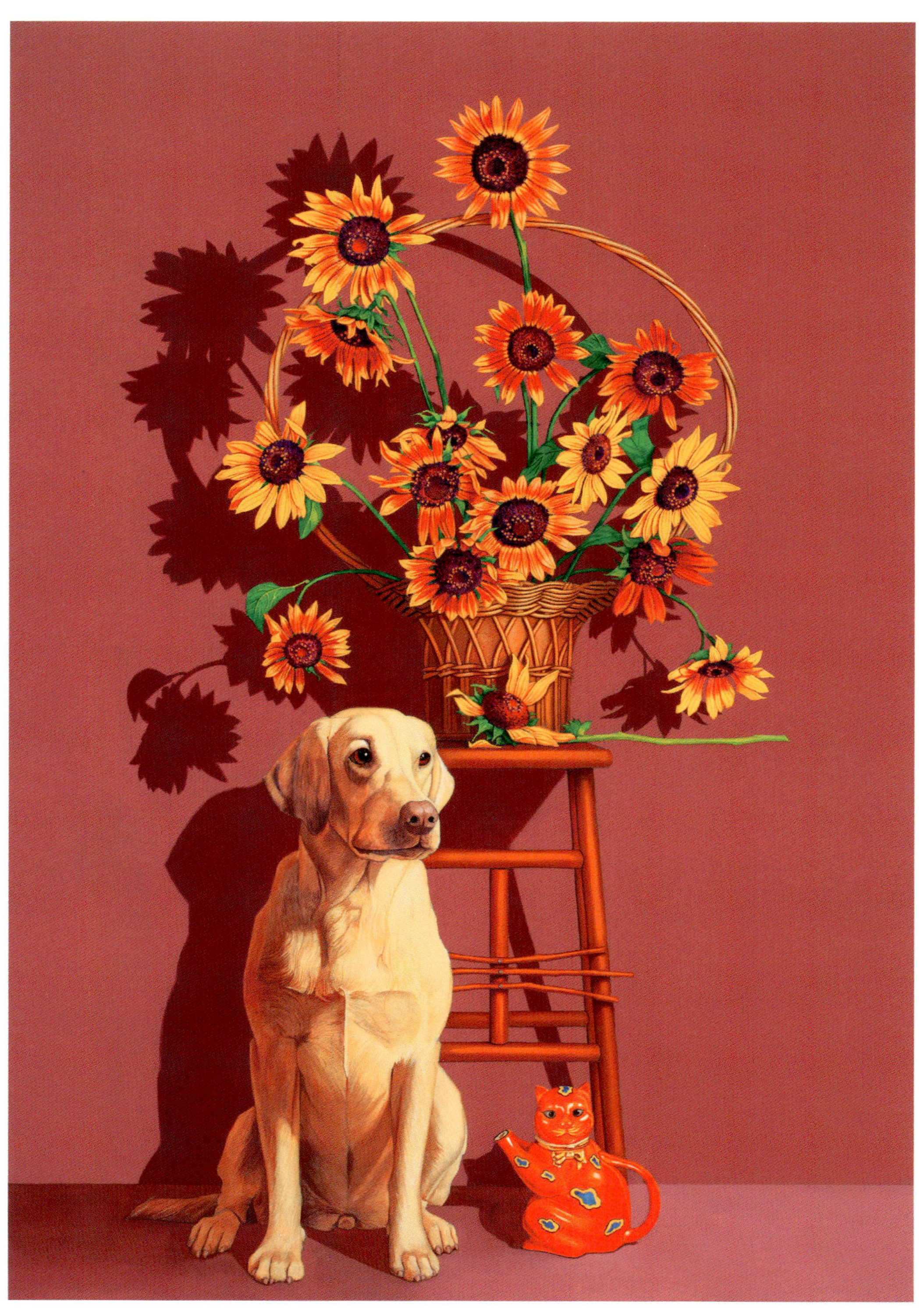

Cat. 58
Midnight Rambler, 1997
Acrylic on canvas
56 × 54 in.
Collection of John Jerit

Samovar and Tomatoes, ca. 1997
Acrylic on canvas
40 × 40 ⅜ in.
Collection of Morgan and Philip Zanone

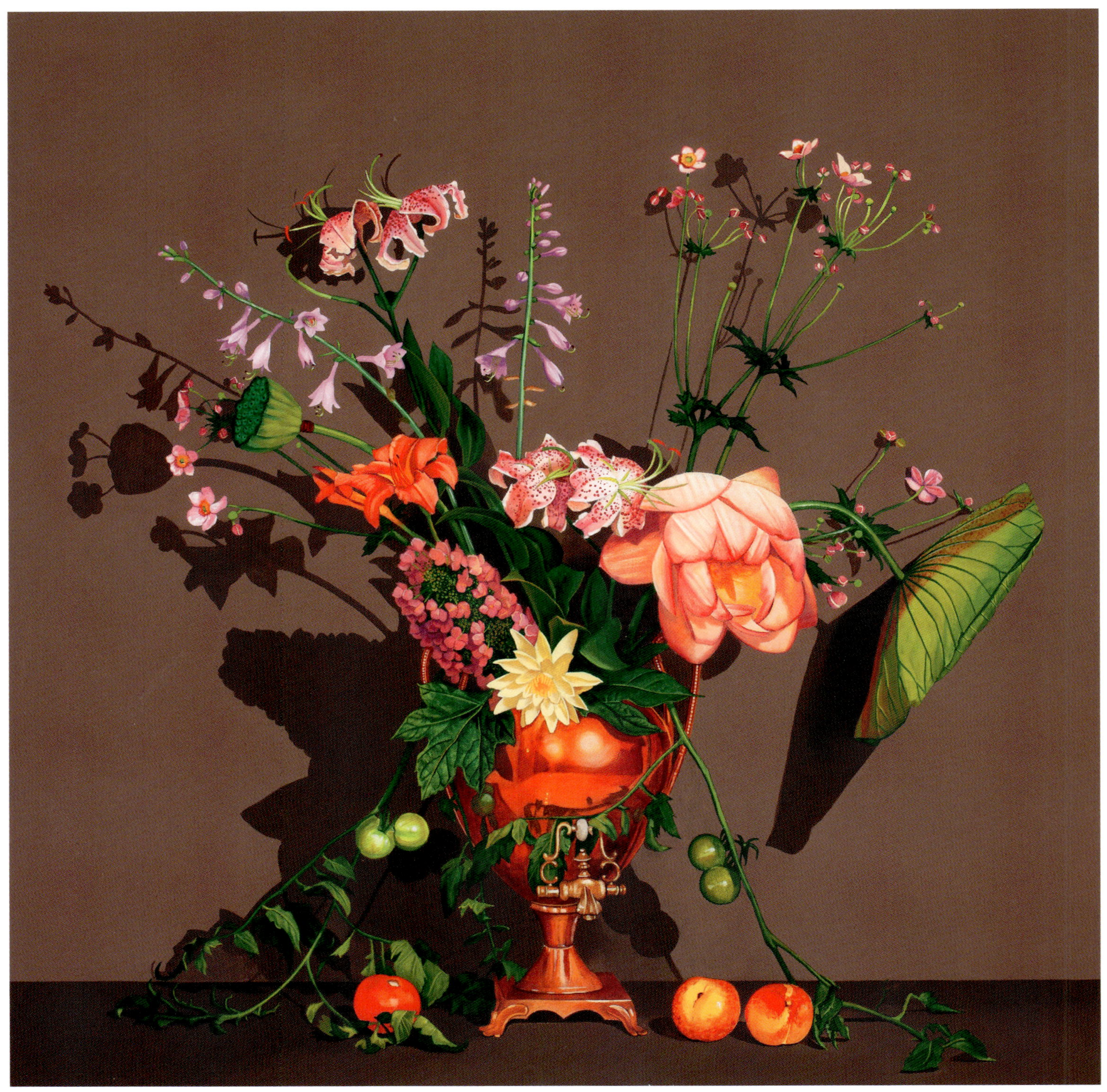

Cat. 60
By Any Other Name, 1999
Acrylic on canvas
44 ⅛ × 36 ¾ in.
Private collection

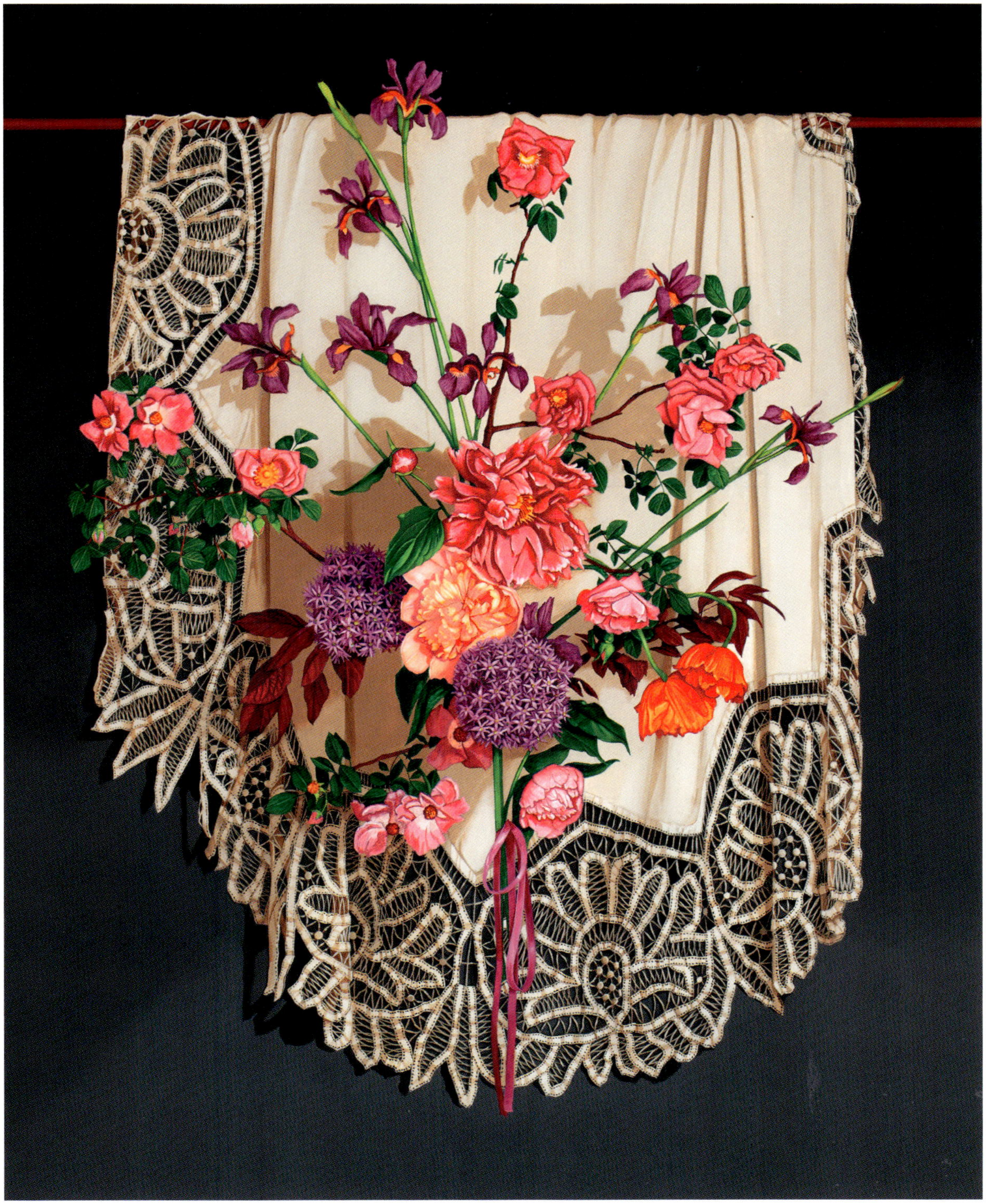

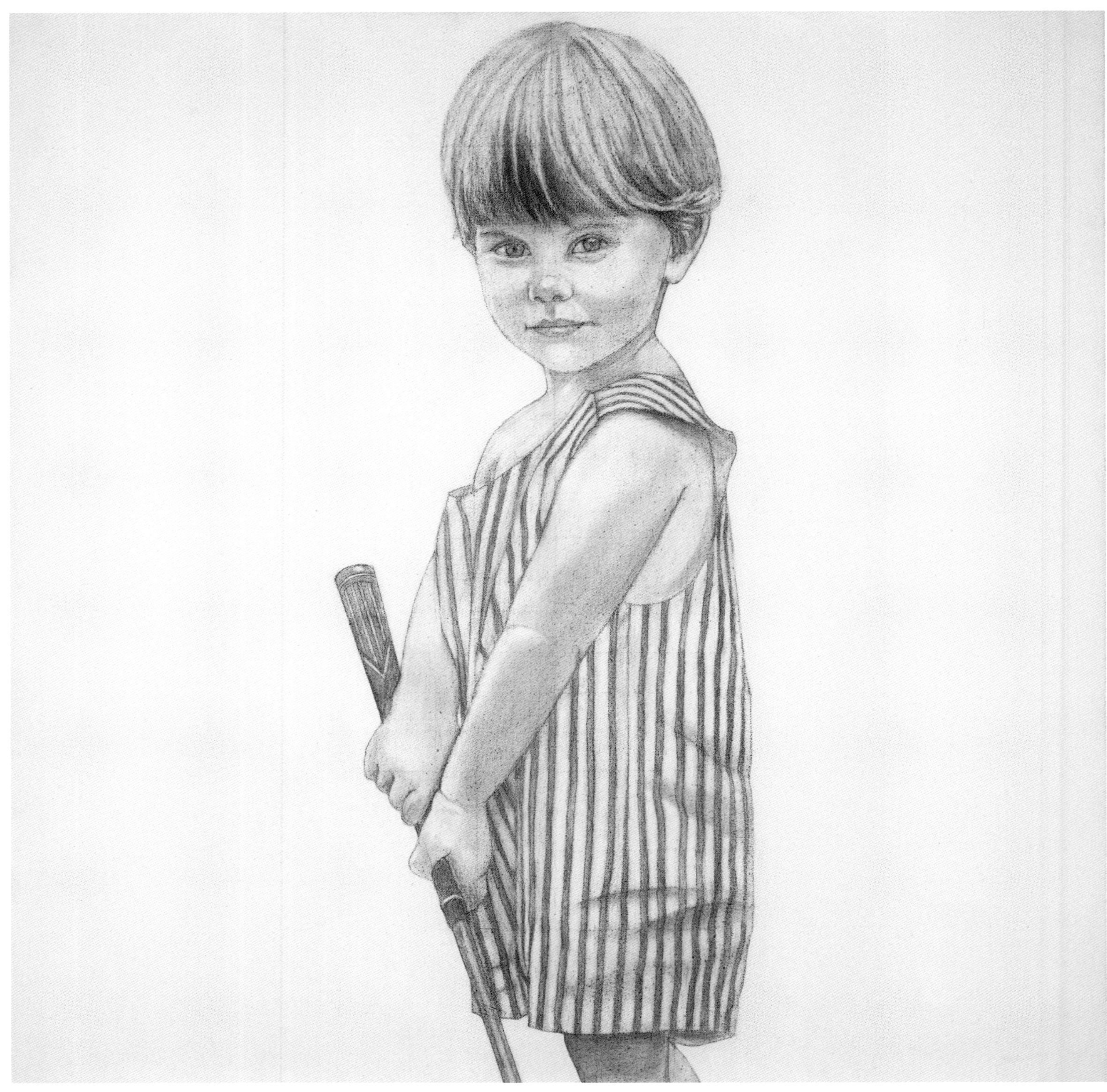

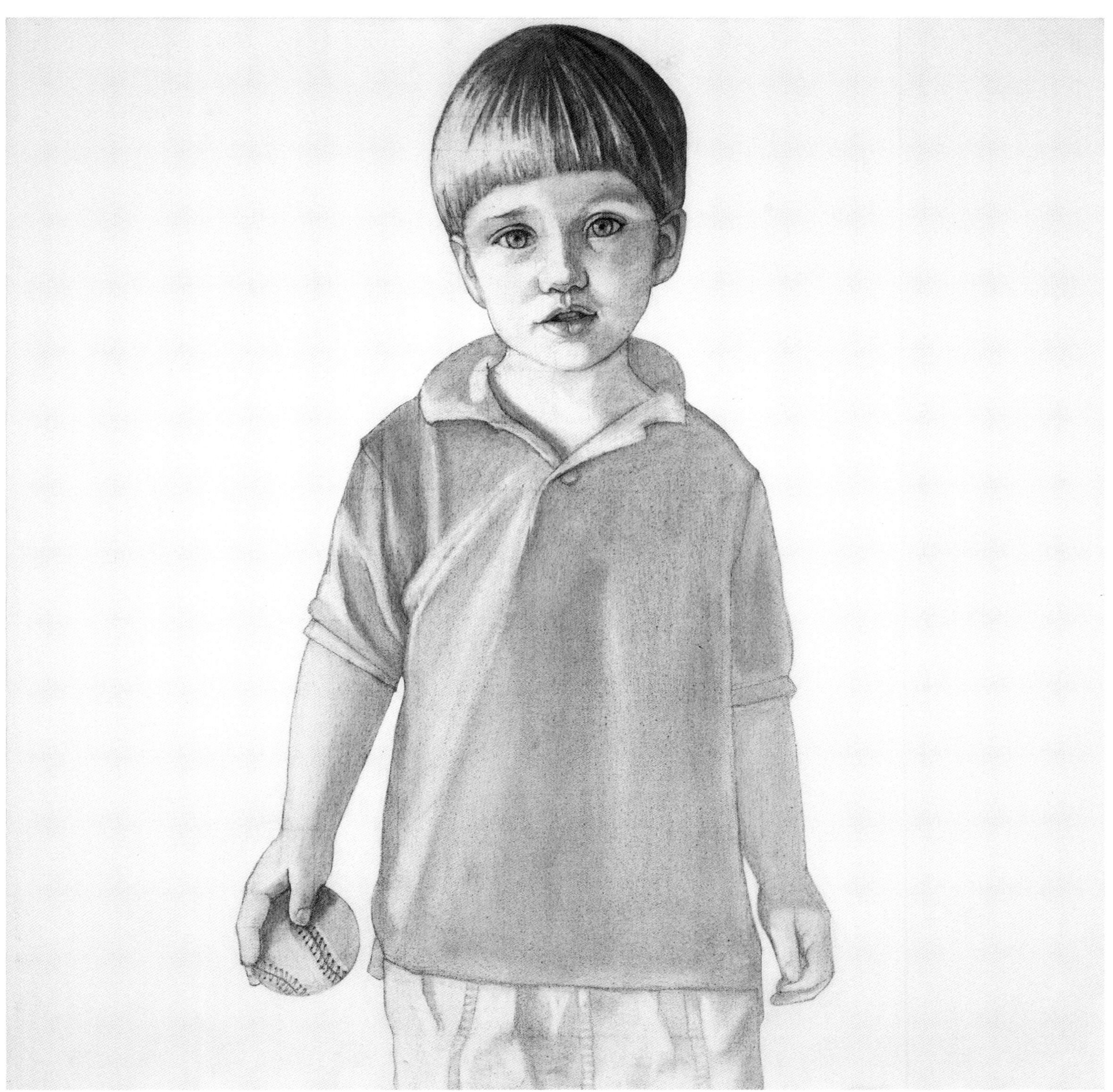

Cat. 62
Out of the Park, 1999
Graphite on canvas
28 × 28 in.
Collection of Muffy and Michael Turley

Cat. 63
The Youngest Volunteer, 1999
Graphite on canvas
28 × 28 in.
Collection of Muffy and Michael Turley

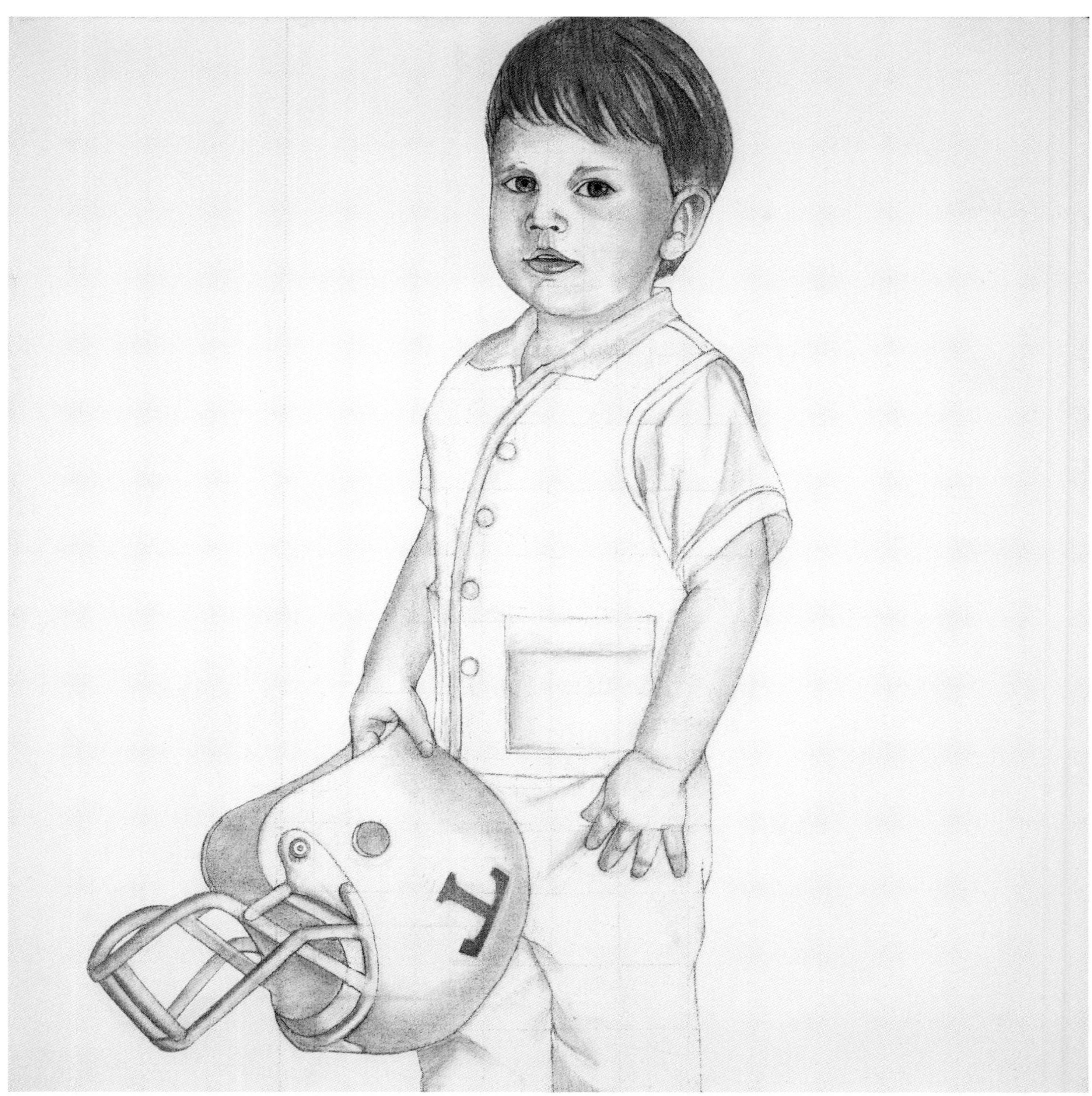

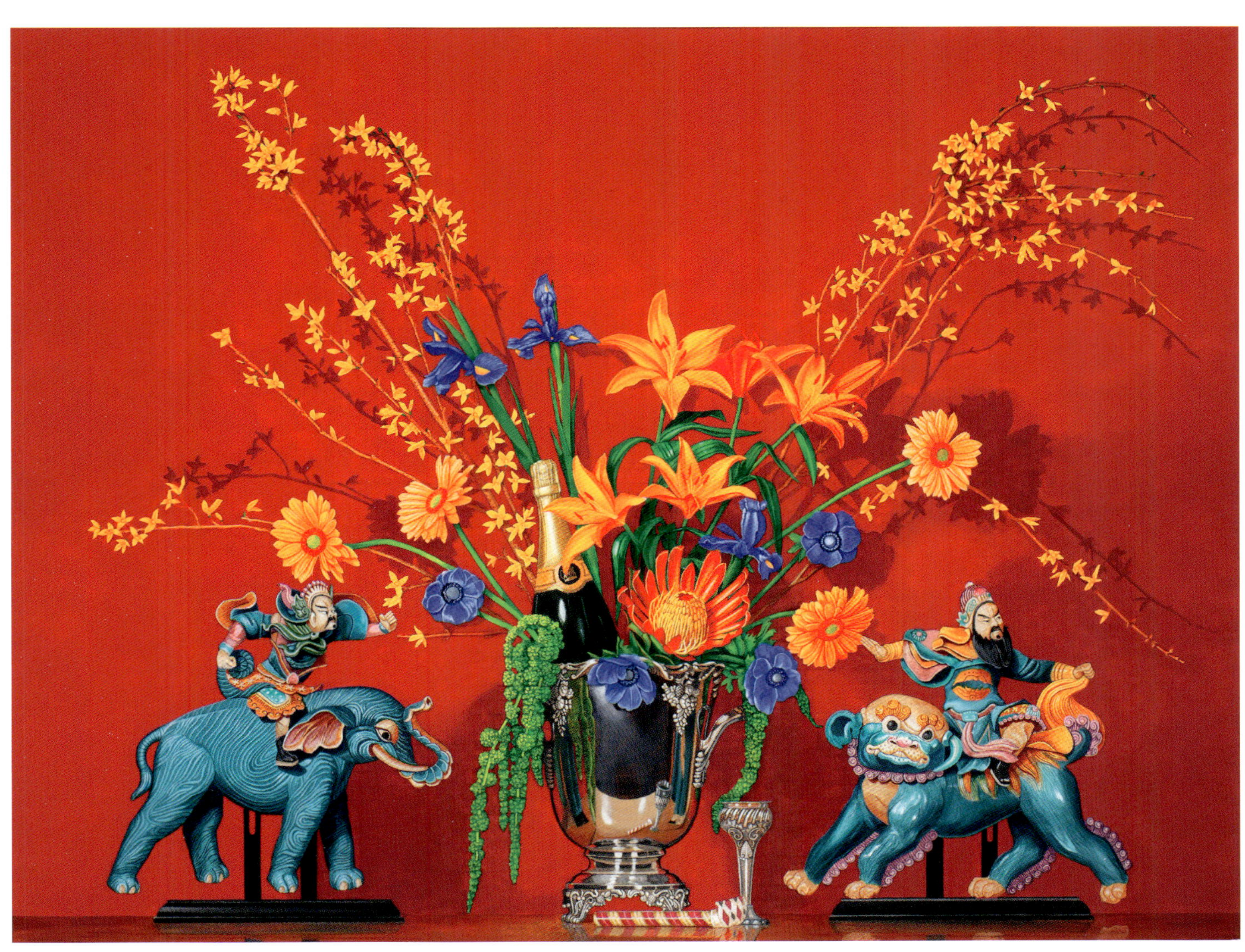

CHECKLIST OF THE EXHIBITION

All works are by Mary Sims (American, 1940–2004).

Cat. 1
Three Birds, 1960
Etching
13 × 18 ¼ in.
David Lusk Gallery, Memphis and
Nashville, Tennessee

Cat. 2
Untitled (Five Children), 1960
Oil on canvas
42 × 40 in.
Estate of Mary Sims

Cat. 3
Alice and Inky, ca. 1960s
Etching
18 ¾ × 16 ⅞ in.
Private collection

Cat. 4
*Untitled (Portrait of Robert
Mezey)*, ca. 1961
Oil on canvas
39 × 31 ½ in.
Estate of Mary Sims

Cat. 5
A Studio Portrait, 1968
Oil on canvas
51 × 30 in.
Estate of Mary Sims

Cat. 6
Untitled (Self-Portrait in Studio), 1968
Oil on canvas
27 × 35 in.
Private collection

Cat. 7
For Cynthia, 1969
Acrylic on canvas
72 × 54 in.
Collection of Cynthia Bringle

Cat. 8
Untitled, 1969
Acrylic and graphite on canvas
34 × 40 ⅛ in.
Private collection

Cat. 9
The Beggared Outcast, 1970
Acrylic and graphite on canvas
60 × 49 in.
Private collection

Cat. 10
Emma and Me, 1970
Acrylic and graphite on canvas
65 × 42 in.
Collection of Katharine
Stanwood Menke

Cat. 11
Miss November, 1970
Acrylic and graphite on canvas
74 × 48 in.
Collection of Lance Oliver

Cat. 12
*Untitled (Portrait of Louise Howry
McRae)*, ca. 1970
Acrylic and graphite on canvas
72 × 48 in.
Rhodes College, Memphis, Tennessee

Cat. 13
All Dressed Up, Nowhere to Go, 1972
Acrylic and graphite on canvas
60 × 34 in.
Collection of Katherine and
Adrian Blackney

Cat. 14
Queen of the Moon, 1972
Acrylic and graphite on canvas
84 × 48 in.
Collection of Audrey Taylor Gonzalez

Cat. 15
Snow White and Rose Red, 1972
Acrylic and graphite on canvas
60 × 54 in.
Collection of Meg Menzies

Cat. 16
Flowerstand, ca. 1972
Acrylic and graphite on canvas
48 × 28 in.
Collection of Beth and David Skudder

Cat. 17
Michael in Purple, ca. 1972
Acrylic and graphite on canvas
71 × 48 in.
Collection of Lawrence and
John Cowart

Cat. 18
*Mutual Consent (Portrait of Jessie
and Dolph Smith)*, ca. 1972
Acrylic and graphite on canvas
72 × 48 in.
Collection of Dolph Smith

Cat. 19
*Untitled (Woman with
Branches)*, ca. 1972
Acrylic and graphite on canvas
72 × 60 in.
Collection of Robert Donovan Smith

Cat. 20
Brier, ca. 1973
Acrylic and graphite on canvas
72 × 60 in.
Collection of Brier Smith Turner

Cat. 21
Untitled (Man on a Park Bench), 1975
Acrylic and graphite on canvas
72 × 57 ¼ in.
David Lusk Gallery, Memphis and
Nashville, Tennessee

Cat. 22
Drop Dead Chic, 1976
Acrylic and graphite on canvas
90 × 78 in.
Collection of Jim Herbst

Cat. 23
*The Blue Cat (Janet's Rose
Garden)*, 1976
Acrylic and graphite on canvas
60 × 60 in.
St. Mary's Episcopal School,
Memphis, Tennessee

Cat. 24
Portrait of Elise, 1976
Acrylic and graphite on canvas
60 × 60 in.
Collection of JJ and Jay Keras

Cat. 25
Virgin Guadalupe, 1976
Acrylic and graphite on canvas
54 × 32 in.
St. Mary's Episcopal School,
Memphis, Tennessee

Cat. 26
Dr. Feelgood, 1977
Acrylic and graphite on canvas
82 × 58 in.
Collection of Roger Ross and
Trae Winston

Cat. 27
Untitled (3 Parrots), 1977
Acrylic and graphite on canvas
40 × 40 in.
Collection of Maggie and
Milton Lovell

Cat. 28
Ship of Fools, ca. 1977
Acrylic and graphite on canvas
72 × 144 in.
Collection of Carissa Hussong and
David Lusk

Cat. 29
A Bride for Hosea, 1978
Acrylic and graphite on canvas
96 × 132 in.
Private collection

Cat. 30
Merlin, 1978
Acrylic and graphite on canvas
72 × 60 in.
Collection of Rodgers Menzies

Cat. 31
Untitled (Flamingo), 1978
Acrylic and graphite on canvas
42 ½ × 42 ⅝ in.
Collection of Neville and
Warfield Williams

Cat. 32
Untitled (Lake Leatherwood), 1978
Acrylic and graphite on canvas
60 × 60 in.
Collection of Katherine and
Adrian Blackney

Cat. 33
Mexican Petunias, ca. 1978
Acrylic on canvas
42 × 36 in.
Collection of Katherine and
Stephen Bush

Cat. 34
Porch Flowers, ca. 1978
Acrylic and graphite on canvas
60 × 60 in.
Collection of Carissa Hussong and
David Lusk

Cat. 35
*Untitled (Blue Wall, Red
Flowers)*, ca. 1978
Acrylic and graphite on canvas
53 ¾ × 42 in.
Collection of Holly and Paul T. Combs

Cat. 36
*Untitled (Lake
Leatherwood)*, ca. 1978
Acrylic and graphite on canvas
60 × 75 in.
Private collection

Cat. 37
*Untitled (Lake
Leatherwood)*, ca. 1980
Acrylic and graphite on canvas
96 × 96 in.
Private collection

Cat. 38
Salute to Egypt, 1981
Acrylic on canvas
55 × 43 in.
Memphis in May International
Festival Collection,
Memphis, Tennessee

Cat. 39
Leda and the Cake, 1982
Acrylic on canvas
60 × 72 in.
Private collection

Cat. 40
Untitled (Napoleon), 1982
Acrylic and graphite on canvas
72 × 48 in.
Collection of Dianne and Myron Mall

Cat. 41
Mama, ca. 1982
Charcoal on canvas
64 × 56 in.
Mississippi Museum of Art, Jackson,
Gift of Larry and Nina Riley, courtesy
David Lusk Gallery, Memphis,
Tennessee, 2003.002

Cat. 42
Let the Wild Rumpus Begin, 1983
Graphite on canvas
24 × 20 in.
Collection of Carissa Hussong and
David Lusk

Cat. 43
Olive Oil and Orchids, 1983
Acrylic on canvas
50 ¼ × 50 ¾ in.
Collection of Grace Megel and
Sarkis Kish

Cat. 44
Old Glory, 1985
Acrylic on canvas
20 × 16 in.
Courtesy of David Lusk Gallery,
Memphis and Nashville, Tennessee

Cat. 45
Easter Parade, ca. 1985
Acrylic on canvas
48 × 48 ⅛ in.
Collection of Carey and Brad Snider

Cat. 46
*Orchid Gut Bomb (Nothing Succeeds
Like Excess)*, ca. 1985
Acrylic on canvas
50 ⅛ × 40 ¾ in.
Collection of Meg and Scott Crosby

Cat. 47
Untitled, ca. 1985
Acrylic on canvas
46 ⅛ × 32 ⅛ in.
Collection of Anne Curtis

Cat. 48
Deborah, Sweet Little Sixteen, 1987
Acrylic on canvas
66 × 60 in.
Collection of Gail Kreunen

Cat. 49
Another Birthday Alone, 1988
Acrylic on canvas
25 × 21 ¾ in.
Courtesy of David Lusk Gallery,
Memphis and Nashville, Tennessee

Cat. 50
Untitled, ca. 1989
Acrylic on canvas
37 ¼ × 30 ¼ in.
Collection of Gwen and Penn Owen

Cat. 51
Spare One, 1991
Acrylic on canvas
40 × 30 in.
Collection of John Jerit

Cat. 52
Andy's Jacket, 1992
Acrylic on canvas
40 × 40 in.
First Horizon Bank,
Memphis, Tennessee

Cat. 53
Beauty and the Beast, 1993
Acrylic on canvas
25 × 26 in.
Collection of Rodgers Menzies

Cat. 54
Busting Out, 1995
Acrylic on canvas
60 × 53 in.
Private collection

Cat. 55
Let the Good Times Roll, 1996
Acrylic on canvas
48 × 60 in.
Memphis in May International
Festival Collection,
Memphis, Tennessee

Cat. 56
A Bird on a Weed and *Sidebar*, 1996
Acrylic on canvas
10 × 10 in. (bird)
44 ⅛ × 35 ⅛ in. (flowers)
Private collection

Cat. 57
Good Girl Kate, 1997
Acrylic on canvas
72 × 48 in.
Private collection

Cat. 58
Midnight Rambler, 1997
Acrylic on canvas
56 × 54 in.
Collection of John Jerit

Cat. 59
Samovar and Tomatoes, ca. 1997
Acrylic on canvas
40 × 40 ⅜ in.
Collection of Morgan and
Philip Zanone

Cat. 60
By Any Other Name, 1999
Acrylic on canvas
44 ⅛ × 36 ¾ in.
Private collection

Cat. 61
Hands of a Champion, 1999
Graphite on canvas
28 × 28 in.
Collection of Muffy and
Michael Turley

Cat. 62
Out of the Park, 1999
Graphite on canvas
28 × 28 in.
Collection of Muffy and
Michael Turley

Cat. 63
The Youngest Volunteer, 1999
Graphite on canvas
28 × 28 in.
Collection of Muffy and
Michael Turley

Cat. 64
Defending the Fête, 2001
Acrylic on canvas
36 ⅜ × 47 ½ in.
Private collection